"AT TALIESIN"

Newspaper Columns by Frank Lloyd Wright

and the Taliesin Fellowship

1934–1937

Compiled and with Commentary by
Randolph C. Henning

Foreword by Bruce Brooks Pfeiffer

Southern Illinois University Press · Carbondale & Edwardsville

Printed in the United States of America

Designed by David Ford

Production supervised by Natalia Nadraga

Library of Congress Cataloging-in-Publication Data

Wright, Frank Lloyd, 1867–1959.
    "At Taliesin": newspaper columns by Frank Lloyd Wright
and the Taliesin Fellowship, 1934–1937 / compiled and with
commentary by Randolph C. Henning; foreword by Bruce
Brooks Pfeiffer.
        p. cm.
    Includes index.
    1. Taliesin Fellowship. 2. Architecture—Study and
teaching—Wisconsin—Spring Green. 3. Wright, Frank
Lloyd, 1867–1959—Homes and haunts—Wisconsin—Spring
Green. I. Henning, Randolph C. II. Taliesin Fellowship.
III. Title.
NA2127.G74W75 1992
720'.7'077576—dc20   91-3501
ISBN 0-8093-1709-5   CIP

The paper used in this publication meets the minimum require-
ments of American National Standard for Information Sciences—
Permanence of Paper for Printed Library Materials, ANSI
Z39.48-1984. ♾

The Fellowship logo is a registered trademark belonging to the
Frank Lloyd Wright Foundation. Southern Illinois University
Press uses this mark with the kind permission of the Frank Lloyd
Wright Foundation.

To Maggie, Michael, and Christopher

CONTENTS

ILLUSTRATIONS

FOREWORD

by Bruce Brooks Pfeiffer

The Taliesin Fellowship was founded in 1932 as a school for apprenticeship training in architecture. The aim of the Fellowship was to develop well-rounded individuals capable of absorbing the principles of organic architecture by working alongside Frank Lloyd Wright. Paralleling work in the drafting room were many other facets of training that, among others, involved building construction and maintenance and participation in the related arts of music, painting, sculpture. This venture into education on the part of Frank Lloyd Wright and his wife, Olgivanna, had its roots deep within the background of each of the two.

Wright was born into a family of educators. His aunts, the Misses Ellen and Jane Lloyd Jones, had founded the Hillside Home School in 1886 in their ancestral valley. As children they had come into this valley with their father and mother, Richard and Mary Lloyd Jones, migrating from Wales to Wisconsin. The Welsh pioneer, as Richard was called, had been a Unitarian minister in Wales, accused of heretical preaching. Determination to seek freedom for his religious expression had prompted his migration to the United States in 1845. As Richard and Mary's family grew (five sons and four daughters), in the valley that they settled and farmed, it became necessary for a school to be built, teachers to be sought, and education to take its rightful place in the family clan. Education became a passion for the Lloyd Joneses. The method of teaching employed by the Lloyd Jones sisters was revolutionary: it was experiential training that focused on broadening the horizons of children of all ages. Specialization was discouraged; application of education and experiences in many fields was encouraged. Wright's mother, Hannah Lloyd Wright—called Anna—also took part in the educational program of the Hillside Home School.

Wright's early life was spent in close association with the school, and his first commission was the Home Building, which he designed in 1886. (It was later demolished by him in 1950). Again in 1896 he designed a structure for the school, the famed windmill tower, Romeo and Juliet. And again in 1902 he designed and built the main school building, containing an assembly room; dining room and kitchen; gymnasium; shops; classrooms; and two galleries, the Roberts Room and the Dana Gallery. These are the buildings standing today that he began converting into quarters for the Taliesin Fellowship in 1932, adding a drafting room with sixteen rooms for apprentices and modifying the original gymnasium into a playhouse-theater. A stone plaque, placed at Hillside, reads: "TO AUNT NELL AND AUNT JANE, THE LLOYD JONES SISTERS, FOUNDERS OF THESE BUILDINGS IN 1886, THE FRANK LLOYD WRIGHT FOUNDATION IN LOVING REMEMBRANCE 1932."

Olgivanna Lloyd Wright herself underwent a rigorous training at the Gurdjieff Institute for the Harmonious Development of Man from 1917 to the time she left and came to the United States in 1924. She first met Georgi Gurdjieff in the Caucasus during the outbreak of the Russian Revolution. Shortly after their meeting, she and a group of White Russian nobility and artists fled Russia under Gurdjieff's leadership and migrated to Istanbul. After traveling across Europe, the group finally settled in Fontainbleau-Avon in the famous Chateau du Prieure. The Institute attracted intellectuals and artists from Russia, France, Germany, England, and the United States. Gurdjieff's method of teaching was forceful, often harsh. But he maintained that man spent most of his life in sleep, living in an unconscious state, oblivious to the forces outside and around him as well as the forces within him. Gurdjieff further explained that man was governed from five "centers," as he called them: the intellectual, the emotion, the physical, the instinctive, and the sexual. His work with his pupils concerned itself with the first three—the mind, the heart, and the body. Gurdjieff's training was often a case of placing obstacles in front of someone, psychological as well as physical, and then watching how that person could overcome or circumvent them. The program at the Institute put everyone into a regime of hard work, physical as well as intellectual. They cooked, maintained the household, did construction work, kept up the gardens and grounds of the Chateau, as well as participating in a form of ritual exercises called "Movements"—dances, many of which were derived from the Dervish rituals of Kashgar, Chitral, and Tibet, where Gurdjieff himself earlier traveled and studied.

By 1924 Olgivanna had finished her training under Gurdjieff; he himself told her, "I have taught you all that I can, now you go out in life and live it accordingly," urging her to go to the United States, where her daughter, Svetlanna, had already been sent to live with Olgivanna's brother and his wife in New York. Following his advice, she sailed to America in November, where two weeks later she met Frank Lloyd Wright in a matinee performance in Chicago's Orchestra Hall. They immediately fell in love. Both were waiting for their respective divorces. After living together for four years—an act considered immoral and under constant attack by an outraged society, only to be sustained by Wright's great physical and emotional stamina and Olgivanna's Gurdjieff training—they were married in Rancho Santa Fe, California, in 1928. By 1932 they were safely established at Taliesin, near Spring Green, Wisconsin. There was no architectural work, the Great Depression having lowered the beam on most building in the nation not funded by the federal government. But despite such lean times, the Wrights decided to found an architectural school.

It was only logical that the pattern of training for this new school be derived from the past experiences of both Wright and his wife. The physical location of the school was the Hillside Home School of Wright's early life, in addition to his own home, Taliesin, nearby. From her own training in the Institute, Olgivanna brought many ideas and applications that molded the Taliesin Fellowship: physical work such as maintenance of the buildings, the kitchen, and the gardens, as well as construction work. The apprentices worked alongside the Wrights more as family members than students under mentors. The Wrights urged and encouraged participation in a great many activities. Music played an important role, with formal evenings and concerts performed by a chorus and chamber ensemble drawn from the Fellowship members. Eventually Olgivanna, through her daughter Iovanna, established classes in the Gurdjieff Movements for further broadening of those apprentices who chose to participate.

Though the life of the Fellowship often seemed unscheduled and hectic, in reality Olgivanna kept a keen eye on all facets of the community life while Wright was at work in the drafting room. A skilled writer herself, one wonders what her role was in the brief period of four years, from 1934 through 1937, when the Fellowship members wrote the "At Taliesin" columns that appear in this current volume. One thing is obvious, Wright himself undertook to edit them. More than five hundred manuscript pages in the Frank Lloyd Wright Archives reveal the typescripts of the columns with his voluminous notes and corrections.

This venture into journalism on the part of the Fellowship had the desired result, no doubt, of providing them with the invaluable chance of becoming articulate and expressive. That it went on for only four years was most probably because by the end of 1937 much architectural work was on the boards in the studio, and Wright needed his apprentices to work on plans and designs.

PREFACE

It began twenty-two years ago, when a near-fanatical interest in the American architect Frank Lloyd Wright was born, growing out of my choice to become an architect; it officially started some four years ago in front of the microfilm reader at the Wake Forest University Library microtext reading room — my quest to "rediscover" the "At Taliesin" newspaper column series.

Little was known of the columns other than that they were written sporadically by Wright and his Taliesin Fellowship apprentices during the 1930s and were printed in several Wisconsin newspapers, more often in the Madison newspaper the *Capital Times*. Any significance of the series was dismissed or forgotten over time. Individually only a handful of the columns, mostly those by Wright himself, have appeared in other books and sources. Wright himself included one in his own autobiography.

Going in, I expected to find only several dozen columns; maybe fifty or even one hundred ("at most"). I was unprepared for what I was eventually to find. It now reminds me of when I saw the Frank Lloyd Wright Drawings exhibit in Phoenix. Walking from room to room, viewing drawing after drawing, I quickly became overwhelmed by the shear number and magnitude of it all. The "At Taliesin" column series also became, for myself (like the Drawings exhibit), an extraordinary and significant discovery that still even now overpowers me with its breadth of information and wealth of insight. I "rediscovered" 285 columns contributed and printed during a time period of slightly less than four years (from January 11, 1934, to January 5, 1938). Only thirty-one of the columns are known to be written by Wright; the remaining were written by more than fifty-five different Fellowship apprentices. There were six different southern Wisconsin area newspapers running the column at various times. In 1936 even an Arizona newspaper — the *Chandler Arizonan* — ran a few installments.

An effort as time-consuming as this could not have been accomplished without the help and cooperation of many individuals and institutions, essential of which were the Frank Lloyd Wright Foundation and the Frank Lloyd Wright Archives, who both gave me their total and unwavering support and assistance—especially Bruce Brooks Pfeiffer, the director of the Frank Lloyd Wright Archives, and his staff of Oscar Munoz, Indira Berndtson, and Penny Fowler. Of the Frank Lloyd Wright Foundation I would like to recognize several individuals for their help—Richard Carney, Charles Montooth, Anthony Puttnam, and Daniel Ruark. It is also important that I express my appreciation to Kenney Withers, the director of the Southern Illinois University Press, for his faith in my unproven ability as a writer and for recognizing the value and significance of the "At Taliesin" column series. Similar thanks are extended to his staff for their professional expertise and guidance.

And I was extremely fortunate to have the recollections and cooperation of those apprentices still living who actually experienced the "At Taliesin" years, and who so generously shared their fond sixty-year-old memories with me—especially Cornelia Brierly, Benjamin Dombar, Philip Holliday, Yen Liang, Marya Lilien, Robert Mosher, and Kay (Schneider) Rattenbury. A few were extraordinarily interested in *"At Taliesin"* and supported its effort along the course without exception and with notable enthusiasm, each in his own way - Abrom Dombar, William "Beye" Fyfe, Pedro Guerrero, John H. Howe, Elizabeth Wright Ingraham, John Lautner, Henry Schubart and, above all, Edgar Tafel, who went more than the extra mile. Ben Masselink, brother of Eugene Masselink, helped with his recollections of his brother's early years at Taliesin. Elizabeth Kassler's 1981 Fellowship Directory was an extremely invaluable source and I thank her belatedly for her effort.

The *Capital Times / Wisconsin State Journal* (editors Dave Zweifer and Frank Denton as well as librarian Ron Larson) recognized the importance of the "At Taliesin" columns by expressing their sincere interest and support in seeing the column series be "reborn." Other institutions assisted me along the way—the State Historical Society of Wisconsin (Harold L. Miller and Myrna Williamson); the Getty Archives (Pamela Johnston); the Spencer Library at the University of

Kansas (Alexandra Mason and James Helyar); the Chandler Historical Society (Scott Soliday); the University of Wisconsin Archives (Bernard Schermetzler); the Cranbrook Archives (Carolyn Texley); the Carnegie Library of Pittsburgh (Maria Zini); SC Johnson Wax (Greg Anderegg and Judy McCrickard); the Alden B. Dow Creativity Center (Carol C. Coppage); the Northwestern University Archives (Kevin Leonard); and especially the Wake Forest University Library (Carrie Thomas of InterLibrary Loan and William Ash of Microtext) for their cooperation over the long haul.

Others who each had a different but considerable impact on me to bring to fruition *"At Taliesin"* are Peter Willoughby, Brian Spencer, Johnathan Lipman, and Stan Mallach; for their inspiration and example, architects Robert C. Broward, Dan C. Duckham, Carlos Anthony Mindreau, Donald Singer, Phil H. Feddersen, James Veal, and especially Larry Wayne Grantham; for his invaluable assistance, support, and guidance, architect and Frank Lloyd Wright author Patrick J. Meehan. Special thanks are extended to friends Brian Hart and Randy Harris for their computer expertise.

Lastly, I would like to thank my parents, Jim and Shirley Henning, whom I owe more than I know I realize; my brothers and sisters, grandparents (God rest their souls), aunts and uncles, nieces and nephews, cousins and friends, who for these many years heard more than they wished to regarding Frank Lloyd Wright (A special thanks to my Uncle Bob and Aunt Sharon Gruber and my cousin Kris who helped by reviewing four years of the *Daily Cardinal* newspaper for "At Taliesin" columns.)

For all the errors, inaccuracies, and inadequacies I accept full and complete responsibility. My apologies also to those that I may have forgotten to mention and whose help I failed to recognize.

To Maggie, my wife and best friend, and to my two sons, Michael and Christopher—thank you for your sacrifice, patience, understanding, and love.

Finally, as Wright knew, "WHAT A MAN DOES THAT HE HAS." This work represents my respect and appreciation for his life and is my contribution to his living legacy.

''AT TALIESIN''

INTRODUCTION

Even if it did seem a shaky time to begin a new work venture, Frank Lloyd Wright (1867–1959) and his wife, Olgivanna, knew it was the right time for the Taliesin Fellowship, when they formed it in the midst if the Great Depression in October 1932. Wright's architectural work was virtually nonexistent and financial responsibilities and liabilities continued to grow. Taliesin, Wright's southwestern Wisconsin home, located on two hundred acres of ancestral, pastoral land near the town of Spring Green, required constant attention. Apprentices would, and could, bring forth the needed physical and financial assistance. More important though to Wright, as he was approaching his late sixties, the Fellowship could renew and enliven the stimulating and creative environment too long dormant at Taliesin. As Wright states in his autobiography, "like fingers on my hand, [the Fellowship] would increase not only my own interest and enthusiasm for my work as an architect, but would also widen my capacity to apply it in the field in their interest."

As the initial 1932 prospectus indicated, Wright's original intention for the Fellowship experiment was "an extension of architecture at Taliesin to the architecture of music, sculpture and painting by way of agriculture, manufacture and building to include seventy apprentices and seven." Soon thereafter, however, Wright abandoned that ambitious idea as being "too far institutional or educational" and turned toward forming a much more informal but creative enclave for "twenty-three apprentices." The textbook used by Wright for Fellowship instruction was the unwritten, "unpopular Gospel of Work." Learning by doing replaced the "book learning" curriculum of the universities. As Wright explained in his "At Taliesin" column of July 13, 1934, "Work has been knocked out of American youth by way of inflated 'education' and it is going to be no easy matter, as I can see, to put the joy back into work that makes it creative and lifts it above drudgery." Two years later, Eugene Masselink provides his own definition of what the Taliesin Fellowship had become in a letter to Hans Koch, dated July 9, 1936, "The Fellowship is this group of us working together for an ideal all under the direct leadership of a great creative brain and spirit—all of us owing allegiance to him and to the principle which he represents and interprets and has taken us in with him to enlarge and extend in work." The Taliesin Fellowship thus soon became a working spirit of devotion and love to an organic way of life. Many apprentices stayed only a short time, some only a year or two, during these early Fellowship years for various reasons (financial, restlessness, disagreements with the Wright's and/or the Fellowship philosophy, family matters, embarking on a career). Some apprentices stayed for several years, some stayed until after Wright's death, and some are still at Taliesin. A few apprentices are even buried at Taliesin in the family cemetery adjacent to Unity Chapel.

The Taliesin Playhouse at Hillside officially opened Wednesday evening, November 1, 1933 (although local newspapers record an earlier October 8). An account of the Taliesin Playhouse building was featured in an article by the *Capital Times* on November 1 (see appendix A), and a report of the opening night festivities was carried the following day, when "more than 200 guests witnessed the first public showing of sound pictures in the unique little theater." Wright and the Fellowship presented four films (*The Merry Wives of Vienna,* a Walt Disney Silly Symphony, *Broken Lullaby,* an Aesop's Fables animated cartoon) and served lunch at an intermission between the second and third films. The article went on to describe the lunch: "the guests were taken to the huge, partially completed draughting room, where barbecued pork sandwiches, coffee and doughnuts were served. At one end of this room, which resembles an old baronial hall, was a huge stone fireplace. On a spit over the fire hung large pieces of pig, from which generous slices were cut for the sandwiches."

The Taliesin Playhouse would thereafter, each Sunday afternoon, offer weekly movies for the public's enjoyment. More often than not in the early years of the Fellowship the feature picture was not an American film but one from various foreign countries. The film, an interpretation offered by an apprentice, and informal conversation, with coffee and doughnuts, were the usual Sunday afternoon fare.

Soon, weekly announcements regarding the next scheduled cinematic showing at the Playhouse began appearing in Spring Green's local newspaper, the *Weekly Home News*. Just into the new year of 1934, the announcements began to also include descriptions of weekly events and visitors at Taliesin.

The "At Taliesin" column series officially began in the two Madison newspapers — the *Capital Times* and the *Wisconsin State Journal*. Coincidentally, each paper ran their first installment (both different columns written by different apprentices) on the same day, February 2, 1934. Obviously, the column grew out of a simple and practical need to advertise the weekly film event to a greater readership. Wright enjoyed a good relationship with the newspapers during the early Fellowship years and often entertained the editors, writers, and columnists from the local area as well as the Madison press corps. William T. Evjue (editor of the *Capital Times*), Betty Cass (columnist for the *Wisconsin State Journal*), Ernest L. Meyer (columnist for the *Capital Times*), and Albert L. Sherman (editor and publisher of the *Grant County Herald*) were frequent and invited guests.

In a letter to William T. Evjue, dated January 30, 1934, Wright talks about his plans for the column: "Herewith is some matter for the little weekly column under the caption TALIESIN of which we talked. . . . There will be a different writer each time selected from among the Fellowship and we hope to make it worth reading every time. I have an idea we should have a number of newspapers hereabouts carrying a similar weekly item—all differently written by different apprentices." And Wright was successful in getting the series in several newspapers. Soon after the two Madison newspapers began carrying the column, it was picked up by the University of Wisconsin student newspaper, the *Daily Cardinal,* and Spring Green's *Weekly Home News*. Two other Wisconsin newspapers would carry the series sporadically (Lancaster's *Grant County Herald* and the Mineral Point *Iowa County Democrat*). Several columns even appeared in 1936 in the *Chandler Arizonan*. The newspapers ran the series as a favor to, and out of their respect for, Wright; neither Wright nor the Fellowship received any money for the columns. Taliesin did not even receive free subscriptions from the newspapers in return for the series. What Wright and the Fellowship did get was free advertisement for the weekly feature film event and a conduit through which they

"More dramatic elsewhere, perhaps. . . . but nothing that picks you up in its arms and so gently, almost lovingly, cradles you as do these southwestern Wisconsin hills. . . . I feel my roots in these hillsides as I know those of the oak that have struck in here besides me. We understand each other" (Frank Lloyd Wright, "At Taliesin," July 20, 1034). *Taliesin Countryside*. Photo courtesy of the Kenneth Spencer Research Library, University of Kansas, "Taliesin Collection."

OVERLEAF:*"Taliesin—The Domain of Frank Lloyd Wright and the Taliesin Fellowship"* (ca. 1930s; drawn from memory by John Howe). Drawing courtesy of John H. Howe, Architect, and Edgar A. Tafel, Architect.

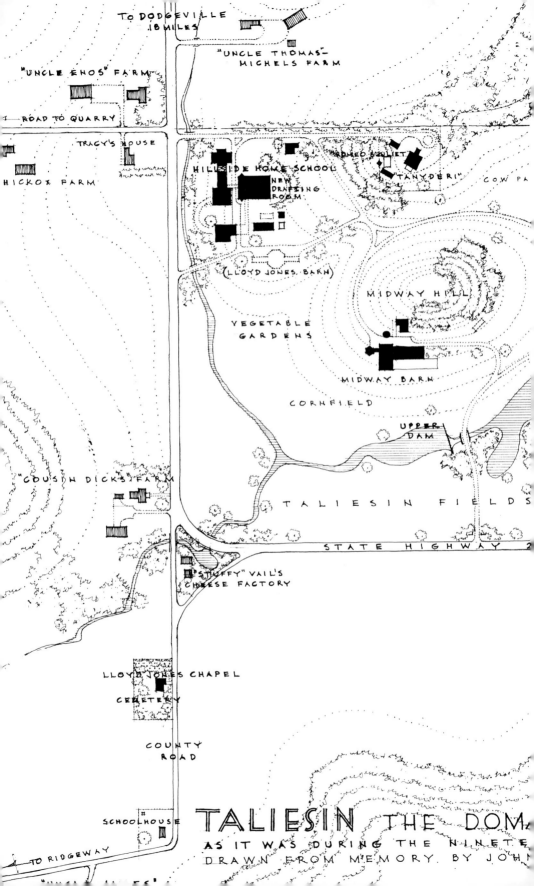

TO DODGEVILLE
.18 MILES

"UNCLE THOMAS"
MICHELS FARM

"UNCLE ENOS" FARM

ROAD TO QUARRY

TRACY'S HOUSE

HICKOX FARM

HILLSIDE HOME SCHOOL

NEW DRAFTING ROOM

ROMEO JULIET

"TANYDERI"

COW PA

(LLOYD JONES BARN)

MIDWAY HILL

VEGETABLE GARDENS

MIDWAY BARN

CORNFIELD

UPPER DAM

"COUSIN DICK'S FARM"

TALIESIN FIELDS

STATE HIGHWAY 2

"STUFFY" VAIL'S CHEESE FACTORY

LLOYD JONES CHAPEL

CEMETERY

COUNTY ROAD

SCHOOLHOUSE

TO RIDGEWAY

TALIESIN THE DOM
AS IT WAS DURING THE NINETE
DRAWN FROM MEMORY. BY JOH

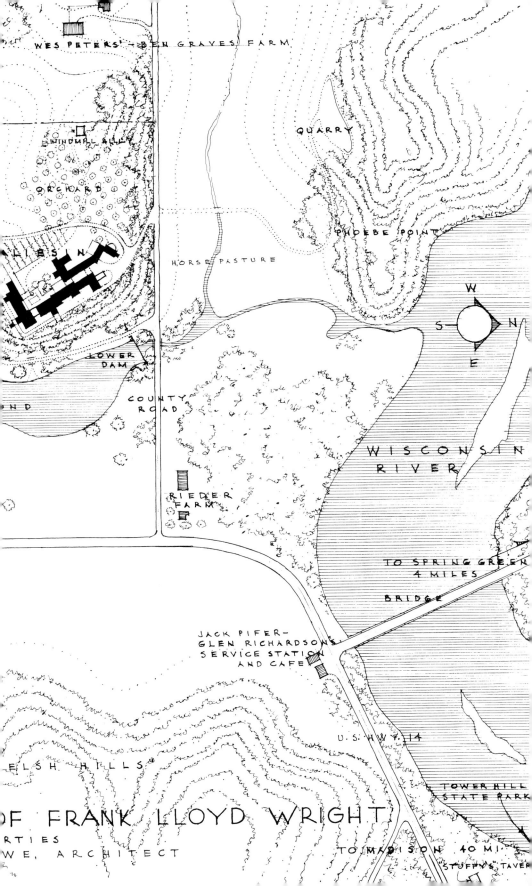

WES PETERS' — BEN GRAVES' FARM

QUARRY

WINDMILL HILL

ORCHARD

PHOEBE POINT

TALIESIN

HORSE PASTURE

W

S   N

E

LOWER DAM

COUNTY ROAD

WISCONSIN RIVER

RIEDER FARM

TO SPRING GREEN 4 MILES

BRIDGE

JACK PIFER — GLEN RICHARDSON'S SERVICE STATION AND CAFE

U.S. HWY. 14

WELSH HILLS

TOWER HILL STATE PARK

OF FRANK LLOYD WRIGHT

...RTIES

...WE, ARCHITECT

TO MADISON 40 MI.

"STUFFY'S TAVERN"

"It was the poet and philosopher Cervantes who said, "The road is always better than the inn." *Frank Lloyd Wright on Road Grader at Taliesin* (ca. 1930s). Photo courtesy of the Frank Lloyd Wright Foundation.

Hillside Home School, 1902 (photo ca. 1910; future Fellowship living room *at right end* and Taliesin Playhouse *foreground*). Photo courtesy of the State Historical Society of Wisconsin.

Frank Lloyd Wright in Taliesin Studio with Apprentices (photo ca. mid-1930s; apprentices *left to right:* Eugene Masselink, Benjamin Dombar, Edgar Tafel, and John Howe). Photo courtesy of the Frank Lloyd Wright Foundation.

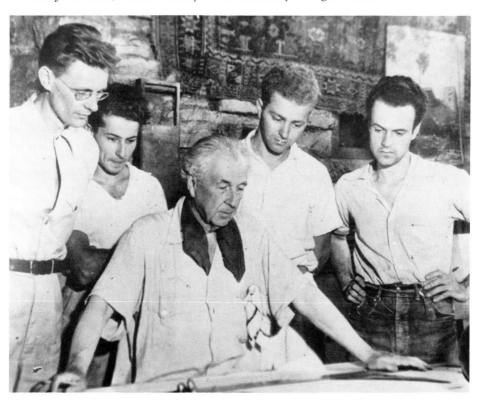

"Greetings from Hillside" (1933 Christmas card designed by William "Beye" Fyfe and sent to his parents; a winter silhouette depicting Hillside Home School; used for the *Capital Times* "At Taliesin" masthead). Drawing courtesy of William "Beye" Fyfe.

Taliesin Christmas Card, 1933 (a winter silhouette depicting Taliesin hilltower wing *in background,* with steps to the tea circle; variation used for the *Wisconsin State Journal* "At Taliesin" masthead). Drawing courtesy of the Frank Lloyd Wright Foundation.

"At Taliesin" Masthead Design for the Capital Times, 1934 (a winter silhouette of the Hillside Home School). Drawing courtesy of the Frank Lloyd Wright Foundation.

"At Taliesin" Masthead Design for the Wisconsin State Journal, 1934 (a winter silhouette of steps to Taliesin tea circle, with hilltower wing *in background*). Drawing courtesy of the Frank Lloyd Wright Foundation.

"At Taliesin" Masthead Design for Three Other Local Newspapers. 1934 (view of Taliesin hilltower wing). Drawing courtesy of the Frank Lloyd Wright Foundation.

Hillside Fellowship Drafting Room under Construction (photo ca. 1934; note piers under construction for connection to dining room wing never completed and Romeo and Juliet *in background right*). Photo courtesy of the Frank Lloyd Wright Foundation.

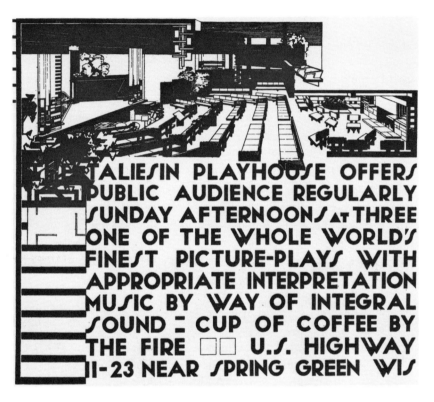

Taliesin Playhouse Advertisement, 1933 (used as a three-column advertisement in the *Capital Times,* as a three-foot-square plywood billboard panel; also incorporated within the December 1933 Fellowship Prospectus). Drawing courtesy of the Frank Lloyd Wright Foundation.

presented a kaleidoscopic anthology of Taliesin life in the mid-1930s.

Wright explained the column series in his autobiography as simply, "Architects, I thought, had need to be especially articulate." Eugene Masselink would later explain "At Taliesin" more completely in a letter, dated November 27, 1934, to the *Milwaukee Journal* (attempting to "spread this weekly column further throughout the state by the medium of your newspaper"). "Each article every week is written by a different apprentice upon a subject of his own choosing relating to the life at Taliesin under the direction of Frank Lloyd Wright. . . . These articles are a living record of this development. Frequently, too, they are discourses on matters of universal interest in fields of architecture, the allied arts, and philosophic and economic issues. Coming from this organic point of view they are significant contributions." In spite of the *Milwaukee Journal* declining Masselink's offer to run the series, "At Taliesin" prospered in Madison for four years, with publication of 285 columns written by more than fifty-five contributors. As almost 20 percent of the columns ran without authorship indicated, it is difficult to assign statistics to the series. However, Frank Lloyd Wright himself wrote at least thirty-one columns, with the remaining being contributed by Fellowship apprentices, Taliesin craftsmen and workers, and others not associated officially with the Fellowship. Wright would usually review and sometimes heavily edit the columns; other times the column was printed exactly as written. Apprentices volunteered to write columns usually of their own choosing; occasionally Wright, Mrs. Wright, and/or Eugene Masselink would seek out volunteers and/or suggest topics. There were times, of course, when a column did not get written because of work pressures at Taliesin or a Fellowship crisis, and thus "At Taliesin" did not appear every week. Three different mastheads were designed to introduce the columns within the newspapers. The mastheads for the *Capital Times* (a graphic depicting a winter silhouette of the Hillside Home School building) and the *Wisconsin State Journal* (a graphic depicting a winter silhouette of the steps up to the Taliesin tea circle with the hilltower wing in the background) were inspired by a Taliesin Christmas card designed and drawn by William "Beye" Fyfe in 1933. A third design (a drawing of the Taliesin hilltower wing) was used sporadically by the *Weekly Home News,* the *Grant County Herald,* and the *Iowa County*

Democrat.

John Howe spoke of the columns in his "At Taliesin" contribution of July 5, 1936, as "these amateur articles, some quite good (?) and some not so good. But all in one direction. And we do 'kill several birds with one pebble,' for, by the pebbles we throw from time to time—we ourselves grow and our neighbors are made acquainted with what we are, what we are doing, and what we intend to do and you who read them are seeing something grow up out of our own soil."

The 112 "At Talieisn" columns included herein attempt to represent the full range and breadth of the entire series. The date listed for each column was the date the column was printed in the newspaper (if the column appeared in more than one newspaper, which happened often in the later "At Taliesin" years, the date listed indicates the date the column appeared first). In only a few instances was the date of the original manuscript used in lieu of the newspaper publication date (some of the original manuscripts still exist, most within the Frank Lloyd Wright Archives, with the majority of the manuscripts not dated). There are four columns used herein (transcribed from their original manuscripts) that were not found printed in any newspaper. The columns have been reprinted in their entirety and in their same form except for the silent emending of obvious misspellings, typographical errors, and oversights and for the italicizing of film, book, journal, and newspaper titles. I have added explanation and commentary only where I felt it was important to the "story" or critical to a column's clarity. Even though several of Wright's "At Taliesin" columns have been reprinted, the columns included in this volume are being reprinted for the first time.

1 9 3 4

We are getting on pretty well with every ten cents doing a ten dollar job.

—Frank Lloyd Wright, letter to Heinrich Klumb, December 2, 1933

INTRODUCTION

It was the year that the FBI finally caught up with John Dillinger, while the entire country was still caught in the clutches of the Great Depression. Even Frank Lloyd Wright and his young two-year-old Taliesin Fellowship did not escape its grip, for outside commissions were few.

Early in 1934 the only architectural commission was the redesign of the Willey residence (as Wright conveyed to Klumb in the December 2 letter, "have redesigned the Willey's House and they will now get poetry instead of drama. Drama always comes high, I guess"). The drawings for the Willey residence were finished and construction commenced in June (the Willeys moved in late December). Other commissions did find their way to Taliesin, but not until late in 1934. The Memorial to the Soil Chapel (Cooksville, Wisconsin) was designed in December and conversation began regarding the Marcus residence (Dallas, Texas) and Kaufmann's Pittsburgh Planetarium and a weekend retreat in Bear Run. Another little-known and mostly forgotten project was executed in April in Oak Park, Illinois, for a long-time friend and previous client's wife, Grace Pebbles. Pebbles operated several restaurants in the Chicago area and opened the Blue Parrot Patio Restaurant in 1931. A room off the main dining room (the Blue Parrot "Celebrity Room") became the object of a Taliesin Fellowship project with walls "decorated" with mural silhouettes of various

Wright-designed Oak Park buildings (seven houses plus Unity Temple and the St. Marks-in-the-Bowery project). These full wall murals took their inspiration from 1933 Christmas cards designed by apprentice William "Beye" Fyfe. Fyfe designed and did the actual execution of the project for Pebbles. (Wright saw the room and expressed to Fyfe in a letter dated November 6, 1934, that "the whole place is a credit to us all."). Finally, it was reported in the *Capital Times* in November that Wright "has been engaged to design a new home for Claudette Colbert," the Hollywood film actress. However, the design never proceeded, and curiously, Wright's son Lloyd received the commission and proceeded to design Colbert a "period" home in the Hollywood Hills section of Hollywood.

The Fellowship was kept busy with many Taliesin- and Hillside-related construction projects in 1934. Modifications related to Taliesin was the addition of "Scherzo" (eight-year-old Iovanna's bedroom) and changes to Taliesin's Hilltower wing (the Fellowship dining room and apprentice dormitories). Massive efforts took place at Hillside with the Dana Gallery and Charles E. Roberts Room completed, the laying of the drafting room stone floor begun, development of the design with construction actually beginning on the foundations for the Fellowship dining room wing, etc., as well as modifications to the Playhouse interior and curtain. Apprentices' efforts also involved reissuing a new Fellowship prospectus early in 1934 and designing and issuing the inaugural "Taliesin" monograph late in the year (which contained various articles by Wright, the apprentices, and others as well as Wright's One- and Two-Zone House designs). They also were repairing architectural models, weaving, farming, cooking, on infinitum — practicing Wright's and the Fellowship's "Gospel of Work" (i.e., "education by doing").

In November 1934 work began on the Fellowship's magnum opus during the "At Taliesin" years—a four-month-long, intensive effort constructing the various models and explanatory panels required to present Wright's Broadacre City concept to the New York public at the Industrial Arts Exposition in April 1935.

Special visitors and the public visiting and touring Taliesin were reported throughout the "At Taliesin" column series. Georgi Gurdjieff visited several times in 1934 as well as the Wisconsin congressman

Thomas Amlie and renowned landscape architect Jens Jensen; others were future clients Edgar Kaufmann, Sr., George Parker, and Stanley Marcus. The newspaper corps visited often, and beginning officially in May, the general public was able to receive a guided tour on weekends by one of the apprentices of the Taliesin and Hillside complex (for fifty cents per person).

The "At Taliesin" column series' most prolific and voluminous year was its inaugural year of 1934. More than 120 columns were written, representing about 40 percent of the entire column series. Wright wrote at least 8 columns, with the remaining contributed by more than thirty different apprentices (one-fourth of the columns printed in 1934 were done so without the contributor's name, so it is difficult to establish exactly how many columns were written by Wright and by each specific apprentice). Subjects spanned world politics and overseas affairs to American universities and education; from agricultural, social, and economic situations and solutions to Russian culture. The Playhouse's weekend planned events continued to receive notice, as did the comings and goings of the Fellowship and visitors. Fellowship traditions began and were continued as described in the columns. The first official Fellowship wedding was reported. Apprentice-given "sermonettes" were created and heard in the nearby Unity Chapel, and Wright began his practice of informal talks to the Fellowship in 1934. Pianist Glen Sherman, Taliesin's first musician-in-residence, came for the summer.

The following representative columns correspond to the majority of those printed in 1934—contributors describing and praising the daily life, experiences, and opportunities for creative growth at Taliesin not only as apprentice members but as actual living extensions of the organic philosophy of Frank Lloyd Wright.

AT TALIESIN
February 2, 1934

The moon casts long shadows of great chimneys on low-flowing roof surfaces—onto flagstone courtyards—to earth. Suddenly the shadowed silence is shattered by the clear ringing of a bell. Human shadows come straggling now—and lights. Fires begin to burn in some of the huge fireplaces. Another bell. Insistent this time. BREAK-FAST. More human shadows come along the moonlit hilltop. Finally a burst of electricity reveals a sleepy group none too poetically breaking fast by moonlight.

At Taliesin the moon is caught napping. In another hour work begins on the road, in the fields, and in the studio. Thirty or more apprentices at Taliesin who are a part of the Fellowship under the leadership of Frank Lloyd Wright (yes, he is also breakfasting at the same time) have wiped sleep from their eyes and are about their business while city folk are still dreaming.

During the day work is conducted in spontaneous fashion under the supervision of the "chief of the fortnight." The chief is one of the apprentices—now Paul Beidler—who is in charge of activities for two weeks with two assistants, his place being taken at the end of that time by an assistant. A rotating system placing each apprentice in full charge in succession. Work is done out of doors until four in the afternoon. At that time tea by the fire in the studio is welcome. Between tea time and dinner at 7, everyone works in the studio—draughting, building models, painting, drawing. After dinner time, relaxation. Lights out at 10 o'clock. There is no routine of work. Each day is an excitement, an individuality itself.

The idea of culture and belief in an organic architecture which is the central line upon which the Taliesin Fellowship is built is enlivened by various activities. The only feature of the Fellowship life to which the public is invited and admitted are the activities at the Playhouse. There, regularly on Sunday afternoons at 3, a program is presented usually consisting of Pathe News, a Walt Disney "animation," and some famous feature picture selected with discrimination from the best the movie world, not only in America but in Europe, has to offer. The program is rounded out by the playing of good music and a feature of the afternoon is an interpretive talk preceding the picture and given by some chosen member of the Fellowship. Last Sunday Beye Fyfe interpreted Sovkino's *Golden Mountains*. Next Sunday Mary Lautner will introduce *Topaze*. To help make the occasion entirely informal, after the incoming guests have deposited their coats and hats in the cloakrooms, coffee is served to them about the fireplace.

Around this fireplace in the past few months have come men like Rockwell Kent, the painter, the traveller and author who showed several reels of film he made while in Greenland; Baker Brownell, author and chairman of the Department of Philosophy at Northwestern University and Ferdinand Scheville, author historian, from the University of Chicago; string quartets from Milwaukee and from Madison have played together with other musicians. Painters have brought their work to the Sunday supper hour gatherings at Taliesin.

Two Sundays ago after the supper hour, Thomas Amlie, former congressman, led a fast discussion on present day social and economic questions in relation to government. Last Sunday Alexius Baas, well-schooled baritone from Madison came to sing a program of Schubert Lieder and gave to the Fellowship two important poetic songs from manuscript not yet published. Franz Aust from the University of Wisconsin came also on Sunday with James Drought and illustrated his talk on the natural beauties of Wisconsin with a collection of beautifully colored slides. At the Playhouse previously was shown a full program of Russian films and music.

A Fellowship play—Piranesi Calico—is in rehearsal at the Playhouse. The apprentices have written it, and the music as well. They are setting it and producing it.

EUGENE MASSELINK

Next Sunday, Feb. 4, at 3 o'clock the feature picture at the Playhouse will be *Topaze,* in which John Barrymore plays the leading role and Myrna Loy is the feminine star. Besides the usual Pathe News, the customary Disney "animation" will be *Traffic Troubles.*

AT TALIESIN

February 9, 1934

Two new rooms added to the pageant of Taliesin's 40 rooms merely by lowering the ceiling of the loggia and raising the roof above it to get the most playful room in the house. The boys call it a "scherzo." This is little eight-year-old Iovanna's room. Until now she was the only apprentice who didn't have his or her own room.

Several new apprentices, with the aid of two carpenters, were working on the job continuously from the architect's first sketch on a shingle to designing and building in of the furniture. And the girls made the curtains. In celebration of the completion of the room we had a "room-warming" in the form of a surprise party for Iovanna. Being quite an authoress herself she thoroughly enjoyed our treat which was a different fairy story told to her by each apprentice as they were all sitting on the floor about the fireplace. The rest is up to her. She will carry the wood for her fireplace and keep the room in order. This will develop her sense of responsibility, a valuable trait that few grown-ups seem to have.

Much of this week was spent in preparing for the Playhouse "warming." A group of apprentices with overalls and wrenches in their hands are seen talking to Scotty, the master steam fitter. He explains to them a few fundamentals, then points out a radiator for them to connect up. They know just what to do and why. They cut the threads on the end of a pipe and screw on the nipple. It is all recreation to them. They enjoy it as much as the models they are building the day before. Relaxation to these fellows merely means changing to a different job.

And when it is all connected these same boys fire the boilers; they hear the crackling of the flames and then the sizzling of the steam and begin to "feel" the steam go through the pipes and into the radiators. And then—Oh! Boy! what a thrill.

Sunday was the first Fellowship wedding. Perhaps the most unique wedding in history. The bride Margaret Astre and the groom Vernon Allen were driven in the old Victorian carriage from Taliesin to our chapel, where the services were held at high noon. The weather was perfect and it was just cool enough to make the rough roads hard enough to hold up under the thin-tired wheels of the coach, two stalwart black horses and coachman perched high on his seat; his boots, wallow-tail coat and high silk hat completing the picture. The moment they left Taliesin the chapel bell began to toll and continued until they arrived. Then the services began. We sang "Oh Comfort Me My Lord" and "Holy, Holy, Holy." Rev. Holloway, Unitarian minister

of Madison, next delivered a beautiful sermon to the couple. He
stressed the importance of friendship between man and wife and the
freedom of the two individuals as individuals and not to over-
emphasize sex. A simple ceremony followed, climaxed by the vigorous
ringing of the bell — then gaiety and laughter.

A little later we had a barbecue lunch right there in the chapel. In
the midst of this Rev. Holloway read "Autumn" from Mr. Wright's
Autobiography. It depicted his boyhood days in that same chapel — the
same altar — the same rocking chairs in which his aunts and uncles
would sit and weep for joy. They have long been lying in the wooded
graveyard on the side of the chapel and perhaps were at our services
Sunday and if so were happy in sensing the sincerely religious emotion
in the hearts of all these youngsters who have taken their places in the
valley. So having them as our tradition and the opening service Sunday
as our precedent we will have a different representative of each faith
come to our chapel every Sunday morning and preach to us. The public
is invited. This Sunday we will have Father Dietz of Milwaukee. And
in the afternoon at three o'clock at the Playhouse there will be a
Sovkino feature comedy *Three Comrades and One Invention* — Sovkino
animated cartoon and a Silly Symphony — a chance to compare the
work of Russia and America.

Franz Aust came again (welcome Franz). He outlined a new scheme
whereby any scientist can evaluate artist phenomena. His plan juggles
changes made in similar compositions compared on a page and you are
asked to make a decision between them. This decision Prof. Aust says,
may consist in choosing "the least offensive." The subjects are a vase, a
house and yard, an abstract, drawing, an advertisement for a hat — etc.
Each picture is a little different and one must decide which picture is
the better.

Of course associated with all this goes a categorical arrangement
adding up all decisions to fit in the "educative" routine. We filed our
names on the date line and dived into the "intelligence test." Under-
lining the plates — choosing the lesser of evils most of the plates were
evil to arrive at the basis of aesthetic judgment invited. Well, the
record on this give-away sheet must give one away as any pedantic test
system whatsoever would do in any case. Juggling statistics can't
discover or uncover artistic values.

Anyway we had fun co-operating. It is a nice game. Earnestly but unfortunately Franz has approached a worthy thing from the usual disjunctive rather than from the constructive side. Where art is concerned the scientist always cuts out the head of his drum to see where the sound came from.

ABE DOMBAR

AT TALIESIN

February 16, 1934

To many of the readers of this weekly column, "Taliesin" is perhaps little more than a pen name. Probably many of you think of it vaguely as a little town somewhere out about 30 miles west of Madison. It is rapidly becoming known to some as the name of a theater where one can go to see good foreign films. But to most of our readers, Taliesin is simply that very exceptional home of Frank Lloyd Wright, and the present residence of Mr. Wright's new group of apprentices.

And you must think, from the occasional reports which get to town what a very odd place it is, (if you think of it as a "school") where classes (if we happened to have any) were interrupted by a recess to help a balking truck up the front hill with a load of firewood, where books are supplanted by drawing boards, and where lectures are postponed for picnics.

And so, I would like to give you some more definite idea of Taliesin and the Taliesin Fellowship. It is true that the Fellowship would be a very odd school, if it meant to be a school at all. It doesn't. And if it did, it would not be "Mr. Wright's school." Our resources, our products, and our ideas all belong to a philosophy of life. This philosophy we call "organic."

The desire for an organic life and an organic art is old, —very old. We are here at Taliesin with Mr. Wright not because we believe he has invented something which we want to learn about, but because we feel that his life and work are an outstanding example of this organic life.

The idea of organic life is not an abstruse one. As I see it, it means a simpler, more natural life, closer to the soil and to the things which always have and always will give men and women greatest peace and satisfaction. Nature, beauty, honesty and a host of other values which you can name as well as I. It is a philosophy which honors sincerity, love, and common sense above material successes.

We think, furthermore, that the world hasn't had enough of this kind of thing lately. That the present economic mess is largely due to the neglect of those aims which should be fundamental. That our country is economically bankrupt now because we are paying entirely too much attention to economics and economies in the 1920s. That spiritual, artistic, and religious insolvencies preceded and caused the 1929 crash, which, I hope I may call without appearing flippant, a minor one.

We are not reformers in the sense that we wish to substitute a new "system" for the present one, because we believe that all the present system needs is men and women trained to do well beautifully and with an eye on human enjoyment, the work which today is being done crossly and carelessly for private profit. Our ambition is to send into the production world people, or the work of people, who realize how complete life can be when ideals of beauty supplant those of material success in terms of the dollar.

And so we are working instead of studying. We study of course, to learn to work effectively, but the study is a means rather than an end. We hope to have at our disposal machinery typical of the most advanced commercial practice in the trades of woodworking, weaving, metal working, pottery, glass blowing, and so on, in order to leave here with knowledge enough to be able to put new vitality into the work being done in those fields and particularly in the field of architecture to which Taliesin believes they all belong.

So far, we have been concerned chiefly with organic architecture as beautiful building. We have built much. But we are also concerned with organic architecture as the beautiful designing of all the appurtenances of our lives, from farming to motor cars. We have farmed much. And we have pushed a great many motor cars up this icy hill out front. And these are some of the reasons why the Taliesin Fellowship would be a very odd school, if it were a school, as it certainly does not intend to be.

The telephone rang and a voice asked for Mr. Wright, who was in Madison. Undaunted, the voice went on to ask, "Are you one of the architects at Wright's. Yes . . . well then, what is a three letter word meaning the cap of the pitch of a roof—the first two letters of which are E-P?"

The voice went on, "Well, have you a student from Mexico—I want a four letter word for a Mexican plant beginning with Q."

Editor Evjue and poet Ernest Meyer came to see us at supper hour last Sunday. Together the two men made a complete evening. Fast conversation and exciting tales. Then together we all listened to the usual music—piano, violin, and singing. Outside contacts like this are valuable and stimulating and good fun.

BOB BISHOP

AT TALIESIN
February 16, 1934

The New Education

For years the founder and conductor of the Taliesin Fellowship has been addressing the world publicly with his architecture. Recently he has added the written word to his medium with such work as *An Autobiography, The Disappearing City,* and *Princeton Lectures.* More recently he addressed the students of the University of Wisconsin particularly in the 1933 Badger. It might be well to read that article again, for essence of it is in existence here at the Taliesin Fellowship.

The article began: "As advocate of an organic architecture for our country I have gradually learned that no architecture genuine or great is possible to us as our system of education stands. Nor great art of any kind. Youth is not trusted."

At Taliesin—under the ever present counsel and guidance of Mr. Wright—one apprentice and two apprentice aides have complete charge of the Fellowship. Each term for a fortnight and rotating through the group, so we may grasp the significance of the entity and grow with our individual experiences. To realize more clearly the relation of the farm unit to the entertainments; of the kitchens to the drafting jobs, of hauling and cutting wood to the Saturday and Sunday evening dinners; of the digging of trenches and laying of pipe lines to rehearsals of plays and Sundays at the Playhouse; it is all tied together, even our filling of silos has its relation to our afternoon teas in the studio. But above all—Youth is trusted.

Taliesin is not an institution. Taliesin is not an art colony. We all aspire to be artists—and who shouldn't—we fledglings, apprentices, hope to become someday by at present and forever doing "whatever befitteth the man."

When living, working, in and for the present, and in anticipation of the future, it is difficult to recall past labors that might share a light on the weekly day as it is lived. Even the results of those labors are not long contemplated when growth is necessary, and we are growing.

At 4 o'clock each day our work day ends. But after a time for tea and conversation in the studio, work begins. Design of the Willey House in Minneapolis; the building of models for exhibition in spring; design of the set for the play; making of posters; weaving; drawing; concentrated Fellowship activity until dinner at seven. After dinner, music or work for a change or a change of work.

It might be of mutual favor to us to choose the stately Romeo and Juliet for a vista of the weekend activities. Romeo and Juliet is our faithful windmill that continues to whirl us the water and chuckle with the wind at the fallen scoffers who odd years ago proclaimed its doom with the first storm and who went down while this animate structure still lives and works.

A group comes sprinting down the incline from Taliesin—boy and girl apprentices—some vaulting the barbed fence, some climbing through. The group that this fortnight's "chief," Paul Beidler, or the next, Phil Holliday, has chosen to clean the dishes for this Saturday's tea and music concert, or to help with the steam-fitting or to work in the carpentry shop. In a few minutes the rip saw will be buzzing. Before long the dishes will be washed and the fireplace be given its nourishment, for wood is already being unloaded near the entrance. And we may be sure that at sometime this morning Scotty, our steamfitter supreme will admonish one of the newer apprentices in such a fashion. "You might well be handling that bloody pick as if you we-r-re a ch-a-r-ristian. You-r-re not thinking it a golf club, ar-re you?" Scotty "did" two years at Oxford and outside of that has lived for about 40 years.

And so the activity will go on, until . . . the clank of the traditional dinner bell summons them to give way to their complementary appetites of food and drink.

After lunch another group will cover the same tracks from Taliesin unit number one, to Hillside, unit number two. A group indistinguishable by its actions; but for a different purpose — to rehearse the play that is apprentice-written, apprentice-directed, apprentice-acted, and the music, apprentice-composed. Our first attempt at the so-called "legitimate" to establish the drama as architecture, where it belongs, and do it indigenously as possible. We believe that although the play be apprentice-produced it could still be a foreigner unless we treat the locale we know the best and the subject we have recognized as the center line of our becoming architecture. This gives us for our field, the universe. For architecture is the basis of all arts — all arts being architecture and parts of the whole.

Rehearsals, steam fitting and ditch digging continue until time for tea and then, at 4 o'clock is the hegira to the Playhouse. Tea and cakes, a fire in the fireplace and in the boiler and concert through our channels of integral sound of Brahms' First Symphony, and Franck's Variations. Then an apprentice-made supper in the theater that preludes our preview of the Sunday playbill. Our way back across the fields is lighted by the moon, or its handy and unpretentious substitute, the flashlight, unless we've all become too accustomed to the moon and the flashlight has been left where we are going — Taliesin.

Sunday afternoon at the Fellowship. From Romeo and Juliet one gapes in wonder at the variety of scenes from which he might choose. Focus is difficult until cars begin to drive up to the theater for the public performance of the playbill that is chosen from the products of the world. By 3 o'clock the bulk of the audience is at ease. In the theater focus is not difficult, it is naturally on the stage, a time for the usual orientation to the quality and environment; to the departures from stiff and antiquated architecture, the ease, the sun pressing through the shades and glowing on the walls, the lighting, the thing as a whole, then, naturally to the stage. The center of interest. The product of movement. The medium of the celluloid strip and the sound track is given full vent in a kind of release as the audience in comfort, sipping coffee and eating cakes and smoking, witnesses one of the world's finest picture plays.

Sunday night—our night with our guests. Ernest Meyer caught the spirit of our Sunday nights when he was here with his wife and the Evjues last Sunday. He transferred it to the Tuesday *Capital Times.* And if tomorrow is Monday, as no doubt one tomorrow will be it begins at orthodox 5:30, with breakfast at orthodox 6, and work after 7— willingly adding tired to tired and adding it again for tomorrow and tomorrow and tomorrow.

NICHOLAS RAY

[As apprentice Nicholas Ray wrote, Ernest Meyer remembered his impressions of Taliesin in his daily column entitled "Making Light of the Times" (reprinted herein, see appendix C).]

AT TALIESIN

March 22, 1934

Now that spring is here—I hope it is—we will begin to prepare for delightful summer months. We don't just go around the corner or go downtown to get our food, we grow most of what we eat here. Already some rows of seeds are being planted in the thawing earth.

Spring must be here. I saw new birds coming from the south, squirrels frisking out, and even a few flies and bees have hatched from their eggs and are buzzing about.

The ice for our cooling drinks has been stacked. A couple of weeks ago the water actually froze thick enough to cut for storage. The air was biting cold, but ice must be had and in the cold was the only way to get it. Saws, axes and tongs were piled, into the truck with a number of fellow apprentices, and were off to get our summer ice supply. Evidently Mother Nature didn't want us to spoil the vitreous surface of the ice, so she didn't make it thick enough to hold the truck. The grand old thing (it has really done its share of work already) broke through the ice to find water and mud below the surface. The ice had to be unloaded and the usual pushing started. The truck moved up and out finally for we have had much practice in pushing cars this winter and the truck—before and after. Now the ice blocks recline side by side with like brethren in the sawdust, to be forgotten until heat comes. Getting ice is one of the stepping stones in our life at Taliesin. It's a pleasant memory (although the work was hard) for it was enjoyed: those ice blocks sliding along on the ice to the truck and the saws gnawing away at frozen water; getting ice is imprinted in my album of memories of Taliesin life. We don't get in our own ice in Brooklyn.

Taking of memories and mentioning plastic art, mud sticks in my mind's eye. It is needed around sand bags when you make a temporary dam and is pushed or rather squeezed between lime rock to make ours. The mud sticks to my mind as it does to my face, hands, boots, pants; everything. Tuesday was a day of mud slinging but artistic mud slinging, mind you. You have to throw the mud so it doesn't splash too much and goes straight to where you want it. It shouldn't hit a fellow worker, for instance, for mud gets excited, and seems to boomerang back to you. Blaine can tell you what mud is like when it comes back at you. He was out in the silt that came down the stream to form our mud. He was on a log plunging in with a long shovel. His white shirt (not long so) was a fair contrast to his surroundings. The muck appreciated the contrast with loud applause and a tossing of water in the air, and that shirt! What a time we had with sloppy mud. It can't be forgotten very soon. We don't have mud in Brooklyn either.

Work on the dam is going on as the breach made by the flood must be filled. And it means work and more work. But we must work! That is part of our life and the best part at that. None of your city regimentation and theory. We work. And like it.

World economics and affairs and philosophy from college are all very well and good in their place, but Unity Chapel on a Sunday morning is best when the Reverend Holloway from Madison is in the pulpit and talks in his straight-forward way on religion.

Mr. Holloway's sermon last Sunday was, I believe, the finest translation of our spheres in architecture and art into the realm of that specialized field of the spirit religion. A religion like the one we heard put into words on Sunday—the way of life—simple, sincere, honest; a life that acts, but acts with thought for neither punishment nor reward in mind; a life that is both hurt and insulted when such reward is offered; such a religion is the solution for a good life well lived—as much as an organic architecture is the solution for a full honest life in America.

ALFRED BUSH

AT TALIESIN

March 23, 1934

Before 30 "fellows" invaded Taliesin there were seven draughtsmen, who were also apprentices in the real sense of the word, working with Frank Lloyd Wright. They had their individual rooms just as we have and had their own little dining room next to the private dining room and the farm dining room, all of which nestled humbly beneath the tower on top of the hill.

Then we started coming. Additions were made, rooms were added wherever possible, and the little dining room soon grew to be the big dining room. The apprentices that were there helped to make it grow. The low ceiling of the old dining room now projected out into the new part to form a deck. Built in lights on this deck reflected onto the new ceiling which followed the slope of the roof.

And then they built a corner fireplace on the far side by the windows. Rudolf Mock, now an architect in Switzerland, laid the flagstone floor. One of the large laboratory tables from the Hillside Home School was put in, and five new small tables were made.

The chairs were some of those from the thousand that the master designed for the Larkin Manufacturing Co. 30 years ago. Large squares were defined on the plaster walls by inch red lines running horizontally and vertically. Each new apprentice was to paint an abstract mural on one of them. It was so planned. And that's the transient way it all remained until several weeks ago.

At that time someone suggested cutting out another door from the partition that separates the serving room from the dining room to create circulation. It was a good suggestion, won approval, and immediately was carried out.

It is a year and a half now that we have been so busy building the new Fellowship buildings that we didn't notice our old dining room never was quite complete. So that new opening was the first step in the force that moved several of us to 'finish' it. These chairs that were built as an integral part of the Larkin Company dining room now had to be made to harmonize with ours.

The high backs were cut down four inches and several other changes were made. The inch edges of the uprights were painted red to harmonize with the red lines on the walls and to make the chairs a part of the wall. We used them with the small tables and built light weight benches like the chairs for the long one. Then they were arranged in the room so that all of us could see the fire in the fireplace while we were eating. One receives more warmth from seeing a good fire than from merely feeling it, so there should be a bench by the fireplace to sit on before and after meals. And it should be built in as part of the wall and at the same time belong to the fireplace so that all three might live together as one. All this was done.

As a protection for the Japanese screen from the Taliesin collection that was above the bench, a small shelf was built between the two and it followed the screen around the corner and continued over the top of the radiators. The coffee cups and silverware are kept warm there and the coffee pot is put there during the meal. Since we wait upon ourselves, this relieves the necessity of our going back to the serving room for our coffee.

Plywood squares have been tacked on the walls in the various places where the abstract murals were to go. The abstractions are to be painted or carved on them instead, and if they are undesirable, they can be removed easily. The lights have been subdued with cleverly designed shades and the lights and the cottonwood branches on the desk cast delicate shadows on the ceiling. Then curtains, the color of the stonework and in the spirit of the Japanese screen, were hung over the windows.

In contrast to the once noisy meals, this new atmosphere that was created, created in its turn an atmosphere for quiet and repose. We were all better behaved. Somehow beauty instills respect.

While all this is going on, the drawings for the Fellowship dining room at Hillside are being completed. The large stone fireplace and part of the foundations were started at the end of last Fall. Soon we will resume our work there and hope to get it "finished" by next Fall, but nothing is really finished at Taliesin. Everything keeps on growing.

Count Hermann Keyserling says, "Hungar and thirst are the most elementary impulses of animal man—so association of these with aesthetic values means more for spiritualization than any intellectual and moral training." And over the opening from the new dining room to the kitchen, in red letters, is this: "WE HAVE POETRY LIKE THAT BECAUSE OF PROSE LIKE THIS."

ABE DOMBAR

AT TALIESIN

April 2, 1934

It has been the fad and fashion of the critics of the theater and other quasi-intellectuals to declare the theater unconditionally dead. But fad and fashion being out of order, and criticism of the type to which we are used being in equally bad taste, I venture the following opinion and take this premise to prove that the theater is not dead, but is rather the idiot child of the sane past.

To me the word theater implies place and performance. A place to which individuals, comprising an audience, go to experience an exalted or singing interpretation of life or receiving inspiration.

The picture frame theater of today (all in Madison including the Bascom are examples) usually a box, prodigiously ornamented, or a cold, glorified classroom as the Bascom, built according to classic errors, and to full seating capacity at so much per head (by now another classic error)—is hideous anachronism.

It is utterly inharmonious with contemporary communication of ideas (few as they may be) instead of aspiring to being what the essence of the theater really is: no moral institution, nor immoral institution; neither temple nor brothel, but a place where stage and audience architecturally melt rhythmically into one, and the performance—the play of the senses—and the audience blend together into an entity because of the construction of the whole.

I wonder how an individual possibly can feel in harmony (not necessarily in moral agreement) with a 20th century play, almost by necessity a series of "stills," produced in a place that is in spirit 17th century construction. Oh is it possible that the aesthetic sins of the fathers inhere also, and we have been born with layer upon layer of dead skin or hard shell over our sensitivities?

Tradition—as a sense of continuity of past into present—is an admirable sense to possess; but when it goes father than that and is personified by institutions that exist as traditions as the only valid basis, it often becomes irritating and is more than irritating, a positive sign of impotence.

The wing stage, picture frame theater that dominates our theatrical landscape is such an institution—seems tradition. Its tradition is as follows:

Created in the 17th century to get away from the democratic seating arrangement that preceded it, and to provide a place where patrons were easily seen, not a place where patrons necessarily could see. Hearing anyone but one's immediate party was barely considered. It was essentially undemocratic, and America's glorious democracy, accepted and recreated this in its own image. Grant 100 years of not-knowing-any-better and we see such an institution receiving added impetus by the typical latter day sentimental longing for the past.

And the theater remains a stamping ground for the showing off of inanities and stupidities and the family's jewels. Buildings are constructed at the realtor's "psychological corner," surrounded with signs and lights and called a theater. Movie "Palaces" with a capital "P" are constructed or rewired, and sound and visibility come under minor specifications if they come at all.

The Greeks at least chose a hill and let nature and the actors provide the inevitable limitations. And, by the way, the principle involved caused less strain on the auditory and visual nerves than do our derivative inappropriate formulas of today.

NICHOLAS RAY

Unity Chapel last Sunday was the scene of a Quaker meeting. Mr. Wright read from the lamentations of Jeremiah, discussing it as he read. General discussion ensured. David Goldsmith, Chicago business man, inventor (of zipper fame) and general authority, spoke of past experiences and future aspirations.

The program at the Playhouse next Sunday will be the great Eisenstein film *Ten Days That Shook the World,* two Walt Disney Silly Symphonies, and short subject.

[Nicholas Ray went on to a storied career as an American film director, writer and scenarist, most remembered for his 1955 film *Rebel Without a Cause.* This column, as well as his involvement with the early apprentice play, a musical farce entitled "Piranesi (or "Pekinese" as it was listed in a different column) Calico" (an earlier "At Taliesin" column states the play was written by apprentice Paul Beidler, music composed by Ernest Brooks, and "is being rehearsed under the direction of Nicholas Ray"), certainly foreshadowed his inner interest and future career pursuit. Director John Houseman remembered in *Front and Center,* "from his (Ray's) year's apprenticeship with Frank Lloyd Wright, Nick had acquired a perfectionism and a sense of commitment to his work which were rare in the theatre and even more rare in the film business."]

AT TALIESIN

April 6, 1934

Enchanted Castle

"Write about the enchanted castle," said the eight-year-old member of the Taliesin Fellowship to whom I frequently tell fairy tales.

"But what has that to do with Taliesin?" I said.

"Everything," was her quick response. "It certainly is not an ordinary house."

She is right, of course. Taliesin is the enchanted castle—not that it is peopled with goblins and elves and other supernatural beings. It is true that Manuel, our master craftsman, who is a Spaniard and deeply imbued with the superstitious beliefs of his race, declared that he had seen the devil peering in his window with "horns, pointed beard and eyes of fire." However, the apparition turned out to be none other than Nanny, our one and only goat, who has adopted the runway of gentle sloping roofs of Taliesin as her especial playground. No, we cannot even boast one convincing ghost. The Taliesin Fellowship is a perfectly normal human being on the whole, not sleeping for 100 years as did the people of the enchanted castle in the fairy tale—"The Sleeping Princess"—even if sometimes they would like to—but one very wide awake indeed in this daily round of striving constantly to live the ideal to which all have subscribed.

Do you remember in the same fairy tale how the idly curious could never get through the hedge of briars surrounding the castle, for "In the place of every twig of thorns they broke, one hundred new ones grew?" So at Taliesin those find welcome who, sincerely interested, come seeking with open mind and heart.

Notwithstanding our youngest member, Taliesin certainly does not resemble a castle in appearance. Its enchanting beauty is essentially its own. Low and rambling, it grows out of and again into the hill on which it is built. It lies just below and encircles the crest of the hill on which it grew. The roof lines follow the contours of the surrounding hills. The architecture has nothing in it reminiscent of battlements and towers. It is so natural and simple and beautiful that inevitably it seems strange, even unnatural, to those who have become accustomed to the trite artificiality of the urban architecture that urban life must live with today.

No, it is the spirit and the soul of Taliesin that makes it the enchanted castle. Here is the magic circle into which all who step believing are suddenly able to see with a clarity of vision undimmed by disillusionment and insincerity. They learn to live at one and the same time in the present and for the future, never again to sink into the oblivion of the world which slumbers and continues to dream of the "globes of the past."

MARGARET ALLEN

AT TALIESIN

April 14, 1934

[This column by Frederick Langhorst has one of the best expressions found in any of the columns of an apprentice's understanding of the purpose and goals of the Taliesin Fellowship. Langhorst also touches upon what the "At Taliesin" column series has come to represent—a kaleidoscopic record of the Fellowship participants, experiences, aspirations, and successes as well as failures.]

Many readers of this column wonder at its seemingly varied nature—one week attacking well-known persons, institutions, the next week mildly recounting the happenings of the week at Taliesin.

It should be explained that in accordance with the freedom of thought engendered here, each apprentice writes what he considers to be of interest, his point of view being relative to his understanding and comprehension of this philosophy of life we call organic.

As the members of our fellowship vary in age, experience, and maturity and besides are widely divergent in their realm of sensibilities, naturally a kaleidoscopic aspect would be first impression of this column.

But underneath the clothing of words which each apprentice weaves (sometimes as his first appearance in print) and in which he often feels as self-conscious as the proverbial farmer boy in his first general merchandise suit, lies a conviction that naturalness, however hard it is for him to attain in a new and strange realm, is the essence of good work.

The artificial and surface sham in all efforts of expression he is learning to abhor. Sad indeed it is, that while fostering and nurturing this inner evaluation of the fine qualities of living, that impotence of expression should sometimes tend to make meaningless the very beliefs which are so full of meaning to him.

We apprentices are like prunings of old city growths which are nearly dead for lack of sunshine, transplanted into the rich soil of the country. Above ground no growth seems apparent but in the rich soil our roots are sprouting to supply us with a sap we once sparsely drained from distant and dying sources. We hope the new shoots we put forth will be healthy and strong, future limbs for a fresh tree of culture, and that if they appear scrubby and inadequate now, you will realize conditions of their growth.

In this building of a Fellowship, both in equipment and personnel we do not face on separate fronts, one physical front plus one mental front, plus one spiritual front, but with a master who believes that only work done willingly and eagerly, is worth contemplating as creative. We strive to reach out in all directions, planning, designing, farming, road and dam building, drawing, weaving, carving, making models of organic buildings, writing these articles expressing our reactions, views and aims and characteristic incidents, making posters and signs for our playhouse, editing and illustrating a monograph of our own work, "Taliesin"—soon to appear—criticizing our movie programs, refreshing our guests with tea and coffee as well as entertainment, when they reach us from the city, brightening our chapel with foliage as well as lifting up our own voices together in music and seeking from our varied guest-speakers such enlightenment as their rich experience may bring to our own.

Mr. Wright believes that only from this complete centering of oneself in true balance with natural, mental, physical, and spiritual endowments of life can any worthwhile individual take his rise.

Full grown, our fellowship will serve a need long felt by sentient people—that of providing organic patterns for living in the way of every kind of building design for industry, glass, textiles, furniture, and printing, as well as music, sculpture, and painting. Each apprentice is a subject for general culture in which individuality is encouraged. The intellect is only a tool here, and not the most important tool.

These are some of the concepts concerning an organic architecture which lived in the life work of our master, Frank Lloyd Wright, and which live in the work of the fellowship:

"Principle is safe precedent."

"The working of a principle is the only safe tradition."

"Human traditions like styles are garments to be put on or taken off."

"Form is organic only when it is natural to materials and natural to function."

"An organic form grows its structure out of conditions as a plant grows out of soil. Both unfold from an inner life principle. It is also necessary for every idea of a good building, statue, painting, or book."

"Growth is a process of becoming. Decay is so no less. Only growth needs or ever finds expression."

"What we understand and appreciate we own and that is all can ever really own."

"A matter of taste is usually a matter of ignorance. The personal idiosyncracy."

"Genuine expressions of principle will always be valuable achievements of growth and should be thrown away no more than books which embodied truth in any age."

FREDERICK LANGHORST

AT TALIESIN
April 20, 1934

We have a joke-boy in the Fellowship. He looks shyly at you with cool, pleasant eyes and goes around a good deal with one — Johannes Brahms.

He — the joke-boy — works like this: Ruth, wife of another "Fellow" is dressing in the privacy of her own apartment — getting ready to go to Madison. The boy discovers this when, wanting to locate Brahms or something, he knocks on her door and is told to go away. Soon another knock. Another boy outside wondering why she sent for him — told emphatically to "go away" — a short interval one more boy, solicitous, "Here I am. What is the matter — "Ruth exasperated shouts "go away." At regular intervals come more knocks from more boys, one after the other — until Ruth is frantic.

Finally the grave Maestro Brooks himself stands at the door, solicitous. And knocks. The door opens suddenly and his sensibilities are shocked by a berating from Ruth. His solid worth does not deserve it. He is innocent. He is offended. But others are innocent too. All sent on some pretext by Johanne's little pal.

Alfie is a new boy from Brooklyn, inclined to be faithful. The joke-boy introduces him to several of the Fellows after whispered confidences in his ear concerning each.

First, rather dignified Paul, chief of the fortnight, who is giving orders to the boys for two weeks — "Nice fellow but, too bad — delusions of grandeur — likes to give orders. Otherwise alright — just pay no attention to him." Imagine the result of that one.

Next Maestro Brooks—"hard of hearing"—Alfie is advised "to shout loud when you hear him"—Alfie does and the Maestro thinks him a queer if not idiotic oaf.

Then Nick—big fellow—"looks strong—but has fits—look out for him." And Nick (previously tipped off) drops to the floor when he meets Alfie in a good enough cataleptic fit to scare a good doctor.

Nick's room is next to Alfie's and Alphie is now urged to keep a pail of water in his room and throw it on Nick should Nick have another fit—Nick unaware of these preparations is urged to knock on Alfie's door and throw a fit. Nick's turn to "get it" this time—etc., etc., etc.

The conductor of the Fellowship is not immune—for he found a heart outlined in soap on the glass of the windshield of his Cord car and inside the heart the names "Frank and Olga." And so it good humoredly goes from A to W.

If there were an X-Y-Z our practical joker would go there too—the limit.

Some say he always was like that. Several cures have, more or less cruelly, been proposed. But it seems so much a part of him, so inalienable to his charm of person and manner, that—like Cupid—who wold have him otherwise? So we have decided to leave it all to Johannes Brahms, himself.

FRANK LLOYD WRIGHT

[Author of *Apprentice to Genius,* Edgar Tafel has confessed that he was the Fellowship "joke-boy" described by Frank Lloyd Wright in this column.]

Sigma Lambda, Art Sorority on the University campus, invited the Fellowship to a luncheon Saturday noon in Madison. The luncheon was the scene of a "symposium of art." Professors Walter Agard, Franz Aust, and W. H. Varnum, Hamilton Beatty and Mr. Wright were the four speakers to debate the pertinent question and we all settled down around the usual after-dinner soiled table cloths half emptied glasses of water, and too many cigarets, to await results.

The professors and Mr. Beatty finished their remarks as briefly as possible—waiting for Mr. Wright to say what he was expected to say concerning Art and Beauty in his own vitriolic fashion.

And it was in the midst of intense interest that Mr. Wright finally arose. A pause while he quietly said he had promised himself not to say one disagreeable word—that he no longer believed in the Art that was eternally hauled over and discussed—and then picked up a little book and read to us a fairy story. Mr. Wright read, simply and beautifully, the fable, "The Nightingale" by Hans Christian Andersen.

Simply and beautifully it told the complete story. It was the living organic art that hours of futile discussion could not have touched. It was beauty—not talked about—but present.

The mixed audience of University people—young and old—and Fellowship apprentices was breathless. Many are still wondering, no doubt, what happened.

Sunday morning the Fellowship, uninjured by exposure to the city, gathered again in the chapel. Mr. Wright continued his talk of the day before—this time in more happy surroundings. He read Walt Whitman to us and then his own sense of Beauty. It was a quiet summation of the nightingale's song.

There were no guests at Taliesin, except Mrs. Lautner and Kathleen, and Sunday evening was very quite. Each of us volunteered to make a program of a more or less spontaneous nature.

Yoshiward, a Japanese production, will be shown at the Playhouse this coming Sunday. This picture is called Japan's outstanding contribution to the art of the motion picture and the most serious effort in films to come out of the east. The film was produced in Japan with an all Japanese cast. We look forward to seeing this picture as one of the outstanding events at the Playhouse. The rest of the program will consist of *Babes in the Woods,* a color Silly Symphony, and *Pencil Mania,* a short subject.

AT TALIESIN

April 27, 1934

Immortal strains from Beethoven's 97th great work, the trio "Grand Duke," sweep down from under a deep roof over a small balcony, diffuse in the midst of a spacious room. A room world-famous, not as a confinement of space but as sympathetic release of spaciousness to space—where the medium of enclosure for two sides is transparent.

This space, a creation spacious with a breadth the inner eye can see and dwell within. But it is evening, the physical vision is limited — confined and reflected to the physical dimensions. The transparent reflecting refracting glass, protected outside by a depth of shelter is seemingly mirror but like water in landscape beyond and below having a deeper content than any mirror may contain and reveals black silhouettes of hills far beyond played upon and patterned over-confused by reflections of a wood fire burning deep in massive stone walled fireplace and repetitions of the soft lights located on wide shelves graced with ceramics of simple contours and iridescent colors.

The floor, wide, well proportioned space of waxed and polished boards, it, too, reflects that plastic graceful rise of ceiling which is above it.

The ceiling, sloped, follows the lines of the roof, for it is the lining of the roof itself.

Color — rich and much of it, but all quiet subdued and profound. Indescribable yellow — a "spiritual" tone of the textured limestone, piers and walls. Pale wood — brown of the floor, textured by wood grain and quieted by hangings. Soft sienna of the natural untreated texture of the ceiling plaster — harmonized and form lightly emphasized by textured strips of pale cypress wood.

All a deep and quiet background for the contents of the room; each and everyone a precious masterpiece and belonging quietly to its place, a part of the whole. As much a part as the tones of the cello of the "Grand Duke" still floating down from above.

All this — the Taliesin living room on a quiet evening, itself symphonic in the same sense as the immortal strains floating majestically parallel with it all.

Soon the lights on the shelves faded out as the finale of the "Grand Duke" ended, its vitrospective tones recording true abstractions upon the mind, the aftermath of great music. All quiet space now, save for the shimmering of the big oak fire-logs. All dark, save the flickering glow from the huge stone fireplace continuing the symphonic movement still upon the ceiling of planes and smooth interrelated slopes and walls placed there for only the reason of spanning and enclosing its need of space. All else cast in long deep shadows upon the flat polished planes of glass — the moon shimmering through.

I, spending the night there on the wide seat next to the fire, a deep fur rug as my covering. A Chinese robe some 400 years old lying at my feet in case of a blizzard during the night. Luxury and such, truly an invitation to sleep. But all this could not be wasted on sleep. It supplied too much food for thought and feeling in an atmosphere of contentment which in this age in our land is one of the rarities of life.

Thought of all the accumulators of spirit down the ages—the works of art—about—and those same deep things that form the underlying qualities which made this, this room just the room it is. Thought of all the things, the darings—faiths—loves that uncovered principles and brought the actions that have gone into this and gone forth from here to stir seekers of truth the world over.

Thoughts came of the conversations between the master and of other masters on the subject of all things, the great breadth of matter that influences mankind; of the organic architecture of which I am a part, of the natural economic order that we have not yet, of the why of this and the why of that, the deeper sense of religion, of art. No, let us no longer say art—all this is not what they talk about when they talk about art as the conversation goes and criticism runs.

Then dreams—perhaps a dialogue between the cast Buddha 20 centuries old on the ledge above and the green porcelain Ming horseman from a temple ridge in Peking in the shelf below.

And at any moment (at least it seemed just that long) gray streaks of dawn, appearing beyond the dark hill masses across the valley whose contours have, at dawn, as much character as Gibraltar and as commanding, cast long sweeping shadows. The calm of the night controlling all, until the sun burst forth from behind "Gilbraltar" bringing with it another day continuing without end this never ending moment we call time.

BOB MOSHER

The Rev. Francis Bloodgood of Madison visited our chapel last Sunday to talk to us. The Episcopalian's text was "The Spirit of God." The young vicar was an impressive figure in his black and white robes and we all liked him immensely. The service was augmented with some of our own music. The Fellowship sang its work song, a Bach chorale, Ernest Brooks played beautifully a Bach organ prelude and fugue.

The Playhouse program next Sunday will consist of a G. W. Pabst film, *The Box of Pandora,* an outstanding German production (English subtitles); *Old King Cole* color Silly Symphony; and short subjects.

AT TALIESIN

May 13, 1934

[This column describes an apprentice-articulated "sermonette" on the subject of "Living," given from the pulpit of Unity Chapel. This was soon to become a regular Fellowship event, with each apprentice assigned to speak on a particular topic that Wright felt the apprentice weak in. "At Taliesin" columns describe "sermonettes" on self-expression, self-assertion, initiative, energy, relaxation, purpose, prudence, kindness, obedience, and intellect.]

In case you have been led to believe that architecture as a mere matter of putting up a building is our only endeavor here at Taliesin, you have been mistaken. Our credo definitely states, "The Fellowship aims, first, to develop a well correlated, creative human being with a wide horizon, but capable of effective concentration of his faculties upon the circumstanced in which he lives." Even the writing of these articles is part of our development—one of our forms of expression. And so with speaking, drawing, music, painting, sculpture and philosophy.

Last Sunday in our chapel it was home-Sunday, the Sunday when some of us try the art of articulation, not that we haven't tried it before. But this was more or less formal from the chapel pulpit. I spoke of "living"—living is the most interesting, bountiful and most important job in one's life. It is a job—it ought to be an art—which has been misbegotten or displaced by the "almighty"—the gold dollar. We are not content with just living—it is not exciting enough. It is too drab.

That is because we have forgotten what living is. We no longer know. We're too busy anyway to care much. We are all time-bound.

Well, I'm not trying to explain what living is, but how it has been lost and what we are doing about it at Taliesin. By way of education and "business" there has been too much cerebration, too much mechanical living and mere thinking. The intellect is not infallible.

Instead it is only a tool of instinct. We have been depending entirely upon the uses of the intellect losing sight of our instincts and the deeper sense called intuition. Bergson says, "The intellect is characterized by a natural inability to comprehend life. Instinct, on the contrary, is molded on the very form of life. While intelligence treats anything mechanically, instinct proceeds, so to speak, organically."

The deeper man is the creative man, the one who alone can know what "living" is, for the creative man is guided by instinct and intelligence at the same time. In his thought and work he lives organically. The creative life in this organic sense is the aim of our life here at Taliesin. We are seeking a true way of life — a growth that few may realize as freedom. We are concerned with fundamentals desiring the feeling of growth from the ground up. We may have something worth expressing where we are — sure of ourselves in this simple sense.

After this small sermon from me, Eugene Masselink read some poetry by Robert Frost that fitted into our simple scene. Then Fred Langhorst read Edwin Arlington Robinson, "The Machine," and Karl Jensen read Nietzche on the environment and then on the "within."

Our chapel service this week was home-made which it occasionally will be — making demands upon our own resources, such as they are. And we find that when we stand up ourselves to speak out in meeting — our meeting is neither dull nor commonplace.

JOHN LAUTNER

It looks as if we've missed spring this year and jumped blindly from winter into summer. The boys are preparing a tom-tom dance to some God of rain — there must not be one, or we would have rain. We are drying up on the hill as the neighbors are in the valleys. If any of our neighbors would like to put on horse feathers or something and join the party in this wild dance we'll be happy to have them. We'll dance around a telephone pole with telephone wires for music somewhere along the road. A quick drying strawberry patch is one of the motives.

The two chiefs of the rain dance squad are Paul and Yen, they went to town Saturday and had their heads shaved for the purpose. Now they are preparing the prayers for the crops. Yen looks like Mahatma Ghandi, and Paul looks like "devil." Here's to a head of hair.

Catherine the Great, the great production by the English director Alexander Korda will be shown at the Taliesin Playhouse next Sunday. With this feature will be the usual Mickey Mouse and other short subjects.

AT TALIESIN

May 20, 1934

Dust migrating from the Dakotas last week through the Wisconsin valley met dust rising from Wisconsin fields and left in its wake great blankets of silt over the entire landscape. Old man Sun rose that day looking, behind that yellow sifty atmosphere, more like the moon in total eclipse, and set that way, too, at the close of day.

Our work that raging day was giving new homes to a thousand conifers—small white pines and Norways planting groups and bunches on Taliesin's 200 acres to carry out this plan for the future. The velocity of the wind increased tremendously and the dust-clouds became thicker. About 4 in the afternoon, with the storm at its height, our planting "safari" had reached that hill-crown on which Romeo and Juliet stands.

To those acquainted with the *Autobiography* of Taliesin's sage, Romeo and Juliet has more significance than the famed Shakespearean pair. It is the windmill on the hill crown, a landmark of 40 years. But why Romeo and Juliet? The romanticism of the name perhaps is misleading. It is more than a name, the name is merely because of it. It is an architectural form formed from its structural circumstance. Romeo, the half doing the work of the windmill, slim and tall, diamond shape in plan, half outside forming the "storm plow," the other half cutting into the very center of the octagon, Juliet, cuddling along side and surmounted with its belvedere, protected, supported by Romeo. Both parts of the whole and each one the "better half." Planned and its shape derived from the purpose that it had to perform on top of that hill-crown against terrific winds.

Yet because it was different, because it wasn't a steel-webbed or trussed and cross-braced windmill, Romeo and Juliet has been condemned and censored ever since its birth. Its architect's two matriarchal aunts, the heads of the Hillside Home School now the home of the Taliesin Fellowship, fought for their tower against the "better judgement" of their five brothers, the settlers of Taliesin's valley who agreed "why build something none of us ever saw the like of in our lives?" It would fall in the first "southwester." Arch conservatism. But it was built. The first storm passed, the uncles said wait for the next. The uncles have passed on long ago, the aunts too, yet Romeo and Juliet proudly still defies all.

The other day the wind blew, strongest in years, the tower swayed as it never swayed before, almost three feet it was estimated. We watched it from below: surely it could not stand this last, it was doomed to go. After all it had lived its life and well, too, nearly 40 years of storms and contrary wills. Ten years ago it should have been renailed, but hasn't been touched for 15. It seemed it could not pass the night upright. We were singing Romeo and Juliet's funeral requiem but neither heard it.

Morning came and in the calm we, too, repeated the uncle's habit of rushing outside to see what God had done. True this time He had done much but the tower had done more. It remained upright. You see, the tower is built like a barrel and is rooted in rock as the trees are rooted in the ground, the staves run horizontally not vertically as in the barrel around the octagon and the diamond. It could not fall for it could not break. Try some time to break a barrel.

BOB MOSHER

Mrs. Max Kadushin spoke in Unity Chapel last Sunday. Her husband, the Rabbi, now doing some literary work in New York City, spoke at our Unity Chapel some weeks ago. Her sermon was magnificent. She spoke of the new movement toward Palestine. The Kadushins visited that country recently, and she vividly brought to mind the many picturesque details of the work there and the revival of the ancient classic Hebrew. She is an eloquent preacher and as she commanded the pulpit this Sunday she made us all feel the new quality of thought awakening among the Jews in this movement as it is awakening in us—a finer sense of man's relation to the soil, a deeper integrity, culture as organic instead of applied.

After the sermon some 18 or 20 members of the Hillel foundation in Madison arrived and spread their dinner out with us at the chapel. Afterwards the party walked about Taliesin and over to the new Fellowship buildings at Hillside.

A new rule to segregate those really interested from those merely curious and protect us from summer crowds was enforced for the first time last Sunday. It kept us busy enough too during the day. We are charging each tourist 50 cents for a tour through Taliesin and the Fellowship buildings. This makes us a guide-agency and if anyone is interested and in need of a good guide we are making them now right here.

Next Sunday we are going popular and have subscribed to *Roman Scandals,* the latest Eddie Cantor picture just to see what the reaction will be.

AT TALIESIN

May 29, 1934

With the coming of summer . . . hot mornings in the fields planting and hoeing . . . cool dips in the river . . . and iced tea on the slightest provocation, fall seems just in the offing, and with it the Fellowship cycle will swing around to its second completion. Two years—almost—and some of us pause now and then along the long row of beans to wonder "Whither Fellowshipkind?"

Well, they have been happy years; and they have been full, intensive years . . . no question about that. "Always something happens, Mr. Wright," a phrase quaintly put by one of the foreign apprentices not yet completely at home with our language, has stuck, it so aptly describes the situation here. And they have been profitable years. Development of the individual, no longer artificially appraised in terms of credits and degrees, is hard sometimes to realize; harder yet to communicate to another. But at odd moments, often coming over the hill with Taliesin laid out below and beyond, gleaming in a rising sun, or at evening glowing in the warm rays of golden sunset there comes a sudden realization of the meaning of these years. They crowd into a single moment of significance, as if seen from the vantage point of the future, psychic, possibly, but of the real stuff of which reality is. And they have been good.

But this development of the individual, at once the reason for our existence and in another sense only incidental to the main program, is an organic development, in that the apprentice is neither coerced nor coaxed into thinking or doing. That which is assimilated, and he may not be completely aware of it at the time, is by way of natural absorption. Infection by exposure, as it were, to a new culture, highly imaginative, tremendously beautiful.

In these 270 acres of hills, fields, woods, streams, organic architecture has combined with nature to make a very wonderful setting for our scheme. There Taliesin clings to the "brow" of the first low-lying hill. It stretches back along a ridge for more than is at first apparent. Then the orchard, and at the top of the ridge, higher even than the buildings, the windmill and water pool. Across a narrow valley another, steeper, smaller hill rises up behind the dairy barns and farmer's cottage. An open air theatre with blue sky for a back drop and trees for the proscenium arch will crown this hill, and lying low, spreading along its short ridge will form a splendid contrast to Romeo and Juliet, the grand old water tower rising so majestically on its own hill several hundred feet beyond to the southwest. And like Romeo and Juliet the theater will be seen from many points up and down the valley. Then down from the water tower the Fellowship buildings themselves, a tremendous project in its final conception, already partially completed. Leader's cottages, guest accommodations, and shops are planned in addition to the stables, dormitories, studios, and living rooms, which are already either started new, or built from the old Hillside Home School. Our one completed unit, the Taliesin Playhouse, a noble exemplar of what is to follow is also from the old school, bringing the old to the new and the new to the old. For there is a fine tradition here, in the life that was this valley and in this school. A tradition which we recognize and cherish. The many flowers lovingly planted in the glen by Aunt Jane and Aunt Nell are once more sanctifying human inhabitation, and on Sunday morning Unity Chapel again calls the valley to communion with one another and with nature. The setting, certainly, is beyond comparison.

But more than anything else there is Mr. Wright, without whom there would be no Fellowship. For in him we have sought a living example of the ideal of "growth of the individual by the way of life called work." We have come to Mr. Wright out of respect for the man and his work, and for the ideal of the Fellowship . . . a group of serious young men and women who apprentice themselves to Mr. Wright because with him and through him the ideal of organic architecture can be brought nearer and made more tangible. And because this apprenticeship is in residence with Mr. Wright it is natural, indeed inevitable, that a good life (organic) suitable to the common endeavor should become a goal in itself. And to some of us at least a goal of far greater importance though more difficult to apprehend, possibly, than organic architecture; an ideal, in fact, in which organic architecture becomes only a constituent part. And so, blessed with the benefits of nature and man—a man, in particular, we are seeking, striving to build a way of life. A way of life which in its search for truth will be more organic, and will be, in that sense, architecture too.

WILLIAM BEYE FYFE

AT TALIESIN

June 8, 1934

Crowds—Music—Lectures—Dinner—Motion Pictures! Taliesin has just had its biggest weekend party in some time.

Our exhibition gallery was finished Friday for the first showing of watercolors and oils by the fellowship group. Each fellow was asked to contribute individual work which he thought worthy of exhibition— and on the whole it is a fine showing, something we are proud to offer our friends.

Saturday, June 2, the fellowship entertained the Technical Club of Madison at its annual meeting. Upon arrival, the Club was escorted through Taliesin, where the house was opened to the visitors. Then followed an inspection of the Fellowship buildings, the Playhouse, the drafting room, the painting exhibit. Dinner was served to more than 150 persons in the Fellowship living rooms. It was a typical dinner such as we might have had any evening—baked ham, scalloped potatoes, cold slaw, cakes, and coffee, with plenty of ice water. After the dinner, the guests assembled in the Playhouse where Mr. Wright spoke frankly to them:

"We are an experiment here; we are seeking a new way of American life—a life freed from all the ostentatious 'ists' and 'isms' of the contemporary life. We are rediscovering that almost forgotten quality in Man—WORK. We have rejected the too many minor traditions in favor of the great elemental Tradition. We are not a 'back-to-the-soil' movement in any sense: we are living a very busy but greatly simplified life here—we derive our pleasure and happiness from things that really count—from doing things; a combination of action and appreciation. We are sensitive to human values with regard to life in the 20th century."

Guests were invited to ask questions about us or our work while Mr. Wright chose various members of the Fellowship for answers. Gene Masselink sang four old English songs, arranged by Leo Sowerby of Chicago, Ernest Brooks playing accompaniment. Glen Sherman, our guest from Chicago, played by Brahms, Scarlatti, Prokofiev, and his own piano transcription of a Schubert song. As a finale to the program came the showing of *The Fall of the House of Usher*—a highly imaginative picture abstracted from Poe's novel by a distinguished amateur photographer, Dr. Watson.

The guests departed and the dishes all cleaned the Fellowship returned to Taliesin to hear Glen play. He is our favorite pianist—a fine technician and extremely sensitive to his instrument and to tone color and shading. Tired as we all felt, we listened until late to Scarlatti sonatas, Bach dances, Chopin, much Brahms and Debussy, Prokofiev, and Schumann. Sunday night he again played for us, this time a fine Schumann "Novelette" in F-sharp minor—seldom heard for it is long and not "popular" enough for concert-goers; Brahms' Variations on a Theme by Handel, Debussy' Suite Bergamasque, Bach, and Scarlatti. After the concert Glen modestly said that he feels he is not mature enough to play Beethoven—certainly a modest and level-headed attitude not often encountered in people who have won scholarships to Julliard and studied with Levine of New York and Thomford Harris and Issador Phillips of Paris.

Sunday morning at chapel we heard Mr. Fernbach, a former member of Dr. Meiklejohn's experimental college, tell of his experiences in Soviet Russia. Miss White, University of Wisconsin, revealed the inspiration for her famous book, *Watch in the Night,* Sunday night.

BRUCE RICHARDS

AT TALIESIN
June 14, 1934

[Frank Lloyd Wright was born on June 8, 1867. This column describes the celebration of his sixty-seventh birthday. Ernie Meyer, columnist for the *Capital Times* and a visitor at this particular event, wrote a poem entitled "To Frank Lloyd Wright," which was printed under his column heading, "Making Light of the Times," in the *Capital Times* on June 7, 1934 (reprinted herein, see appendix C).]

Birthday celebrations would be really celebrations if we became one year younger instead of older each time — that is, if we didn't start too soon. We really celebrated last Friday when Mr. Wright became one year younger and said that next year he will be in his fifties. Equipped with everything possible and impossible we drove through the country to a rocky pine-covered hill and had a magnificent picnic. Steaks, potatoes baked in the coals, apples, plums; bananas, pineapple, ice cream, cheeses, and hot towels (Japanese fashion) to clean our faces and hands afterwards. And music. Afterwards to the Playhouse where we saw a pre-view of *July 14th*, the delightful Rene Clair film.

Ernie and his wife stayed through the afternoon for the Playhouse program and for supper in the evening. After supper everyone went up to the hill garden to let the beautiful evening make the music.

The Meyers love the country and especially our country about Taliesin. They were out once before and this time hitchhiked ("bummed," for short) out.

Mrs. Robert Bitsey Gilham left last Saturday for Hollywood for three weeks with her husband. She left Nickie and Janet, his nurse, behind and now Nickie is getting the education of a prince. At tea he makes his daily bow to society and drinks from all the tea cups regardless.

Bisser Lloyd Jones and Peg Helen Seiffert have deserted the now completely dead university and are staying at Taliesin for a week or two. We wonder if they consider this a post mortem?

Paul T. Frankl and son Peter arrive at Taliesin this Saturday. Mr. Frankl is a well-known New York designer and writer and is leaving his twelve-year-old son to be a member of the Fellowship.

The Playhouse offers this Sunday a recent Hollywood film, *By Candlelight*. Elissa Landi and Paul Lukas star in the film and all rumor says that it is an excellent and entertaining film. In the near future *Pamir,* a Russian documentary of a great expedition into the Pamir mountains and *The Passion of Joan of Arc,* the famous Dreyer film, will be shown at the Playhouse.

AT TALIESIN
June 28, 1934

Three cheers filled the studio Tuesday when a telegram was received telling of the breaking of the ground for Mr. Wright's design, the Willey House in Minneapolis. Dean and Mrs. Willey are to have a unique house mainly because of its utter simplicity and material use of local materials. Brick comprises the major portion of the structure, used for interior walls and floors, as well as exterior walls. Another feature of the one floor house is the glass partition between the kitchen and living room, so constructed that shelves are put against the glass to make a screen between dining alcove and kitchen. Until the union saw the plans for the house we were afraid that the building strike would cause considerable trouble. They then backed out shyly and the strike settled itself.

Rev. Holloway of Madison came out again to preach us a Unitarian sermon, bringing with him a great many of his congregation who picnicked in the chapel yard after the services. So his sermon was doublefold: to the Fellowship on one hand and his congregation on the other. However, although the sermon was a strong one, it lacked the peculiar force and character of his previous talks as applied to us because of the divided attention. We like our lectures straight.

The members of the Fellowship are becoming excellent guides as the visitors swarm Taliesin over weekends. Jack Howe thinks of dropping architecture in order to be a guide in Washington to those interested in

The Hilltower at Taliesin (photo ca. 1930s; kitchen and apprentice rooms in tower portion, Fellowship dining room in single-story section *at left*). Photo courtesy of the Frank Lloyd Wright Foundation.

"The darings — faiths — loves that uncovered principles and brought the actions that have gone into this and gone forth from here to stir seekers of truth the world over" (Bob Mosher, "At Taliesin," April 27, 1934). *Taliesin Living Room,* photo ca. 1937. Photo courtesy of Hedrich-Blessing Collection, Chicago Historical Society.

"The boys are preparing a tom-tom dance to some God of rain. . . . The two chiefs of the rain dance squad are Paul and Yen, they went to town Saturday and had their heads shaved for the purpose. Now they are preparing the prayers for the crops. Yen looks like Mahatma Ghandi, and Paul looks like 'devil.' Here's to a head of hair" (John Lautner, "At Taliesin," May 13, 1934). *Apprentices Yen Liang and Paul Beidler* (photo ca. May 1934). Photo courtesy of the Frank Lloyd Wright Foundation (Henry Schubart Collection).

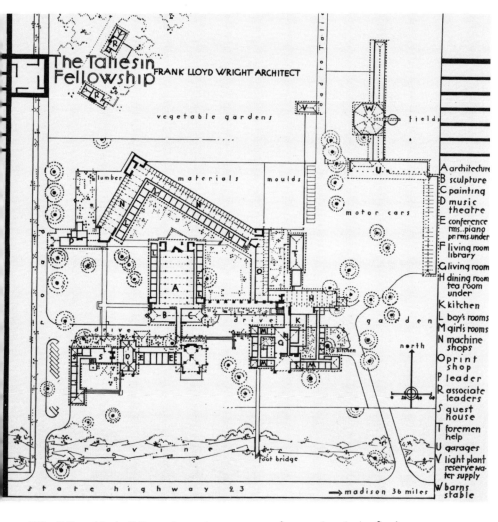

The Taliesin Fellowship — FRANK LLOYD WRIGHT ARCHITECT

vegetable gardens · fields

lumber · materials · moulds

motor cars

A architecture
B sculpture
C painting
D music theatre
E conference rms..piano pr. rms. under
F living room library
G living room
H dining room tea room under
K kitchen
L boys' rooms
M girls' rooms
N machine shops
O print shop
P leader
R associate leaders
S guest house
T foremen help
U garages
V light plant reserve water supply
W barns stable

drive

north

garden

ravine · foot bridge

state highway 23 · → madison 36 miles

"The Fellowship buildings themselves, a tremendous project in its final conception, already partially completed" (William "Beye" Fyfe, "At Taliesin," May 29, 1934). *Fellowship Complex Master Plan at Hillside,* 1932 (partially executed). Drawing courtesy of the Frank Lloyd Wright Foundation.

"The whole becomes a simplified machine, as efficient, as beautiful and as economical as the machine it serves, the motor car" (Bob Mosher, "At Taliesin," July 6, 1934). *"Village Type" Roadside Service Station,* 1932. Photo courtesy of the State Historical Society of Wisconsin.

"The Dana Gallery is an exhibition room for architectural displays and renderings and work of the Fellowship" (Bob Mosher, "At Taliesin," July 12, 1934). *The Dana Gallery at Hillside* (completely remodeled as the Dana Gallery in 1934). Photo courtesy of the Frank Lloyd Wright Foundation.

"To Abe—am sure the stone is much the prettier. Put my face into it for remembrance. Affectionately, Edgar [Tafel], 1938." *Fellowship "Cornerstone" Carved by Abrom Dombar,* ca. 1933 (originally placed in low retaining wall outside Hillside; now integrated within east wall of Hillside drafting room). Photo courtesy of Abrom Dombar.

"Charlie Curtis is our master stone mason" (Abrom Dombar, "At Taliesin," September 11, 1934). *Charlie Curtis* (photo ca. 1934; construction at Hillside in background). Photo courtesy of the Frank Lloyd Wright Foundation.

"Imagine a spiderweb. . . . building expressed in glistening steel and its complimentary partner—glass. Together these elements offer limitless possibilities of light and space consciousness" (Cornelia Brierly, "At Taliesin," October 19, 1934). *Steel Cathedral Project, New York,* 1926. Drawing courtesy of the Frank Lloyd Wright Foundation.

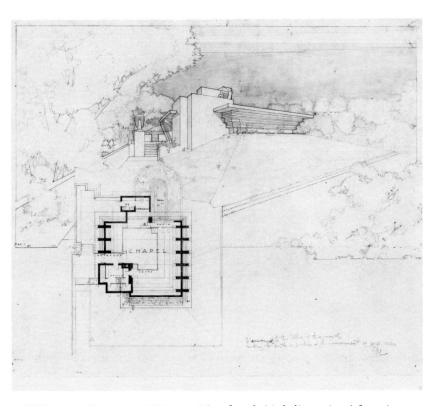

"Whitman's 'Pioneers! O Pioneers!' has found third-dimensional form in architecture here" (Bob Mosher, "At Taliesin," December 9, 1934). *Memorial to the Soil Chapel,* 1934. Drawing courtesy of the Frank Lloyd Wright Foundation.

Taliesin Playhouse Playbill, December 1934. Courtesy of the University Archives, University of Wisconsin, Madison.

the New Deal. Prof. George Beal of Lawrence, Kansas, one of our newer apprentices, tried to get a worm's eye perspective view of life last week when he fell off the running board of John Lautner's car and landed head first on the hard ground. Although George was partially unconscious for twenty-four hours, he came out of it all with a broad smile, figuring that life had some new aspects with every fresh idea. We were all greatly relieved when George came through again with his infectious laugh.

Paul Frankl, the well-known interior decorator of New York City, visited us for a week and made Mr. Wright a present of a beautiful reed reclining chair designed by himself. The chair has only one disadvantage — students stand in line for hours to get a chance to recline in it.

Florence Lloyd Jones of Tulsa, Oklahoma, is resting at Taliesin for a spell, and is joining the painting group. Her latest mural was done on the wall of her room, in silhouette, and is called "shadows against the wall." Miss Jones draws beautifully and was shown for the *Tulsa Tribune* prize design of 1934: "The Fife and Drum Corps."

Messrs. Lautner, Mosher and Beidler are working overtime and furiously with Mr. Wright to complete the sculpture studio at Hillside. A general exhibition is planned for the near future to include the work of the Fellowship up to the present time.

The Fellowship is glad to announce the showing of the extraordinary film by Carl Dreyer, *The Passion of Joan of Arc* this coming Sunday. Since this film was released no screen production has surpassed it, or it reaches the highest peaks and will live indefinitely. The treatment of the film is devoted almost entirely to close-ups. Moving at a slow pace but never lagging it is a photographic study of the great French actress Falconetti that unwinds the story of Joan of Arc in her last hours — her imprisonment, her delusive trial and her condemnation and execution at the stake. Such a vital picture ought to be of great interest to the people of Spring Green. The opportunity to see it or anything similar may not come again soon.

AT TALIESIN

July 6, 1934

[Frank Lloyd Wright toyed with the design of a more appropriate (to the user — the motorcar) standardized gas station in these early Fellowship years (Corner Station prototype, 1930; Monolithic Filling Station, 1931; Standard Overhead Service Station, 1932; Automobile/Airplane Service Station, 1932). A model of the "Village Type" Roadside Service Station found its way into the Broadacre City exhibit. It was 1956 when Wright was finally given the opportunity to execute a derivative of the 1932 Standardized Service Station for R. W. Lindholm in Cloquet, Minnesota.]

Perhaps one of the worst faults of mankind is criticism without cause but even worse than that is criticism of something without a better solution to that something. Critics of the things that are criticized in the world today should be even greater in knowledge of that thing than the creator himself. If they are not, they have no right to criticize.

So when we criticize a certain thing here at Taliesin it is because we not only feel that it has just cause for criticism but only by way of a better solution our criticism becomes valid. In architecture we criticize freely because we have a natural solution for the problem in place of the superficial. Our solution is shown by accomplishments and therefore we become legitimate critics.

One of these problems, which cover all means of endeavor in the world today, is the modern gas station. We thought the gas station being a result of this machine age had never come up to its function in being an actual working part of the machine in which it serves. That it was merely a temporary thing nothing more than a glorified shed placarded with signs for greasy oils and gas, a memorial to the accomplishments of the House of Rockerfeller. That being strictly a service to the auto-riding public that it must blare to attract attention so that "four out of five" city blocks have it and to the motorist the countryside has been somewhat obliterated by the approaching glare of the gas station and grease palace.

Because all this was unnatural and therefore open to criticism, the standardized gas station was designed in the Taliesin studio. A solution to the problem. Standardized because of repetitious machine efficiency and prefabricated because it was standardized and had to be flexible in order to fit its particular site and limiting purpose as well as rigid economy. Here the old principle of "form follows function" is at work. By taking all those things that make up the gas station as a machine for the machine and letting them be the gas station we find our problem actually planned before it is designed. Gravity-flow pumps, tanks, ample protective covering, service space and rest rooms. These things insist that it takes form to fit them and their function. Therefore how could it be a brick box, let alone a Chinese temple or an Indian wigwam as the ones that so disgrace our country-side and Madison itself.

Concrete, metal and glass . . . our materials. Concrete of the back structure which contains the tanks supplying the gravity-flow pumps located at the ends of the two long arms of pre-fabricated metal coverings cantilevered at right angles to each other from the concrete structural mass. This allows four cars to be serviced simultaneously without interference. The fulcrum of the cantilevered covering extends through the roof forming the neon signs still a part of the structure. Advertising, not vulgar but in its proper place to be seen from every point of view. In the angle formed by the cantilevered arms as they intersect the concrete is the service room in direct view of all approaches and midway between the pumps. Rest rooms are directly under the roof coverings with the concrete form as its back and allowing storage space and attendant space beneath.

To fit all conditions of business enterprise the solution has been divided into three units. The first just described the second, an addition of garage unit and greasing court, the third, composed of kitchen, restaurant and shops. Each added when desired by use of unit construction. This freedom for addition makes the roadside station a natural centering for all the requirements of the motorists and thus an advance agent of the decentralization that is coming. The whole becomes a simplified machine, as efficient, as beautiful and as economical as the machine it serves, the motor car.

BOB MOSHER

AT TALIESIN

July 12, 1934

Extensive operations at Hillside have added two new studios to the Fellowship's list of accomplishments and they have been named after two of the old Hillside Home School patrons — the Dana Gallery, named for Mrs. Susan Lawrence Dana of Springfield, Illinois, who gave to Hillside the north wing of the school and the Roberts Room dedicated to the patronage of Mr. Charles E. Roberts of Chicago. These rooms, in conjunction with the large architectural studio and the sixteen apprentices' rooms, compose the studio wing of the Fellowship buildings. The old building, in ruins when we started almost two years ago, is slowly coming into its own and is slowly taking on an atmosphere that is to make them a showplace here in the country. Truck loads of works of Oriental art, architectural models and drawings have been removed from their storage at Taliesin and have at last found their place. The Dana Galley is an exhibition room for architectural displays and renderings and work of the Fellowship, while the Roberts Room will contain exhibitions of Japanese prints and Momayama embroideries dating from the sixteenth century.

BOB MOSHER

Last Sunday, after showing of *Thunder Over Mexico* at the Playhouse, our virtuoso, Glen Sherman, played a number of selections on the Beckstein to a large audience. Wednesday evening he gave a concert over the Madison radio station and next Sunday he will give a full-length concert after the feature showing of *Storm Over Asia* at the Playhouse. Next week Glen leaves for a concert tour in the east.

AT TALIESIN

July 26, 1934

[Georgi Gurdjieff was a most-celebrated and special visitor to Taliesin during these early "At Taliesin" years. Wright, in another "At Taliesin" column entitled "Georgi Gurdjieff at Taliesin," wrote: "There is only one Gurdjieff. His career is as unique as is the man himself. . . . He rather impressed me as being something of a Walt Whitman in Oriental terms." With a different viewpoint, Eugene Masselink remembered a Gurdjieff visit to past apprentices George and Helen Beal in another letter, "Gurdjieff is here feeding us salad and soups that would knock the roof off Corrells Drug Store if ignited."]

Taliesin was much honored last Sunday by the visit of Georgi Gurdjieff, the noted philosopher and leader of the famous work at the Prieure Fontainebleau, France. In the evening we heard some of his music and the introduction to the vast series of books which he has written. His powerful personality affected us all strangely. It seemed as though we had an oriental Buddha come to life in our midst.

His music, of an extraordinary simplicity and clarity, was played by George Hansen from manuscript. The philosophical readings were also from manuscript. After our usual movie performances at the Playhouse, a remarkable Russian satire on Buffer States and Kingship, a group of summer school students from the university gave us a series of sketches on the stage of the theater entitled "Romeos and Juliets." Shakespeare is dead. And it is his good fortune where this performance is concerned. But we are mildly thrilled to see how far his masterpiece could be fetched and distorted, without being completely boring. Nevertheless, the afternoon was exciting as we looked at the remodeled theater — remodeled by ourselves, the interior changed considerably to simplify the spacing and add new balcony seats. There are new lighting devices, too, unique in construction and effect, and twelve good new seats. Judging from our Sunday audiences we will need many more than we can get.

Jack Howe and Bob Mosher are being awarded the 1934 Taliesin Weed Prize. The two aforementioned cultivated bigger and better weeds than even the author, who humbly feels that the Howe-Mosher combination deserves national recognition. The prize-winning pig-weed is on exhibition in the studio, entitled "our life's work." Miss Barnsdall came a close second, but was not conferred the second medal as she was en route to California for a short visit — incidentally — with her mother.

This Sunday the Playhouse offers a Viennese musical comedy, *Liebeskommando* (*Love Command*). It is a recent continental release. U.F.A. filled with "rich romance and irresistible music." The picture is produced by those who brought out *Zwei Herzen* and *Der Raub der Mona Lisa* and is undoubtedly a musical comedy of similar "distinction." Someone will play the Bechstein after the picture. And maybe our new trio—piano, violin and cello—will be ready to play. They have got the missing E and A strings and have been rehearsing.

We are repeating our Sunday afternoon performances, now complete, every Sunday evening at eight-thirty.

[It should be noted that John Howe developed a particular relaxation in pulling weeds; his own therapy for when he grew tired of drawing.]

AT TALIESIN
August 2, 1934

[Frank Lloyd Wright began his practice of giving informal talks to the Fellowship during these early "At Taliesin" years. They were on Tuesday evenings within the newly completed Dana Gallery at Hillside. Topics were, of course, varied and usually spontaneous. "At Taliesin" columns mention talks given on many subjects — the interrelationship of structure and space, the third dimension, critics and criticism, the Japanese print, glass and steel, as well as discussion of his architectural work (Hollyhock House, the Doheny Ranch and Lake Tahoe projects, and Unity Temple). The following one was an early talk regarding "form research."]

"The more awkward the moment, the better the speaker's chance to make an impression." These were Mr. Wright's opening words in his lecture to us Tuesday evening on form research in the Dana Gallery at Hillside. To feel and express the inner spirit of the drawn object whether it be pine or oak tree or hollyhock flower, rather than the outer aspect was the main theme of Mr. Wright's talk. "The Egyptians and Orientals have come closer to interpretation of the spirit of these materials than the Greeks, Romans or other cultures of the western world." Realization and expression of structure is comparatively unknown in Western Art. We have most always indulged in an aspect for view of the exterior. Mr. Wright increased the meaning of what he was saying by illuminating his words and drawings by the great Japanese artists, Korin, Kokusal and Hiroshige. He also used illustrations, abstractions by several members of the Fellowship and abstractions and drawings of his own. This talk is the first of a series which will take place every week in our new gallery.

This week brought visitors to Taliesin from all parts of the country: Mrs. Maginel Wright Barney, visiting Mr. Wright, her brother, and her daughter Mrs. Robert Gilham, who is "roughing it" as Mrs. Gilham says. Hank Schubart's mother is here too, for a two month stay. Mr. and Mrs. Ernest Meyer and bairn Karl are also visiting with us for about a week. Mr. Meyer doesn't write articles for the *Capital Times* while at Taliesin and won't look at a newspaper for the week. Instead he has been tarring the drafting room roof with a crew of the boys, and taking a hand at masonry. The last we saw of Mr. Meyer was when he was under a six-inch stone, making heavy of the times.

Mr. Wright went to Madison Tuesday, and our secret service agent unearthened valuable information as to a brewing revolution right here in our own midst. From an authentic manuscript of the revolutionary forces the general setup of the new liberal government officials was to be as follows: Chief Commander, Karl E. Jensen; Secretary to Commander, K. Edward Jensen; Dean of Work, E. K. Jensen; Dean of Women, Edward Jensen; Architect General, Jens E. Jensen; Mulch Expert, Jensen Jensen; Chief Secret Police, Oscar Jensen. Minor Government officials to be appointed by Jensen. The existing government suspects Karl Jensen as one culprit in this revolutionary force Jensen has a long criminal record, and was involved in the well-known Jensen Affair and the Jensen Putsch. Jensen refuses to talk.

The Playhouse this Sunday will be the scene of a grand revival. The curtain will ring up at three and eight P.M. on the greatest of Rene Clair's pictures—the new classic satire, *A Nous la Liberte*. This picture was shown in the early days of the Taliesin Playhouse and is brought back again for this Sunday to give our friends, the public, another chance to see one of the greatest of contemporary motion pictures.

[In a letter written to Wright on July 24, 1934, Ernest Meyer requested, "If it suits your convenience, could the Meyer family— wife, one bairn and myself—come to Taliesin Sunday. . . . It's my vacation week, and I know of no place I had rather visit. On our side there is one condition: that we put up in the dorms and pay for keep, for we know that your hospitality is enormous but the Fellowship coffers are not." His weekly column featured a three-part description of their stay (included herein, see appendix C).]

AT TALIESIN
August 8, 1934

A child's sailboat floats across a patch of light falling from the electric bulb set into the soffit of the long overhanging eave above. Nearby the fountain plays against a darkening sky. Crickets chirp their evening song in neighboring fields, as darkness blots out faces. I join the little group that has come to rest on the ground and steps before the studio door . . . that pause "between the dark and the daylight" when everything seems at peace with itself and with the world. A few more join the group, conversation flows and dies. Then the master speaks—with one thing suggesting another. Gurdjieff has been here recently; the conversation turned on him, a difference of opinion quickens the tempo and we hear of the relation of the disciple to the master, of Orage to Gurdjieff, Saint Paul to Jesus . . . Lights go on in the house. It is still early, and yet tomorrow starts early too. The group gathers itself up and slowly disperses.

The four o'clock tea bell brings the Fellowship together for a welcomed respite from the day's work. Cooling sounds of ice rattling in tall glasses fall on ear as we climb the steps to the circular stone bench the "council ring." What was shortly a deserted courtyard and hill top soon becomes very much alive as people appear from all directions. King, Mrs. Wright's beautiful police dog, comes to bite playfully at protruding feet and arms. Mimi and Nicky, aged three and two, quite suddenly find it great sport to splash in the pool at our feet and occasionally even the ducks come over the hill to see what it's all about. This day a guest arrives for tea. Miss James from Richland Center is paying us the honor of a visit, and soon she has captured the hearts and interest of every one. The story of the work which she is doing in her county with the mentally deficient is a startling revelation to most of us. Startling that the conditions could be so bad. Startling, too, that such conditions could continue to multiply, were it not for a few undaunted souls like Miss James. The subject is one close to Mr. Wright's heart. They discuss its further implications, and he volunteers his support. Then the shower which has been threatening all afternoon begins to fall and we leave to go to the studios, our rooms, the kitchens, or wherever the next task calls.

Usually it is on Sunday afternoon, but there's no telling just when it will come. Maybe there is a schedule, but I don't know what it is, and I'm glad I don't, for it is always a pleasant surprise to hear Mrs. Olson's cheery voice coming through the courtyard. And I'd rather keep it as a surprise. Mrs. Olson does laundry for several of the fellows. Does it well, too, for they all swear by her. But her greatest service is free to all who will be on hand when she comes — you don't even have to have laundry to do. Just be there and say hello, or just be there and hear her say hello to someone else; it all amounts to the same thing, for Mrs. Olson is one of those gay, kindly women who have a great secret in life which makes the world a little brighter wherever she goes.

Today Mrs. Wright's bed of moss roses was a blaze of color.

Bud Shaw, world traveller and adventure's own boy, returned to the fold on Sunday last. Mr. Shaw says he is not being interviewed. He seldoms talks for publication.

We will see at the Playhouse this coming Sunday the much heralded French film masterpiece, *Foil de Carotte,* or as it is called in America, *The Red Head*, a triumph dramatically, aesthetically, and technically. It unfolds in a poignant drama the story of a very young French lad detested by his mother and misunderstood by his father, who really loves the boy but is in a quandary as to just how to act in the midst of a family feud. *The Red Head* is something more than a moving drama of adolescence; a study of human nature in its various phenomena of inner conflict with the chains of environment.

The picture has been highly successful in New York. The director, Jullen Duvivler, ranks with Rene Clair as France's foremost motion picture director. There will be two performances every Sunday beginning in the afternoon at three and in the evening at eight.

AT TALIESIN

August 19, 1934

By the light of a match I found his house — the devil appeared in his shorts. I gave him a bottle of beer and he gave me a bed. I slept a little and drove a little and came to Taliesin — the end of my journey. The place where life is lived, where life is loved, where life is used and not abused.

We are adapting the nature of reality to the resources of spirit, mind, and imagination. It is time we go beyond adapting the nature of reality to the resources of animal, instinct, and rationalization. We are getting inside of the thing. Taliesin is the match that lights the way. We are not content to live outside — on the surface, we must get in — experience and feel; then create, project, a product of a new reality.

Why does a house have to be colonial? Why not something of the environment, something organic and beautiful? Is every oak tree the same, is every leaf the same? Why does life have to be the same daze day after day? Why not a new light every time the sun comes up?

We must grow bigger and taller every day — just as the tree reaches up and stretches out. The philosophy working from the inside out instead of merely reacting to the environment applies not only to the large but to the small. Not only in architecture but in every bit of life. If you don't like what you can buy in stores — change them, or better, make them yourself to fit your sense of things.

Things don't have to be ugly to be practical or ornate to be beautiful. Man invented the machine, but, unfortunately, his animal nature controlled it, he didn't know how to use the machine. When spirit, mind, and imagination controls, life will be worth living again.

JOHN LAUTNER

The course of theatrical events at the Playhouse brings us from the tragic French *Foil de Carotte* last week to an English romance, *The Constant Nymph*, this Sunday. It will be welcome after satire and tragedy to see a picture heralded as an idyllic drama.

The book by Margaret Kennedy has stood for some years as the shining example of poignant writing. It was produced both as a play and as a silent motion picture, but the talking version of the famous story places it high above any of its previous interpretations. A great part of the picture was made in the Tyrolean Alps and the playing of a symphony concert in one of London's big concert halls is a high point in the picture's drama. Special music for the film was made by Eugene Goossens and John Greenwood.

Performances will start at 3 and 8 P.M.

AT TALIESIN

August 23, 1934

After the lecture—what?

Last evening Mr. Wright gave another one of his penetrating talks to the Fellowship. Quite a number of the apprentices claimed this for the finest talk so far in the series of Tuesday night meetings. It was filled with a sense of reality and spiritual interpretation of what is. It dealt only in passing with form and function in architecture, lingered on the nature of materials in relation to art and then sounded what was, perhaps, the basic note of the evening by discussing the "Third Dimension" in architecture and all creative works.

After returning from the Dana Gallery most of the Fellowship went quietly to bed with their thoughts, to ponder before sleep shut all out. But to a few, this was impossible—ideas had to be expressed in words. First two started the exchange—here sounded the different points of the painter and the architect—others, one by one, joined in the argument until seven voices had taken sides. Some, hearing the reckless way that words were being wasted, could not continue undressing so pulled on a sweater or wrap and entered the group in order to give their words which were more understanding and plumbed the depth of the argument without waste.

So ran the argument: "Institution is the fine thing. Don't give me intellectual analysis which is dead before it issues. But institution unschooled or directed is but a start not a place to rest. Painting made through institution is complete in itself and filled with the freshness of Spring."

"Yes, most paintings are made to be complete and thereby expose their most evident weakness, that of incompleteness. Institution is a fine instrument but it is the first, not the fully symphony."

"Paintings have just as much completeness as architecture and consume the whole attention of the observed."

"Organic painting is complete in the same sense that organic architecture is complete. But paintings made on an easel out of the menial half thoughts of the moment have no place to live."

Then a long shuu—. "You are arguing too loudly and will disturb the Wrights. Best to move further away."

"The tea circle will be all right."

After the group is quietly seated and additional architectural support has joined, the argument continues.

"When one looks at a painting or reads a book, it consumes the whole attention and a sense of completeness is there."

"You have the wrong psychology. The whole environment enters into the observer to alter the picture."

Tossed into the wing by an architect came this: "The whole trouble with an architect is that he is a sensitive individual. Just imagine a colonial house placed right here, next to Taliesin. The physical materials would remain the same, but organic quality would certainly take a setback."

Thus, continued the argument far into the night. It's good thing for apprentices that Mr. Wright does not lecture every night, for sleep is a valuable quality and quite necessary.

"THE THREE"—BEAL, TAFEL AND LAUTNER

The program at the Taliesin Playhouse this Sunday, August 26th, at 3 and 8 P.M., will be *Czar Ivan the Terrible,* a silent film made in U.S.S.R., and *Lullaby Land* one of Disney's best color cartoons.

The story of *Ivan* revolves around the serf Nikita, who is punished by his master as being in league with Satan because of his attempts to make wings and fly. The outstanding Russian actor of the Moscow Art Theater, L. M. Leonidoff, plays the czar. This film has received the most extravagant praise as a masterpiece by New York critics. And no wonder, for it is a great historical document of the tyrannical czar and his time, told with the dramatic power and technique characteristic of the best Russian productions.

AT TALIESIN

August 30, 1934

["Taliesin," vol. 1, no. 1, was the inaugural monograph of the Taliesin Fellowship. This particular issue contained Wright's designs for both a

One-Zone and a Two-Zone House, as described briefly in the following column. These small-house studies preceded the early Usonian Lusk and Jacobs houses. "Taliesin" was completed and sent out to it's initial subscribers around Christmas 1934.]

The small-house problem has invaded us again at Taliesin through the work on the soon appearing "Monograph." The Small House— price ranging between $3,500 and $5,500—has been one of the most neglected architectural fields. The "big architect" could not make a living at building small houses, so his thought has run to other directions. But now, there is a definite need for careful study of the small house. This is the only type of work there is for the architect, since the era of plenty has vanished. He can make it worthwhile if he thinks along the new line of thought, not only from the financial standpoint, but beauty as well. We have only to look at the new Tennessee Valley projects to see a new 1934 architectural blunder. These architects have flooded the valley with a poor offshoot of the worn-out Colonial style; the style that is neat and clean looking, which in reality is a continuous "swipe." It always borrows. This Colonial house, painted white, with lovely pea green shutters that are never used, sells for $3,500 on long-term credit. Cheap enough. But what about is functioning? Its relation to the terrain? Its workability for the family? Its growth? Materials? These phases have been sadly neglected.

In designing this new house, Mr. Wright is keeping in mind firstly the plan workability for the whole family. There must be three zones in the house—work, quiet and slumber. These zones grow out of the housewife's need to keep the house within easy command, as to children, quiet and cleanliness. There must be inexpensive units for kitchen, bath and heating, close together in plan. These units can be shipped to the building site at low cost. Around this, the house is designed. Its materials are brick, concrete, or prefabricated composition.

Work on the stone floor for the Hillside draughting room is being carried on through the cold weather with coats and gloves. Our master-mason, Charles Curtis of Mineral Point has returned to stay indefinitely. Mr. Curtis is one of our major inspirations in stone cutting.

Mr. and Mrs. Wright have been in Chicago visiting and John Lautner has returned to Marquette to drive Mrs. Lautner back to Taliesin. Mrs. Lautner has been visiting her family. Mrs. Gillham and Mrs. Beal have

been visiting the orchard this week. H. Fever has been visiting Quincy
Beal. On Thursday evenings the Fellowship visit Mr. and Mrs. Porter for
a round of the Virginia Reel Ghost and nice hot chocolate.

China Express is our picture for the coming Sunday. This is a new
sound picture from Russia, based on a dramatic revolution on a train's
run through China.

AT TALIESIN

September 11, 1934

Charlie Curtis

Charlie Curtis is our master stone mason. He is 78 years old now, but
he still has that quality of youth that makes him eligible for apprenticeship at Taliesin. Still active, he works with an agility that is
positive in its results.

In years past he did much of the stone at Taliesin—and much of the
best of it at that. Having worked with him off and on for the past two
years I have come to know him not only as a man whose character is a
reflection of the sterling character of the stones he works with, but I
know he is an artist and a philosopher, too.

He was born on the Cornish coast. He father was a stone-mason by
trade and as a child Charlie played among the stones as his father worked
and soon learned to love "stone." It was natural that he should have become a mason. "Handle the stones like they were eggs," his father re-
peatedly told him, and Charlie passed this important axiom down to me.

Granite was abundant nearby in Wales and in these days each block
was cut by hand. Just as the early American pioneers had to cut down
huge trees and pit their personal power against raw materials and
naturally developed robust characters—(man in tune with nature)—
so is there something noble that gets into the character of a white-
haired stone mason by way of his work.

The best masons we have had here were usually old in years and still
working away for the love of working and usually with something of
the salty philosophy of a Walt Whitman or a Thoreau in their minds.

Many times as I stand admiring Charlie's work I involuntarily say,
"Charlie you're a real artist." In his humble way he goes on working

pretending not to hear me—sometimes he naively says, "Well Abe him doin' the best h'l know 'ow." Charlie doesn't realize that his work has the characteristics of art and that his simple philosophy is parallel to that of the true artist throughout history—he just knows that he does his best in everything and will never do a bad job even though it is to be out of man's sight. He says, "h'l know it's there and h'l don't want to be on bad terms with myself. No."

Charlie is five foot nine, lean and slightly stooped. He weighs but 140 pounds. Has snow white hair and a long white mustache over a firm jaw. He and his old corn cob pipe are inseparable except during work. He never smokes when he works but will stop several times a day when the spirit moves and sit down for a smoke. He advocates work so that he can rest, work so that he can work, and work so that he can sleep. And he rises with the sun as a master man should. He loves to eat and to walk and to be among men as to be among his stones.

He says, "There is nothing like the rock" and holding both arms out and shaking his hands up and down "h'l like to get the feel of the rock into me 'ands." Each stone has a strong individuality of its own—one can be split—you must use the point on this one—a set will break this one, you will have to use the stone hammer 'ere, etc. And he can tell by a glance at a man what his character is just as he is able to tell it in the stones.

It is refreshing to hear him talk with his "H'l say there boy." And speaking of a stone beautifully cut, he'll say "h'aint she the berries?" or "Oh, say, h'it's a bird." Then he chuckles, his eyes glistening and apparently to himself says "yes" and chuckles again nodding and saying "yes." Then he is likely to repeat, "Yep, she's a beauty, Abe."

"Well Charlie are you happy?" Mr. Wright asked one Sunday. "I don't know how not to be happy." And then his eyes twinkling with a chuckle repeats, sotto voice, slow, his "yes."

He believes heartily in what we are doing here at Taliesin—has as much respect for Mr. Wright and is determined to stay with us until the buildings are finished or he is laid away. We are putting up a home for him nearby where he can oversee the work and Mrs. Curtis, his good wife, can oversee him.

ABE DOMBAR

[Abrom Dombar obviously enjoyed a close relationship with Charlie Curtis and developed a serious interest in his craft. This is evident in two very visible examples of stonework by Dombar—the carved "TALIESIN" at the eastern entry to Taliesin off Highway 23 and the Fellowship "cornerstone" at Hillside.]

AT TALIESIN

September 19, 1934

Japanese Prints

[It has been well documented that the Japanese print was an important inspiration and love of Frank Lloyd Wright. He shared his vast collection of prints and rare Oriental artifacts with the Fellowship often through talks and exhibits; even integrating many two- and three-dimensional priceless pieces within the very walls of Taliesin and Hillside. Japanese prints from his collection often found their way to apprentices as gifts from Wright at holidays. They were just one of many abstract morsels of inspirational and creative nourishment that he offered the hungry Fellowship apprentices at Taliesin.]

Japanese prints were a mirror of the floating world—of the popular life and scenes of the daily existence of the Japanese common people and today they are the only record we have of Japanese life at that great period which began with the Momoyama and prevailed through the succeeding periods up to 1840. The print came to us via France, the habitual discoverer. The de Goncourt brothers first discovered them, brought them to Paris in bales as waste paper and ripped them out on the floor of the attic of their home where Beaux Arts students used to come and rummage about in them and study them. The French have written many books since upon Japan and Japanese prints.

So large a body of the prints were destroyed in the succession of fires which have burned Tokyo to the ground five times that what remains is a mere fragment—and this fragment we have owing only to the care with which the country people cherished the prints as souvenirs of the visit to the capital. The print is one of the greatest expressions of the nature of materials as fine art, a creation in perfect accord with the materials of which it is made and the process used in the making. Not only were the prints a full record of a unique civilization, they were also the impetus and motivation influence of our so-called modern art and so have intrinsic value.

Hiroshige and Hokusai, whose work is represented so completely in Mr. Wright's collection, were the greatest interpreters of landscape perhaps the world has ever known. They were worshipped by the people because of their sympathetic understanding of Japanese life and their ability to show it to the people as beautiful. Hiroshige especially achieved a sense of breadth and continuity of scene of which the actual print is a glimpse without limiting the sense of environment. Sometimes this effect would be achieved by a portion of a tree truck at the edge of the print or end of a trailing gown as the Geisha left the room giving an importance to the thing suggested and not seen greater than that seen in the drawing. Such an achievement in delimitation is a tenet of modern architecture. By the use of the simple convention called notan they arrived at a feeling of atmosphere — distance without destroying the convention and the limitation of the flat. Simple conventions like the seals and title labels aid the sense of the third dimension or sense of depth — volume — as contrasted with the labored and conscious modeling of French methods to achieve what is called "volume."

Shigemasa and Shunsho were early artists who depicted the popular figures of the stage. Their fine prints have preserved the character and environment of the people of the earlier times. Utamaro and Toyokuni were later artists — leaders in this movement and lived and worked in the Yoshiwara itself. The prints were not only portraits of the places and characters portrayed, they were interpretations and were all that is called "decorative." This decorative quality is a very great quality in art as it springs from something internal of intrinsic value. The Japanese were also masters of what we call "composition." Black was always used, conscious of its pattern, as were all the other colors and in perfect rhythm and correlation each to each and all in all.

The *Hundred Views of Edo* was Hiroshige's last and probably greatest work. The series, *36 Views of Fuji* — extended to 46 by his virtuosity, was the last work of Hokusai. Degeneracy had already set in around them and after Hiroshige and Hokusai, came to the exaggeration and loss of respect for limitations that is degeneracy. The succeeding artists became more and more extravagant, less restrained and imaginative.

Truly, the great art of the Japanese prints were, as the name given the school by the Japanese, "Ukiyo-e," would indicate; a mirror of the floating world that was the popular life of Edo, the great capital of Japan, in the 18th century. America possesses the finest collection of prints now extant Japan herself waking up to their great art value too late.

WILLIAM ADAIR BERNOUDY

AT TALIESIN
September 20, 1934

[Music permeated many aspects of the daily life of the Fellowship and imbued many apprentices with an understanding of its place among the arts. Not only was music omnipresent and important, its performance so too was an event looked forward to— from performances at the Taliesin Playhouse, classical pieces "broadcast" over the Taliesin Hilltower speaker to impromptu piano accompaniment to drafting work in the studio. Betty Cass, a frequent visitor to Taliesin and columnist for the *Wisconsin State Journal,* captured in her column an initially tense but then wonderfully humorous moment between Mr. and Mrs. Wright, subtitled the "affair of the stringed instruments" (reprinted herein, see appendix D).]

The Fellowship is so music hungry it will even take *The Tales of Hoffman* on the piano or sit in at grand opera. Sunday evenings we make music among ourselves; Yen, violin; Edgar, piano; Gene, baritone.

They bring us Brahms, Handel, Bach, Beethoven and Cesar Franck. We begin by singing together a Bach chorale— "Joy of Our Desiring," the words altered to suit our own desiring. We sing it on various occasions whenever we get together. It is our "for he's a jolly good fellow." And it is our work song.

We sing it in the little old shingled chapel Sunday mornings when the bell stops tolling. We might all get up and sing it in public gatherings in which we happened to be. And we may broadcast it soon:

Joy in work is man's desiring,
Holly wisdom. Love most bright;
Drawn by hope our souls aspiring,
Soar to uncreated light,
Nature's love our strength that fashioned,
With the fire of life impassioned,
Striving still to Truths unknown,
Working, striving, though alone,
Through the way where Hope is guilding,
Hark what inspiration rings,
Where the man in life confiding,
Drinks to joy from deathless springs,
Ours is beauty's fairest pleasure,
Ours is wisdom's greatest treasure,
Nature ever leads her own,
In the love of Joys unknown.

Several of our fellows — a girl too, is a fellow here — play occasionally as the spirit moves. We very much want to have an ensemble "a la camera" as a regular feature of Taliesin life.

And if we could find a young man or woman cellist, violinist, pianist or viola player who was not satisfied to be just that only, but wanted to broaden their basis for playing by broadening their general culture, we would be tempted to give them the equivalent of scholarships elsewhere and make them one with us. It is difficult, however, to find musicians who care about or are able to be anything more than mere players.

Last Sunday afternoon Jane Dudley brought her quartet — with a quintet attachment, to our Playhouse and played as Dohnanyi — the allegro from a difficult quintet the quartet has just put into rehearsal, a Beethoven quartet of great beauty — beautifully played be it said, and Smetana's "Aus meinen leben?" a personalized tone-story of life and grief, making effective use of cello and viola, the two instruments richest in pathos, it seems to me, in any ensemble.

Somebody told Jane to pronounce Smetana, "Smettna," which she did in announcing the number, and will blush with annoyance if she reads it here, or, more likely, will insist that she was right. But never mind, she can play astonishingly well. A girl as handsome as Jane can usually do little else than take up all her time just being handsome. In fact, we may say that Jane Dudley plays better than several "virtuosi" who have turned up lately and for this, thanks, I believe, to her master Leopold Auer who turned out Elman, Zimbalist, Heifetz, Erica Morini and several others who, violin in hand, hold the center of the violin-world stage today.

Nor do I see why the populace—"the eye of the vox populi is upon us"—should be afraid of Beethoven.

As Jane's ensemble rendered this second number of the famous Beethoven Opus 59, one of a group of superb quartets, everything music can humanly bring poured out richly from this work and was sufficiently objective to please even a native or any natural who really loves music.

Next to Jane's performance in these numbers was the fine cello playing of Janette Wieder. And now we must pick up the vogue of the reporter to say that Ruth Mortonson as the viola player (the viola is a fine instrument and I'll be damned if I can understand why it is so neglected by soloists) was able and effective. The second violinist, Rosalind Paykel (should be Paquette—such is philology) gave admirable support. Mrs. Henrietta Buell Mortonson was the quartet's hastily improvised quintet—attachment for the Dohnanyi at the piano, Mrs. Carpenter being absent. She played remarkably well for a charming mother of babies playing at the same time at home.

On the whole, the Jane Dudley quartet-quintet can and does make good music very well indeed. They are going on tour and a good thing too. They will bring a fine performance to thousands. But you should just hear our trio-quartet-quintet when we get one.

More and better music "a la camera" (music in a room—room at home I say) is a necessary factor in more and genuine culture.

In fact, next to architecture such music is the thing homo sapiens—genus Americana—most needs always, of course, an organic economic system excepted. But musicians all tend toward the psychosis, psychopathic because they are just players, or just "composers."

They have neither time nor will to live even for what they call their "Art," and seldom succeed in being anybody at all in their own right. Especially when at home or off their job.

FRANK LLOYD WRIGHT

Madisonians and Wisconsinites missed a real treat if they did not see the charming English picture at the Playhouse last Sunday. *Heart Song* was a beautiful musical comedy.

This next Sunday, the 23rd, we shall see another picture of the same caliber called *Paris-Mediterranee,* or *Romance of Paris.*

This is a very recent French film in which the famous star Annabelle plays the leading role. Coffee and cookies will be served as usual, and the performance begins at 3 in the afternoon.

AT TALIESIN

September 27, 1934

[This column describes another Tuesday evening lecture given by Wright, which concerned two of his more unusual, to-date, projects — the Doheny Ranch Resort (1923) and the Lake Tahoe Summer Colony (1922). The Doheny Ranch predated and foreshadowed the San Marcos-in-the-Desert project. The Lake Tahoe cabins were romantic and still logically creative responses to use and site. Both projects were exceptionally suited for their particular sites; each evidence of Wright's genius for appropriate integration of the built environment within Nature.]

Mr. Wright's Tuesday evening lecture this week was concerned with two of his most beautiful projects, the Doheny ranch and the Tahoe cabins. The Doheny group is planned for the mountains near Los Angeles, and is so arranged that the natural beauty of the site is preserved. So far the Californians have mutilated the hills by cutting the roadways like gashes and slicing off the rounded hilltops, planting lawns where grass does not grow naturally, and bringing in exotic trees and shrubs to beard the houses. Mr. Wright planned his houses so that there is only enough excavation to make firm footings and so that the trees and sagebrush are not disturbed, keeping the natural beauty of the country intact. Each house is of concrete block construction, with flat roofs flowing into the hills and forming terraces, and placed in ravines, on the hillside, ever boldly on the top. Looking down from the terrace of one building, instead of a series of closed, forbidding roof tops, there seems to be a terraced garden stretching endlessly to the valley below. The road rises to a level on a short easy grade, and approaches the group through tunnels and bridges, which are part of the scheme of construction. For the highest house, there is a garage on the road level and a self-service elevator to the house itself. By means of this plan, there is privacy and beauty in abundance for the residents, with no sense of being crowded.

The Tahoe project is planned for Emerald Bay on Lake Tahoe, in the Sierra Nevada. Being again a site of great natural beauty, the cabins are made to blend with the landscape, instead of forcing themselves into view. There are several types, each planned for its particular hot, the wigwam, the fir tree, the shore type, and the floating barges like houseboats. Here again there is no excavation, and the camps are built of the materials found on the site, wood for the superstructure and concrete blocks made with the glistening beach sand for the sub-structure. As many as two hundred cabins could be built without destroying the landscape.

Neither of these two projects has as yet been built. Mr. Wright says that an architect's best projects are never built, and that a half-finished, nearly-ready drawing is always immediately constructed. Each building is during the actual process of construction, an education in itself for that particular building, so that when it is finished, the architect knows how it should be done—not always the way it was completed.

Three new apprentices have appeared during this past week. Cornelia Brierly arrived fresh from the halls of Carnegie Tech to learn with the rest of us the meaning of organic architecture. Edgar Kaufmann, also of Pittsburgh, came to see if we lived up to all that he had read about the Fellowship and wound up by signing up for himself and for one of his friends. He has only recently returned from studying painting in Florence and Vienna, so now he is coming here to learn something about it. Mr. Davidson, promoter of Mr. Wright's farm project, came for a day and stayed two, telling us all about the house Mr. Wright built for him in Buffalo. Today we have a young Englishman as guest, a student at Harvard.

MARYBUD LAUTNER

On Sunday, September 30th, the Playhouse presents the latest picture in which George Arliss stars, *The Last Gentlemen.* It is a whimsical comedy revolving about a crotchety old millionaire's sly effort to pick a worthy heir from his many relatives. This American film is one of the few Hollywood productions which we show at the Playhouse and should hold great entertainment for our patrons. Come and enjoy a cup of coffee during the performance.

AT TALIESIN

September 28, 1934

The Apprentice Who Built One Fire Each Morning

Starting fires on brisk fall mornings when the brilliant sun was just coming over the long line of hills, or on cold winter ones when it was so dark that you couldn't see to find matches, kindling or fireplace was just a sideline with him. He wasn't a "regular." He didn't have five or six fires to make each morning and great piles of kindling already cut and stacks of wood waiting for him in the right places. These luxuries were provided by others for themselves.

These "others" were legitimate fire-makers and behaved as such. There was a certain sureness in the way they got their wood; in the way they carried it in. A certain authority about the lighting of the match. They had aplomb. Their fires were sure, always, to start and if there seemed to be the slightest hesitancy on the part of the fire to cooperate there was always the hidden can of kerosene handy.

But he had no aplomb. None whatsoever. He had never even been a Boy Scout. Each fire was to him a different problem—a new creation. In the first place the kindling—gathered from far and near—was most of it wet and too large to break. Of course there was no axe. Not for him anyway. That was in hiding too. So the kindling would appear in every shape and size from fragrant grape baskets to old brooms. Sometimes egg crates helped along and there were gala mornings when wonderfully dried shingles were found like a nest of eggs—stowed carefully away by some other firebuilder.

But whatever the provender—be it egg crate or broom—it was all assembled nicely over a scramble of newspaper. The precious match breathlessly struck. A flash—a sputter—a tiny burst of flame and at once the entire structure would gasp, tremble and fall in a heap. A cloud of pale blue smoke would rise and grin over the ruins. Once more and then several times again. Finally there would be the triumphant mastery of wood, dried by this time, over the mind and the room would light up with the most beautiful fire it had ever held. The apprentice would gaily go off to breakfast. This was success.

During the darkest and coldest part of the winter he became a trifle exasperated over the evident superiority of the regulars and began taking (it wasn't really stealing) a very little of the beautifully cut and assembled wood from the holy of holies—the kitchen-stove pile. Such a little could not have been noticed but for the tracks in the snow. And a chance remark dropped at dinner that "The next time anyone meddles with the stove wood, there's be a bullet through"—this, from the regular "hired man" who husbanded the cook—stopped all adventure in that direction immediately.

But undaunted each morning regularly there came the final burst of fire—each time more beautiful and brilliant. Egg crates and grape baskets gave way to sticks which stuck through the rest of the winter.

Until one morning the warm sun shone onto the windows of Taliesin and the apprentice, whose one right to fame lay in that his fire had been built in the inner studio office of the Master himself, cleaned out the fireplace and opened wide the doors to let in the warm fresh air of the Spring.

Now—again—the brisk fall mornings with the brilliant sun just over the long line of hills and the fire constantly built and constantly warming and cheering the heart of Taliesin. The studio fire is now a morning masterpiece and a pattern for all other fires on the place, if I do say it myself.

EUGENE MASSELINK

[The building complex of Taliesin had a total of sixteen fireplaces.]

On Sunday, the Playhouse presents the latest picture starring George Arliss, *The Last Gentleman.* It is a whimsical comedy revolving about a crotchety old millionaire's sly efforts to pick a worthy heir from his many relatives. This American film is one of the few Hollywood productions which we show at the Playhouse and should be extremely enjoyable. Come and enjoy a cup of coffee during the performance.

AT TALIESIN

October 19, 1934

And the apprentices said to Frank Lloyd Wright, speak to us of steel. And our Master answered his apprentices.

Before you would know steel you must find the qualities that distinguish it from all other metals. These properties of the material are its ductability, rigidity, continuity, adaptability in welding, and, above all, its great tensile strength.

Previously there has been no material that could carry great weights in suspension. Because of this tensile attribute of steel, cantilever construction is a possibility and the system of the post and lintel becomes archaic. Nevertheless, our sluggish public, unable to grasp the possibilities of so revolutionary a material, use it in antiquated building forms and only for a few valid purposes such as for railroad rails and machinery and when we do build with it the building looks like machinery.

The first time expression was given to its real nature was in the steel suspension bridge — Roebling's Brooklyn bridge. In its own right steel should be a beautiful expression and used with glass comparable to the spider web in the dew-covered grass of early morning. By visualizing the possibilities of continuity and tensile qualities of steel, imagine a spiderweb . . . building expressed in glistening steel and its complimentary partner — glass. Together these elements offer limitless possibilities of light and space consciousness. Contrast such a vision with the depraved buildings called "modern" where the grace of steel structure is camouflaged and encrusted with veneer slabs of stone or other unrelated materials that add nothing — save a crushing load and unnecessary expense. There is today no building that approaches the ideal of an organic steel structure.

All attempts to roll steel into new forms have been efforts of manufacturers to suit its integral qualities to existing "stick" construction methods that should have become obsolete with the advent of a material that allows for such plasticity.

We admit that in building with steel there are problems as yet unsolved; for instance it is found in combining steel and glass, that their coefficients of expansion are so different that glass used in larger surfaces is liable to be crushed by the steel. Since every problem carries in itself its solution this is not an unsurmountable difficulty. Neither is the problem of rust. We have stainless steel, expensive because of patent laws that allow ideas to be held from the public, and because of prevailing economic processes, the shelving of which would cause financial disruption.

Perhaps it is impossible to introduce the realism of our organic steel architecture to an existing system so mongrel as ours. If this ideal is attained, it may be through such a group as our Taliesin apprentices whose ambition is to experience the building of an organic unit in each available material—stone, wood, clay, brick, wood, pulp, glass and steel, etc. As a means to this end, we have the Taliesin workday wherein by combining mental and physical labor, we learn to correlate the energy that stimulates organic thought. We believe in the experience of work for "what a man does that he has."

CORNELIA BRIERLY

We have a pleasure of presenting at the Playhouse Sunday, a picture made and produced by Dr. Arnold Fanck, the director of the *Hite Hell of Pitz Palu*—one of the greatest films of recent years. This latest picture by Dr. Fanck is called *Avalanche* and was made on the topmost heights of Mt. Blanc, the very highest peak of all Europe.

On this monarch of all the Alpine range the director staged the story of this photoplay, and the mountain itself was cast in the principal role. The film is a great achievement because not only did camera equipment have to be carried to the top of the famous mountain but also all the sound apparatus. The famous aviator, Ernest Udet, plays the important role in the film and many of the greatest pictures are made scaling the sides of the mountain during his daring flights. Udet makes the thrilling rescue of the hero who is cut off on the mountain top from the rest of the world by a tremendous story.

Mickey Mouse will also appear on the program in a film called *Moose Hunt.*

AT TALIESIN

November 22, 1934

A Taliesin weekend usually brings guests from far away or strange places. Last Sunday came one of Wisconsin's bravest and best with his best girl—George and Mrs. Parker of Janesville—he who made a quality pen outsell a cheap one and leads the field in consequence. Traveling is his passion. Far and wide the Parkers have gone about the world as a sort of avocation, bringing back all manner of trophies—not the least of them the tale he told to the Fellowship Sunday evening of his trip up the Yangtse River. And, he told the Fellows, too, some nice things about themselves. It is upon the character and vision of such men as George Parker that the Fellowship bases its hope for a more creative America.

The usual Sunday morning picnic—this morning wet and misty with sun streaks coming through—found the senior Parkers standing on top of "Sugarloaf" the highest point hereabouts—looking down at the gay picnic below and the scene on the plains beyond the keen eye and zest of true youth. When we stood together to sing our worksong, as we usually do Sunday evening just before supper, there was the suspicion of tears in the Parker eyes. Taliesin covets more contracts with men like George Parker and women like his good wife.

Side by side with the Parkers at Taliesin last Sunday were Edgar Kaufmann and his wife. Merchant prince and princess of Pittsburgh. Mrs. Kaufmann helps her husband manage the 13-story department store covering a block in the heart of the city and employing some two thousand five hundred people. And the talk he gave us Sunday evening, after we had got safely back from the Yangtse with the Parkers, showed that romance has not dropped out of merchandising just because Marco Polo is gone. Mr. Kaufmann gave us the most encouraging view we have had of the hand the enlightened merchant is taking in improving the product he sells. The merchant is naturally the anterunae of the maker but, more than that, now under leadership like Edgar Kaufmann's he is banding together to make actual experiments to improve the maker's output. Make it intrinsically better worth buying.

Good design in industry becomes more important every day in every way. And the modern merchant of the Kaufmann type is the "runner-up" for more organic performances in that line than just stylizing of "stream-lining" a product.

Just as every problem carries within itself its own solution, so every article of use in industrial life has a form and color and quality to be found in its own nature. So he believes and says.

This is good "Fellowship" faith also. A merchant like Mr. Kaufmann invariably takes a hand in the development of his city as a better place in which to live and he is a power behind official and journalistic Pittsburgh, working for city improvements on a large scale. No citizen who gets that far in can ignore the changes taking place in the state to make it a better state for the city to live in and the nation's policy to make the nation a better union of better states.

The short in men like George Parker and Edgar Kaufmann, as different in themselves as men ever are, is united the great impulse that will build a new and better way of American life for the American people.

The strength of Taliesin hope lies in this unity in diversity—his vision and purpose in the apparently mundane affairs of a better pen and better clothes and finer home fixings.

Art as we know it is something supremely useful to such men. Their appreciation and encouragement is vital, now, to anything worth the name. Last Sunday again came helpful encouragement from the outside—from sources where it should be found but so seldom is found. There is not much encouragement for us to come, directly, from other workers in the field of art. They all need encouragement themselves too desperately to give anything of the sort away.

FRANK LLOYD WRIGHT

[Both George Parker and Edgar Kaufmann, Sr., were to become clients—Parker commissioned Wright for a detached garage (1937), which was not built, as Parker died July 19, 1937 (Wright attended the funeral in Janesville and subsequently wrote an "At Taliesin" column eulogy, dated July 30, 1937); Kaufmann becoming a patron of Wright's for years to follow. Betty (Willoughby) Cass, columnist for the *Wisconsin State Journal* noted in her column on February 7, 1937, that Parker ("of the Parker Pen fame") had once offered free paint to Wisconsin farmers provided that they would not paint their barns red. She continued, "but immediately Frank Lloyd Wright, who was a Wisconsin farm boy before he was the world's most famous architect, wrote to the newspapers that farmers SHOULD paint their barns red because that was a color very much needed in the landscape. . . . and, so far as I can find out, very few farmers took up Mr. Parker's offer." In fact, Wright was said to have arbitrarily demanded that the Wisconsin legislature pass a law to require every farmer in the state to paint his barn a bright red. Lest it be misunderstood, this was obviously only a friendly argument, as each was known to have had a great admiration for the other.]

The Taliesin Playhouse will present *En Glad Gutt* (a happy boy) on this coming Sunday, the 25th of November. This picture is adapted from the immortal story of Norway by Bjornstjerne and is filmed in the beautiful valley of Gudbrandsdalen, with a cast of Norway's foremost players. When we saw the Swedish *Varmlanningarna* not long ago we were impressed particularly by the strong rugged character of the people. They were people of the north—a quality that came out in their faces, their action, their dancing and their music. Even the photography of the picture itself had a distinctive clearness and cleanness. We are looking forward to seeing in *En Glad Gutt* this same purpose and vigor and hope that the Scandinavian people in the region will avail themselves of the opportunity to come "back home" to the songs, the stories, the customs, the people and the language itself of old Norway.

AT TALIESIN
December 9, 1934

[The following column is of interest for several reasons. First, the newspaper article referred to was written by the then *Milwaukee Journal* staff writer Herbert Jacobs who, less than two years later and writing for the *Capital Times* newspaper in Madison, became a Wright client and recipient of the first built Usonian house. Jacobs recalled in his book, *Building with Frank Lloyd Wright: An Illustrated Memoir,* that his interview of Wright for the 1934 Journal article lasted "a little over ten minutes." Second, this column is the first to mention that work was under way on the Broadacre City models for eventual exhibit in New York. Last, the Memorial to the Soil Chapel project mentioned herein establishes the client and location (heretofore unknown) as well as a design date of 1934 (heretofore listed as 1936).]

A short while ago there appeared in a Milwaukee paper one of those lengthy résumés of a reporter's visit to Taliesin. Stock headlines reported the glorious news that "Wright's Apprentices Cut Dreams Out of Stone." Stock because the work gone forth from Taliesin's workshop these many years and of the work being done "on location" the last two years has been to the newspaper only "dreams." But why in terms of "dreams?" Because neither the dream nor the formula plays lord and master here, is that why the misrepresentation? Or is it because when anything comes from the creative artist, from clear thought uncontaminated by fashions, by the power of money and the majority (and the majority is the mob) it must seem to the newspaper, which is the servant of all these, in the category of a "dream." If so, then the work is a dream and we workers are merely dreamers? But we "deny the allegation and refuse to marry the girl." Actual work does not come from dreams but from pure creative thought put into action. That eliminates "air castles" for us. If by any chance the life and action here seemed to lie in a different world outside the category of the newspaper reporters it is simply because of our attempt to live.

And so here now is growing an actual model in terms of recent work by Master and apprentices. No, not dreams. Objectified ideas in concrete form. You may touch them and handle them and use them as patterns.

To memorialize the Wisconsin pioneers: a chapel of reinforced concrete and glass (broad and sturdy) for the early settler family of the Newmanns at Cooksville came to the drawing board from the master's hand last week, soon to be turned over to eager apprentices for working drawings. Whitman's "Pioneers! O Pioneers!" has found third-dimensional form in architecture here.

"Moved in yesterday. You have made another masterpiece. Thrilling beyond word"—came a wire from Dean and Mrs. Willey of Minneapolis. The Willeys had moved in time to serve Thanksgiving dinner before their large living room fireplace. This long low simple-lined dwelling is the latest completed work of the Taliesin studio. Complete, too, furniture and all. To Mrs. Willey goes the laurels of the world's best client.

Two years ago Mr. Wright's *Disappearing City* appeared from the press. Today this treatise on the decentralization of the present city has become extremely vital. Washington is slowly realizing its importance as inevitable. Early next year an important New York exhibition sponsored by the characteristic "big-boys" will present Taliesin's pattern for a New America in form of the Broadacre City. So a visitor to Taliesin within the next few months will find all working night and day on a twelve-foot-square model of Broadacres. Its scale will cover four square miles illustrating the principle that the city of the future will be everywhere or nowhere. As auxiliaries to the large model will be numerous larger scale models of specific buildings. To attempt such a project within less than a year's time would be futile were it not for the fact that much already has been designed—contained in most of Mr. Wright's work in recent years. They contain such projects as St. Marks Tower, organic solution of the tall building problem; large and small factory units; gas and mercantile unions; the farm units of prefabricated steel; the new theater; the tourist camp. The houses will range from the machine-age-luxury House on the Mesa, the Doheny Ranch Houses, the Tahoe Cabins down to the Prairie House, the Two-Zone House, the Medium House, and the Minimum House.

Structure to be designed and modeled include the County Center which is the only tall building in Broadacres, school groups, hotel and chapels, market centers and art center, hangars, clubs and outdoor or automobile objectives. An acre to a family is minimum and all land utilized in a general scheme natural to life.

All this also is not dreaming nor is it planning ahead of the times. If America were up to the times, the times wouldn't be going down hill.

Last Spring the Lloyd Jones Chapel down in the valley was the scene of many fine Sunday sermons by many of Madison's "brethren of the Cloth" and many University personages. To them we give many and heartfelt thanks. But all the time we felt that we were becoming too dependent upon the performances of others, becoming too much the "much and mediocre" congregation. So this year we are each in his turn and all in time, both congregation and pulpiteer. Throughout all the Fellowship assignments have been given that particular assignment going to the individual who most needs the specific knowledge derived from it. Last Sunday Gene Masselink opened the Chapel seen with "The first shall be the last first." Next Sunday comes "Purpose" with Bill Bernoudy pulpiteering, later on Cornelia Brierly on "Prudence," the rest will follow.

A short time ago John Gloag, of London, well-known author and publicist spending a few days at Taliesin brought us all very close to the London scene and last week our own Jamesway James and wife brought Mr. Gareth Jones also of London and private secretary to Great Britain's once Prime Minister David Lloyd George took us much closer not only to London and Lloyd George but to the men of current fame all over Europe due to his personal contact with them. Of Russia, he has been barred four times from Russia and now finally, of Stalin, of Lenin's widow, etc., etc. His charming manner in personation of Europe's greatest combining each with the salient features of their own outlook made Gareth Jones a splendid actor as well as great journalist.

BOB MOSHER

You will see at the Taliesin Playhouse this coming Sunday the most exciting and most thoroughly western picture that the distributing company in Milwaukee could send us. Even the tin cans in which they were sent were painted red and might have contained explosives. So the Playhouse will explode with a red-blooded American picture — with Buck Jones as hero and the Western plains as the scene. Even our favored foreign productions could give us nothing that even approximates this, our two-gunned, roaring, rip-snorting cowboy picture. To finish the program in truly American style there will be Mickey Mouse again in another later production, *Steeple Chase*.

AT TALIESIN
December 10, 1934

We, at Taliesin, were awakened the other morning by the usual 6 o'clock breakfast bell, knowing by the peculiar, dulled and muffled sound of the snow-covered bell that we awoke to a new season. The harvest time had passed along with the turkey of the day before, although it was the sentiment of the group that the spirit of thanks and appreciation characteristic of Thanksgiving day was to be felt each day each year.

Daylight gave us Wisconsin in sharp pattern of black and white, ushering in nature's rest time, winter. Forced inside and drawn closer to the great fireplaces we gather to work each day in the studio on the Broadacre City model. An imaginary landscape is taking shape in plywood. The courses of rivers and the forming of lakes which were first determined by the sweep of a pencil in hand are now being cut by the bank saw. Plans and elevations in the flat are taking on physical form in balsa wood and cardboard yielding to the straight edge and sharp blades.

The work of the week was pleasantly interrupted by the eventful weekend which began when the Fellowship and close friends gathered at the chapel to open this season's Sunday morning services. This year each member of the Fellowship has a Sunday in which to conduct the service and preach the sermon on an assigned subject which has to do with some phase of human character. Gene Masselink conducted the service this first Sunday by singing and giving a fine, thoughtful, and sincere sermon of a quality which would be quite enviable among many church leaders. We remained after the singing of the "Fellowship's Work Song," which closed the service, and had dinner there in the chapel.

Guests last weekend were Mr. and Mrs. James, who brought with them Gareth Jones of London, England. Mr. and Mrs. Stanley Marcus, Dallas, were our guests also. Mr. Jones afforded us joyful entertainment with dramatized stories in dialect of his experiences in Russia, England, and Wales. Being in the employ of David Lloyd George, he gave us a fine character study of this important and famous Welshman. Welsh characteristics were brought to light in his humorous, quick-witted dialogues.

[The visit of the Marcus' came at a period of genuine enthusiasm and renewed activity with actual outside architectural commissions. As Abrom Dombar expressed in a letter written late 1934, "So there is activity in the studio again and everybody is happy." There was finally (after so little so long) studio work for the apprentices at Taliesin—the Broadacre City model was commissioned the month prior; the Stanley Marcus House in Dallas (a close "cousin" of the earlier House-on-the-Mesa project); the Memorial to the Soil Chapel and the Kaufmann project proposals under way (a Pittsburgh planetarium, an office for Kaufmann as well as the Kaufmann "retreat" in Bear Run).]

AT TALIESIN

December 20, 1934

Despite the unceasing flow of energy that manifests itself in human lives there is one energy, that cosmic spark, that the Universal Spirit reserves for great men. Two such great men have just met at Taliesin—our master, Frank Lloyd Wright, and the poetic naturalist, Jens Jensen. With different words these two strong men sing a freedom song for the beauty of America. We apprentices are at Taliesin to build our master's song into our lives. Jens Jensen offered to our score a new theme to aid in the building. This Dane, with all the strength of his powerful vitality, is trying to help Americans be Americans by conserving their regional foliage and intelligently replanting where men have scarred the landscape. Each section of the country, Jensen says, must be kept true to the nature of the region by using native plants, for the aggression of foreign trees and shrubs, by vulgarizing the country, reduces it to mediocrity. Foliage is part of the organic makeup of its natural habitat. Birches have in them the essence of the north—their trunks are of (and out of) the snow; Hawthornes by their horizontality express the repose of the plains. To feel the emotion of the land, plant foliage in sweeping masses—acres of wild plum blossoms that float like clouds over the plains. Let the shadbush grow with the birch so that in the spring the pink tinge of the shad buds creates a spirit that only a Hiroshige or a Hokusai could interpret—and did—in the Japanese print. It becomes poetry among the silver birches.

When a certain park commission asked Jensen to set the boundaries for a state park he said, "Take me to a hilltop." From there he viewed the country. "You see that range of distant hills? Take all of it—as much as can be seen and yet a little of the part hidden by these hills in front."

It may mean more than 100,000 acres but when a highway is built the poor starved city folk can drive along that ridge and learn from the breadth of this sweeping view how to become Americans. For each group of people must have or develop a feeling for their own land before they can express their character as an American nation.

Jens Jensen is of Danish virility. Erect, ruddy, white haired. In conversation his "w's" are pronounced "v's" and his flow of pictorial speech is interspersed by a firmly accented, "By Jove!" His experiences are to the listener as fresh as ice crystals on pine boughs. He tells us that when the leaves of the lupine begin to unfold they are tinged with pastel colors and have the appeal of a baby's palm. And, he says, the most touchingly beautiful sight in nature is to see that leaf with a drop of dew upon it.

CORNELIA BRIERLY

On Sunday the 23rd — just before Christmas — we are showing a British film that ranks with the beautiful German musical comedies that we have seen. *Waltz Time* is filled with the music of Johann Strauss and was made in England. Evelyn Laye plays the leading role in this light opera which in spite of its English direction has captured the true Viennese flavor. It has played in New York with great success and should continue at the Playhouse likewise.

[The "naturalist," "conservationist," and "world-famous" land-scape architect Jens Jensen, whose Taliesin visit this column described, wrote to the Fellowship on January 30, 1935 — "Dear Friends: Days have passed — weeks have gone by — more than one moon has come and gone since my long to be remembered days spent amongst you. I can still see, in the fading light of a late December day, Taliesin peacefully coming out of the ancient cliffs of which it is a part. What a delight it was climbing over the hills with a new found friend. And the Sunday walk to the Chapel; the early morning bell and dawn slowly rising over the valley of the Wisconsin: Sunday evening, when your lovely hostess, mother to you all, ruled supreme. And last, the friendly farewell — thanks — a thousand times thanks."]

AT TALIESIN

December 23, 1934

Last Sunday John Lautner spoke at Unity Chapel, continuing the series of services the Taliesin Fellowship is having there. Speaking on "Energy," he said that to be doing something is better than nothing but you may be doing something all your life and still have done nothing. It is again a matter of quality rather than quantity. What is energy? No one knows much about it. The Scientists have been studying its aspects for many years trying to get the cause or the nature. They have split atoms and drawn pictures of them — developed electricity — but what is this force? The world is a bundle of energies in one form or another. Just as the dog cannot comprehend man, so man cannot comprehend the universe. No component part can see the whole or is the whole. To study the physical aspects, at least, of the working of energy in the body of man; we all know that we breathe air and eat food and these fuels are converted into energy. We know something about the chemical processes involved. But when we get to the endocrine system and the controlling factors we are bewildered. Each individual has slightly different developments of each of his glands and his entire makeup — so he is an individual and acts and reacts in his own way.

No one knows the essence of energy — therefore we should consider one of its most important aspects — direction. There is a natural direction for all energies in this world. The animal's energy is directed by instinct; plants just grow as strong as their environment permits. But man, claiming to be above instinctive behavior, presumably directs himself and his energies.

John continues saying:

"Concerning the direction of myself I have always proceeded from generals to particulars. Instead of jumping this way and that way and from one thing to another I have been endeavoring to establish a broad base and then to narrow down or to concentrate my energies in one field of life."

"That is why I do not have the habit of being energetic. In school instead of energetically sitting down and writing the lesson, I wondered if it was of any value — what was the meaning of it or did it have any? Some courses I believed stupid, so I just forgot about them and took a passing grade. Others that were good I would study. I believed in using my energies on things which I considered important in life — in living."

"At any rate I have been growing every year and intend to keep on growing. Trying to grow like a tree, taking what food or fuel I judge good. But as all life consumes energy in growth so do I. I don't feel that I have the right to produce until I have attained more growth. Of course, I consider what little I do produce as part of my growth. Taliesin is the perfect soil in which to grow. I believe when I have attained more growth I will have more strength and energy. I think my energy is latent or potential and is gradually coming out. However, we are learning to see the essence of the abstract here at Taliesin and this joy of work — in truth — in beauty is making me stronger."

"But talking on energy is like talking on what makes the world go around. If anyone thinks they know — I would like to learn."

And the meeting broke up in discussion and dinner.

Taliesin invites you to the Playhouse to attend the western premiere of *The Blue Light* on Dec. 30. *The Blue Light* is the most significant experience in drama, music and photography that has come to the modern screen for years.

The film is co-operatively produced, acted and directed by Leni Reifenstahl and Bela Balacz. Greatest credit, however, must be given to Schneeberger, master photographer, who does his work so well that in New York frequently the audience responded with applause. It is a non-commercial production, the dialogue is in English although the film as a hole is international in character.

Taliesin brings *The Blue Light* for the first time to this part of the country. On this occasion there will be added music, coffee as usual, and discussion, if you wish, by the fireplace afterwards. The admission charge will be the same as ever, 50 cents.

It has just played for five weeks in New York City where all the critics spoke enthusiastically about it. The *New York Herald Tribune* writes, "In the magnificent setting of the Italian Tyrol a picture has been woven from the strands of an old folk tale which, for sheer pictorial beauty, is perhaps unexcelled. Shot against sifted sunlight, the streaming spray of cascades and webbed shadows of nightfall, these vast horizontal peaks pushing their way from the farthest Alpine boundaries have a deeply moving grandeur. And, even more, the legend of the Dolomite village holds one captive by an eerie strangeness."

The critic of the *World Telegram* says, "Couched in photographic masterpieces made for the most part in and about the Italian Dolomites, *The Blue Light* is one of the most beautiful pictures I have ever seen. Nor is it lacking in drama and suspense, either."

Many months of devotion on the part of the Taliesin Fellowship—the young men and women who unselfishly made time—has brought the models here, where their worth for the future may be judged.

—Frank Lloyd Wright, "At Taliesin," April 26, 1935

INTRODUCTION

Where, in 1934, the "At Taliesin" columns covered a range of topics that included not only the Fellowship, Taliesin, and Frank Lloyd Wright but the world at large as well, the 1935 series concentrated more on specific work-related matters. The first trip to Arizona (Taliesin West to-be) and events there, coupled with the intense pressure to complete the Broadacre City exhibit models in time for their April 15 New York debut, quite completely monopolized the Fellowship's time and attention for most of the first half of 1935.

Architectural commissions were still only trickling into Taliesin. Wright and the Fellowship worked on the Marcus residence project (Dallas, Texas) and the German Warehouse remodeling in Richland Center (a pioneering adaptive reuse project of Wright's only warehouse design, done twenty years earlier). Discussions also began with Edgar Kaufmann concerning his office remodeling, while the drawings were being prepared in the latter half of 1935 for "Fallingwater," his Bear Run weekend retreat. Even Taliesin- and Hillside-related "reconstruction" projects were kept to a minimum with only slight modifications at Taliesin (expanding apprentice rooms and the rebuilding of the dam) in the summer.

Wright traveled noticeably more in 1935: the Arizona trek, the Broadacre City model exhibit, the architectural commissions, and the effort to expand his lecturing (to improve his still dismal financial picture). He was in Dallas (Marcus House) and Kansas (lectures) in January; New York (Broadacre City exhibit) and at Northwestern University in Evanston (lecture) in April; Dallas (Marcus House) and Washington in May; Pittsburgh (Broadacre City and Kaufmann) in June; Washington (Broadacre City exhibit) in July; North and South Dakota (potential client) in September; New York, Pittsburgh, and Yale University (lectures) in October; and East Lansing, Michigan, and Oshkosh, Wisconsin (lectures), in November.

Throughout the year and in spite of the extensive traveling, Wright found time to write (he wrote at least five "At Taliesin" columns with one being a three-part column regarding his trip to the Dakota Badlands and contributed several articles to various magazines). He also completed a book review at the request of the *Capital Times* on a book written by a local university professor, Walter Agard, entitled *The New Architectural Sculpture* (coincidentally, and obviously unknown to the *Wisconsin State Journal,* as they also asked and received an entirely different review from Edgar Tafel, both reaching similar less-than-praiseworthy conclusions).

The "At Taliesin" column shrank from 120 installments in four different newspapers in 1934 to half that number printed in only three newspapers in 1935. As previously stated, many columns deal with Broadacre City and the columns written during the Arizona stay reflect the Fellowship's experiences and efforts there. The columns also continue to paint a vivid picture of the sometimes colorful, sometimes colorless Fellowship life at Taliesin, presenting various unpretentious and natural stories of the Taliesin kitchen, cooking, eating and mealtimes, dishwashing duty, and even loading buckwheat. Education was the topic of several columns and various apprentice "sermonettes" also were written about more frequently in 1935.

What had been in 1934 a lone musician-in-residence, with the presence of pianist Glen Sherman, had now grown to four musicians by the summer of 1935. From New York, pianist Anton Rovinsky, violinist Edgar "Eddie" Neukurg, and the Russian cellist Youry Bilstin played together many times for Wright, the Fellowship, and the public that chose to travel to Taliesin. Their coming created the need for an expansion of several rooms within Taliesin into what was referred to in the August 23 "At Taliesin" column as "The Maestro Suite. . . . the rhythms they understand in music turned in upon their daily lives as environment."

AT TALIESIN

January 3, 1935

Christmas broke at Taliesin as a bubble — the well-rooted were separated from their work only for a short time; the rest were blown to all parts of the country. Materially our progress suffered, but the hardest half of our purpose has nothing to do with the things one can touch. Interest in ideas for the improvement of life seems smothered by "social inertia." There are people discontent with the artificial life led around them who turn nowhere because there seems nowhere to turn. Among such, one with a way can do a great deal of good. Even during the holidays when everyone is bent on enjoying themselves there are a great many questions to be answered. Every fellow who temporarily leaves Taliesin is a healthy seed and it seems to me the further he is carried the better.

As material work plays a large part it is not possible that members of the Fellowship should be spread about the country for long, or frequent periods. Written articles must play a large part in our getting to people. The "Taliesin Monograph" as seen in its first number is a vehicle worthy of the job. It is unexcelled by any magazine I know of in its unity — each part being necessary to the whole and yet an entity in itself. The monograph contains no advertisements and will depend for its existence on the number of people that it can reach.

The picture shows at the Taliesin Playhouse are necessary as contacts with perhaps a smaller range of people, but a circle within the radius of forty miles is a large nucleus on which to build. The pictures shown are chosen for their beauty and the part they should play in the trend towards a truer representation of something real rather than the extravagant display of superficial life.

More and more people must be reached in order that the worth that is Taliesin may be spread. The job is not as simple as lifting the basket from over the candle but it must be done in order that we should never become just "Bohemian."

JIM THOMSON

For the first time since its opening, a year and a half ago, the Taliesin Playhouse will close its doors to the public after the afternoon's program next Sunday, the sixth of January. The Fellowship will leave shortly after that for Arizona via auto-caravan. Upon our return the doors of the theater will again open on April 7th with the showing of *Man of Aran*.

This coming Sunday we are showing a French film based on the immortal story by Alexander Dumas, *The Three Musketeers.* This picture which is twelve reels long (125 minutes playing time) is an accurate reproduction of the novel from beginning to end. The dialogue is in French but the story is so familiar that it is like meeting old friends to see D'Artagnan, Porthos, Athos and Aramis as well as Milady de Winter and the Cardinal de Richelieu and the lovely Constance act and talk on the screen.

AT TALIESIN

January 10, 1935

Even Ulysses and the children of Israel could not have left home and most of their possessions with more preparation, more excitement and more prayerful anticipation than the Taliesin Fellowship when it leaves Taliesin and Wisconsin for Arizona and the desert. The shining new painted truck loaded with one half of all the canned fruit and vegetables; with all of Broadacre City—four square miles no less (75 feet to the inch); with drafting tables and beds; with bedding and tracing paper and beds and drawing instruments; with sauerkraut— barrels of it; and then with every conceivable thing that will fill every corner and crevice. And on black and sophisticated; Carrots the top of all sit the cats: Shan-Kar, playful; Peter, stern; Tussy, aloof—totally unconcerned. All of them looking with disdain and sitting in judgement on each item and the way it is packed and the whole idea anyway.

Then after the truck has left in advance as emissary into the wilderness — ten cars will follow each other, red banners flying — the Cord or a Ford leading and then the various denominations: Fords, Plymouth, Hudson, Graham-Paige (Egyptian gray) and maybe one or two thrown in for good measure — they follow each other in caravan down the hill — out of the front gate and from Dodgeville to Dubuque to Kansas City to Chandler, Arizona, we go.

Mr. Wright has returned from his preliminary skirmish into the southwest with work to do with long and fascinating tales of orchards of grapefruit and oranges at our disposal, swimming pools around the corner, a cactus garden that has no rival — and then the desert itself, as vast and tremendous a space as our Wisconsin hills are intimate; all this will be around us and under us.

Arriving just in time to make the trip, Hulda Brierly, sister of our million-dollar Cornelia, is the newest member of our Fellowship. Her daily life during her first few days in this new life will be comparable to nothing else whatsoever — at least that is our guess.

While we are gone Taliesin and the Fellowship buildings will be fully occupied and under constant and adequate supervision and care. But the Playhouse itself will discontinue performances until we open again on Sunday, April 7th, with *Man of Aran* — the film that won the highest rating at the international film exposition in 1934 in Venice. We will continue our articles from the road as we go along and from camp after we arrive.

AT TALIESIN

January 22, 1935

[The Broadacre City exhibit project is aptly described in the following column. This, of course, was the Fellowship's magnum opus during the "At Taliesin" years. Under the guidance and direction from Wright, and based on his book published in 1932, *The Disappearing City*, the exhibit models were enthusiastically constructed during the period beginning in November 1934 at Taliesin until they were packed up in the courtyard of La Hacienda and trucked out on the last day of March 1935 to their New York debut. Wright, in a letter to Alden

Dow, dated March 14, 1935, emotionally stated, "the magnum opus, Broadacres, which grows into something very beautiful and we all hope and believe, something useful. You'll see it at Radio City which it is capable of blowing up into thin air."]

Visitors at Taliesin these days (and we still have them despite all the snow on the hill) are confronted and confounded upon entering the studio with a huge sheet of plywood, variously taken to be a movable stage, a dance floor, or a ping-pong court. They are usually surprised to learn that this platform is the beginning of an architectural model. It is easy to understand the surprise, for it is indeed something new in models.

Twelve feet square, the model will represent four square miles out of the center of Broadacre City, if a community so outspreading can be said to have a center. Designed to be typical of many such cities, the model will not be a replica of any one of them. It will include such public buildings as a hospital, university and county administration building, designed to serve a community several times the size of the residential districts within the scope of this piece of plywood. The land-planning basis of Broadacre City is based on the minimum of "an acre to a family." So while the 2,560 acres of the model would contain to scale one-fourth of Manhattan Island, they would house only about 10,000 Broadacre City inhabitants.

On the scale of the model, a house plan is as big as a penny — an acre the size of a playing card, and a tall skyscraper as long as a pencil. We might start up a typical wide-as-your-thumbnail highway and see a few of the sights of Broadacre City.

We come along one edge of Broadacre City on the super highway, a many laned speedway which more than any other factor makes this city possible. With no intersections, with one-way traffic unencumbered with trucks, which have there own lanes, and with curb lighting to eliminate glaring headlights, such high speed thoroughfares at once make possible a new sense of distribution and create a new field for architecture. In fact, with the successful and beautiful solution of the traffic problem, half the battle for a beautiful city is won.

In the Broadacre City the glare of the concrete is dulled with iron oxides to a restful, brick-like red. At each important highway inter-section, a large warehouse forms an integral architectural unit with the highway. The through-trucking traffic has unloading access to these warehouses, which form the centers of distribution in the city, where trucks pick up merchandise.

Taking a cross-town road from the highway, we first pass the tourist camps, convenient to the super-highway for motorists going through. The industrial section, too, is here, near the transportation centers. We notice that none of the houses are crowded together, but always with at least an acre of land around each, and occasionally larger farms. Tall buildings are the occasional sight, never in groups, and surrounded always with enough land to prevent shutting off useful light.

There are no dangerous highway intersections, as the through traffic goes up or under at every crossing. Garages open into multiple private lanes, so there is less danger from drivers coming in from unexpected angles.

We see office buildings, apartment houses, hotel, stadium, theaters, the cathedral, and in between and among all, homes — all well out in the open.

Most of the country is flat. There is one typical hilly section, farthest from the highway. Here is the university, the zoo, a large hotel, and the hospital. At the top of the plywood mountain and on the extreme corner of the model, we reach the automobile objective and an excellent view of the city itself, stretching out in a simple and natural pattern — a conscious pattern, but made with respect to the natural beauty of the country, its hills, rivers, and woods.

Broadacre City was conceived and christened in a small book of Mr. Wright's written three years ago, called *The Disappearing City*. In this book, a prophecy of and a sermon for decentralization, Wright sketched the outlines of Broadacre City. He is now asked to put it into the concrete form of a model to be the chief architectural display in the Annual Industrial Arts Exposition in Rockefeller Center, New York.

Accompanying the large model will be 12 or 15 smaller models of Broadacre City buildings. The gas station, theater, tourist cabins, highway intersection, several houses, and a model farm are among the representative buildings to be shown on a larger scale.

All Taliesin is humming with Broadacre activity. Typical of the enthusiasm was a comment of a youthful apprentice, who is familiar enough with Mr. Wright's books, but sometimes gets the names confused. She pointed to an elegant riverfront site and said, "When I move into Disappearing City, I want to live right there!"

BOB BISHOP

AT TALIESIN
February 10, 1935

The Arizona Trek

[The Fellowship's first excursion en masse to Arizona began at noon on Wednesday, January 23, ending in the evening of the following Tuesday, January 29. Prior to establishing Taliesin West as their permanent Arizona "camp" in 1938, they would travel to Chandler twice (February 1935 and January 1936; they did not go to Arizona in 1937, as work kept them in Wisconsin), each time staying in La Hacienda in Chandler. The following column describes this inaugural trek.]

It grew—the idea, that is—during the coldest and most bitter storms last year while Taliesin was cutting and burning the deepest holes in the forests to keep its boilers and fireplaces and its studios warm. The idea began in the back of Mr. Wright's head and first became action when he announced during the early summer that next winter we would go to Arizona. We would go by caravan he prophesied—cars and a truck. That was last summer and although it sounded alluring it was not until the sound of a saw cutting its first cord of wood on the hill at Taliesin and the first flurry of snow covered the roofs that the promise of the Arizona desert became a remote reality and a really longed for dream. There was a long period of speculation, of frustrated plans and delay after delay. First we would be going "next Sunday" someone would say bravely. Then it was "sometime early next week." And we never said it convincingly enough to make our listeners really sure that we were actually going at all. Some of them even thought that it was just a tactful way of closing the Playhouse for the winter, I guess. But if they thought that and if we did not sound convincing than they did not know Frank Lloyd Wright and neither did we. Because the Fellowship is in Arizona; the sun is shining endlessly; the woods around Taliesin are safe.

To start 30 people in one direction—all at once—and keep them going for 2,296 miles over ice and through mountains was the problem.

Gradually cars enough to haul these 30 were assembled on the Taliesin hill. Mrs. Wright became the very proud owner of a new Ford sedan; Marybud and John drove around in a red and grey Graham Paige convertible; Jim and Edgar simonized and repaired their Plymouth and Ford cabriolets each; Fred brought out the family Ford; the Schwankes turned up the Nash; the long grey Cord was painted until it shone like new—a red square on the right side of the hood near the radiator made it sing; and certainly not least, the giant new red truck was decorated with a giant red swastika. It was a family Fellowship of cars and the car owners aired their views on every other car on the market freely.

Mr. Wright returned with Mrs. Wright from a lecture tour on Sunday; the deadline for leaving was Wednesday. The truck was packed to the very top brim—10 feet from the ground up; the caravan cars filled with luggage. The Cord—last to be ready—stalled on the icy road up the hill when the wind blew 30 degrees below zero at 4:30 in the morning—the day upon which we left.

But its familiar roar was the first to leave the front gate at high noon on that Wednesday and the eight other cars and the truck followed it out of the gate and on the road south to Dodgeville. The day upon which we left was brilliant sunshine. Great clouds of glistening snow swirled back of each car as they curved and swung and dipped on the icy road. Snow was banked ten feet on either side of the highway. Everything was shining white. Wisconsin barns were redder through the white, and the blue above it was deep cobalt.

First stop was in Dodgeville. The big round table in the back room of Parsons & Hocking meat market groaned with hams and sausages and doughnuts and cakes and coffee as our old friends, Etta and partner, Hocking, filled us with a great lunch. Encouraged—on we went following the truck this time in close caravan through Dubuque and into the College Inn in the college town of Mount Vernon, Ia., carrying roasted turkey and chickens and calling for hot coffee to finish our dinner. Cedar Rapids, a few miles away, was our first night away from home.

Here in this little town in the midst of Iowa the Cord was introduced to the best mechanic it had known in its career and was put on the road again with the vim and the beautiful roar of its youth in its motor. The rest of the caravan traveled on into Lawrence to stay with the Beals but those of us who were lucky enough to be in the Cord and the boys who were driving the truck spent the night with Mr. Wright in a meager hotel of glorified name, "Mecca," and in other words—a sort of "flop house," but our midnight supper of steaks and beer was delicious, our cook and waiter a "Scotch" Greek.

From the bottom to the very top we went the next day when we traveled from Missouri into Kansas, breakfasted with our former-fellows, George and Helen Beal, in Lawrence, and from there to Emporia where we had luncheon with Mr. and Mrs. William Allen White. Luncheon? Mr. and Mrs. White walked around their luxurious home loading our plates until our eyes bulged because there was everything anyone could want to eat spread upon tables set about the big living room, and our generous and illustrious hosts treated us like sons and daughters. In a dream we drove onto Wichita and there the Henry J. Allens served us dinner at tables also in the living room of their home—a house in which we felt at once at rest and "at home"—its quiet and reposeful beauty making us aware of a kind of hospitality that we had not known before. Kansas hospitality was the "top" of the entire journey to Arizona. There is nothing quite like it. William Allen White and Henry Allen are two great Americans.

Already ice and snow had disappeared and the warm sun seemed like days in May. We went from Wichita to Tulsa and to the Richard Lloyd Jones home. He lives in Mr. Wright's most recent concrete block house. Pictures of the house had given no suggestion nor any idea of the atmosphere it really creates. It is the color of soft mother-of-pearl. It glows in fading sunlight. Walls in this house do not exist. There are only screens of piers and glass separating the inside space from the outdoors. The rooms inside are stately and noble. I fell asleep in my sleeping bag on the floor of the tall dining room—30 of us slept like that that night, all over the house. The house had feted 120 people at one time, they said, but this was the first night 30 besides the family had slept there.

The next day we headed due south and started the longest run of the journey down through Oklahoma and Texas and spent the night in

Abilene, Tex. Monday for the first time we began to see what the great floor of the west was like as we drove for mile after mile over unbroken stretches of Texas and finally toward sundown approached the foothills of the Rockies. The sun sank behind the mountains as the Cord wound its way into them. It was very quiet and night fell as sharper curves and a hot motor made us realize that we were in new country. We broke the ride; rested the night in the "swell" hotel of El Paso—continued on the final day's drive on Tuesday.

All my life I had been brought up on Fords and Buicks and such. This was my first experience in driving a solid Cord a great distance. I needed much coaching—and got it—during the first part of the trip. But now on this last day I realized at last the thrill of handling the great heavy motor and the light long swift body along a straight perfect road and over and down and through narrow curves without losing speed for an instant. The sensation is a long undulating movement that never ceases momentum. Curves and hills and straight levels become as one and the car is a shooting thing upon them. Shooting but none the less fastened firmly to the ground by the great well-balanced weight.

The straight road became a winding one, then a slightly hilly and winding one and finally mountainous—the curves swifter and hills steeper. Fascinating. The road a ribbon—nothing but the road before me like some deadly serpent from which I could not move my eyes (a good thing I didn't). At last we reached Globe. Mr. Wright took the wheel through "Devil's Canyon"—more dangerous and narrower curves, mountains towering above us (I could look now)—tremendous masses—gigantic rock surfaces flung upwards. Unrest and intense emotion.

Magically we came from the mountains as the sun was nearing the horizon and we rode out upon the Arizona desert. Tall ancient saguaro and graceful waving ocatillo and the vivid green on the floor of the desert and the purple mountains beyond. A garden like none I had ever seen. A desert like something I had never dreamed. The mountains were softened by the distance and the fading light and the desert plants stood out strong in the long low streaks of sunlight. The new forms, the vivid green, the purple shadowed rock masses and the blue sky and the movement of the car winding in and out and around.

Suddenly a quick stop—Mesa, eight miles from Chandler and with startling theatrical rapidity all the cars of the caravan caught up with us and there the truck which had proceeded was waiting. The procession was resumed and as we started from home, so we entered the destination of the long journey. Night now and the lights were gradually turned on revealing to us our new home, La Hacienda, a rambling spacious building that could not have been better built to suit our life. Rooms facing the open patio, living room with piano, large dining room, kitchen, bathrooms and showers, 28 rooms about a patio, an automobile court, and the final touch when the model was set up in the center of the covered section of the patio. Drafting tables and work benches surround the model and we work all day long out of doors in and out of the sun—wearing shorts as if it were the hottest summer in Wisconsin. The thermometer has been 85 degrees in the shade.

There is a quiet repose about the atmosphere and a freshness in the air. Never have I breathed or lived such boundless purity of space. Mountains surround us but they are far off—50, 60 miles. We see them clearly all around the horizon. And the sky is brilliant blue with white clouds and spaceless. I asked Mr. Wright why this quiet and this repose and this undisturbed silence and he said, "It is because of the eternal and the everlasting smile of the sun."

EUGENE MASSELINK

AT TALIESIN

February 24, 1935

[The *Baraboo Weekly News* printed two letters (February 28 and March 28, 1935) from a local Spring Green carpenter, W. C. Schwanke. Schwanke and his wife went along with the Fellowship to Arizona as "carpenter and advisor on construction" (as he described his position) of the Broadacre City models. In the first letter he listed the twenty-five apprentices that were there to build Broadacre City—"Eugene Masselink, Grand Rapids, Michigan; Edgar Tafel, New York City; Edgar Kaufmann, Pittsburgh, Pennsylvania; Alfred Bush, Brooklyn;

Burton Goodrich, Princeton, New Jersey; Mr. and Mrs. Don Thomp-
son, Richmond, Virginia; James Thomson, Watertown, Connecticut;
Mr. and Mrs. John Lautner, Marquette, Michigan; Mr. and Mrs. Bud
Shaw, Los Angeles; Fred Langhorst, Elgin, Illinois; Abe and Ben
Dombar, Cincinnati; Robert Bishop, Philadelphia; Robert Mosher,
Midland, Michigan; Bruce Richards, Phoenix, Arizona; Blaine Drake,
Ogden, Utah; Mabel Morgan, Dodgeville, Wisconsin; John Howe,
Evanston, Illinois; Cornelia and Hulda Brierly, Pittsburgh; William
Bernoudy, St. Louis; and Peter Frankl, Los Angeles."]

In the courtyard of our Hacienda the master and his apprentices are
working on the model of Broadacre City. The model comprising an area
of 12 square feet is placed at the head of the court and around it the
apprentices have grouped their drafting tables. On these tables lie
materials such as Japanese wood and bright palettes of oil paint, with
which the workers build Mr. Wright's and their own ideas into third
dimensional models. Because of the scale of the city (75 feet to the inch)
we have learned to create methods for presenting flowers, vegetable
gardens, wood lots. When the model is given to the public, the
abstracted forms such as those of the wood lots can't mean so much to
them as to the apprentice who evolved them. It is an exciting experience
to create a landscape — to determine its orchards, fields of blooming
clover, tennis courts, swimming pools, its reservoirs, its forests. We live
in this future city. Speed in the shady lanes of its super-highway. Know
the repose of its floating lake-cabins and when our backs ache and our
eyes smart from bending over this finely detailed work we loose our pent
up energies by romping in the grass of the courtyard. The intense draw of
the sun gives the feeling of exhilaration that must be the lot of the cattle,
who in the spring are loosened from the musty warmth of the winter
stable to stomp across the early thaw of the pasture.

But unlike the cattle, we are not confined by the fences of a limited pasture. From our courtyard we look to the mountains. There is old superstition that holds, deep within her mighty womb of rock the golden ore
responsible for the legend that gives the mountain its name. While we work
we watch these mountains during their spectacular changes. They draw
towards us. Great rock masses and crevices purple with shadow. Then they
recede — become phantom forms in the repose of clouds.

On Saturday afternoons work on the model stops and we travel
towards these mountains. We pile ourselves and our sleeping bags into

the gorgeous new truck and as we speed toward the desert the wind beats at our foreheads and whips through our hair.

To arrive in the desert in the evening; to see the sun flame like volcanic fire from the western mountains, then smoulder until the great rock furnaces become cold stark outlines; to feel the power of the saguaros silhouettes—these are the experiences of the Fellowship as the red truck slackens its pace to take us across the desert floor. At the foot of Old Superstition we stop to camp, build our fire, and eat our roasted mutton. When the full moon rises to cast grotesque shadows from the ocotillas, the sahuaras and make eerie playthings of the treacherous cholla barbs, groups of four or five hoist their sleeping bags to their backs and leave the fireside. Some climb over the boulders and through sage brush to higher rock ledges and others pick their way through the shale and cactus of the desert floor to find a sleeping place in the open or at the foot of a mighty cliff.

Our group lies in the moon shadows of an ocotilla—sinuous shadows like the tentacles of an octopus. Throughout the silence of the desert night all hear the same magnified calls of solitary owls or lone coyotes. In the morning we brush the frost from our sleeping bags, tie them into bundles, hurry them back to camp and briskly climb to a high peak to see the sun rise above the restless pinnacles. By the time the sun is high, apprentices call to one another from different mountain tops. Although the voices are clear and the echoes long-lasting, the mountains are so great in scale that the boys look like stick-figures. At the top of one peak, Iovanna and I watch a coyote cross and recross a crevice with a graceful trot. And nearby the sun blazes on a mountain side covered with the gold of California poppies. Far up the slope, coming down from the stone peaks, we distinguish the form of our master, Mr. Wright, for he has salvaged the old flower stalk of a century plant and carries the 15-foot pole with its dried flowers, over his shoulder. The great grey stalk is in the courtyard now—near the model of Broadacre City, for our master said, "Something told me that if we get it home, I'll live a hundred years." But his apprentices know that he will live forever—even as the desert.

CORNELIA BRIERLY

AT TALIESIN

March 1, 1935

Three left the Hacienda in the big car—open to the sky, one driving, two in back. It swiftly moved along the straight road directly into the morning sun to the foot of Superstition mountain. Then on to a winding road that slowly crept up and through the increasing grades toward the mountains. It was a wonderfully planned road built by the Indians long ago, called the Apache trail.

A field of yellow poppies—some say "California poppies"; others say "Arizona"—who knows which way the wind blew—stopped the car. Yellow poppies and yellow rock and yellow-green moss. The one said "dead moss;" the other said, "alive." The splash of sunlight upon a giant saguaro against the mountainside stopped the car. The undulating rhythms of rocky ledges stopped the car and it would stop for the sheer wonder of seeing cliff pile upon cliff; now black, now glistening gold as the traced clouds in the delicate Arizona sky played across them.

The two in back stood and towered over the one in front just as the mountainous masses towered over the road and the car. One in back with majestic sweeps and waves of his arm and hand directed the car's rise and fall and constant turning. He directed the road's tortuous direction and it almost seemed as though he were creating the mountains themselves as the car swung gracefully into the very midst of them. Near the highest top the car stopped. The two walked to the very top and came back again very slowly through the garden of ocotilla and tall century plants of the desert.

Then the three sank slowly down with the car and the road into deep shadow from the heights and the sun. The two in back saw the tremendous cliff ascend higher and still higher as the road descended. One said, "See that up there is where we were standing just a few minutes ago"—then with a twinkle in his eye—"it was a fitting pedestal, don't you think."

The one in front saw the twinkle, saw the other smile, saw the road curving and descending, saw the straight cliffs of the canyon, saw the distant sky—all at once.

The other in back said, "God never seems to have stopped working at all."

The one in front felt himself in the presence of greatness such as he had never experienced. Before him and around him and over him this black and gold splendor. Behind him two great men each expressing the power and beauty that is their's and each accepting, sometimes silently, sometimes by exclamation, the power and beauty that is Arizona.

He who drove saw enough of the twisting road to continue the trip beyond Roosevelt dam — through "Devil's Canyon" — and in the complete silent blackness of night — home.

THE ONE WHO DROVE

AT TALIESIN
March 10, 1935

Bridges for Broadacre

The motor car and the aeroplane characterize Broadacre City. Provision for leisurely enjoyment of the countryside by car, as well as for the faster travel which distance demands, has resulted in a system of wide local roads integrated with the super-highway: the old railroad right of way. The aeroplane of the future — a self-contained mechanical unit — which can rise and descend vertically, has determined the hanger with doors in the roof through which planes leave, and the short landing field for short easy descent. Space and freedom from congestion are thus made possible by generous provision for these two forms of fast personal transportation.

Safety in surface travel is assured by ample width of roads which are not crowned but slightly dipped toward the center, and the elimination of all grade crossings at intersections. From the short feeder lanes which abut the group garages, through the local roads to the super-highway, sound design has made traffic hazards non-existent, ditches unnecessary, and visible light either on cars or alongside the roads unnecessary also.

Next to the arterial, the basis of the roads system is the local road, fixed at a width of four car lanes, two in each direction. Only in a case where traffic does not and should not demand speed or volume, as in the roads to the general acreage dwellings and to the automobile objective, is a general road narrower than four lane width used. With two lanes in each direction, safety even in passing is assured.

The super-highway — the railroad right-of-way — is the main artery of all traffic through the decentralized countryside. This super-highway is the carrier of large volume at high speed, and is essentially for the long haul. A super-highway would not occur, depending upon the character of the country, oftener than 20 to 100 miles apart, as is now the case with the railways.

Where it passes Broadacre City, the super-highway cares of each class of traffic separately. There is a roadway in each direction for fast passenger traffic, depressed roadways in each direction exclusively for long truck hauling, and, because access to the super-highway is had only at comparatively long intervals, a local road paralleling it on either side. The elevated center section carrying the passenger car lanes and the speed-train roof over all necessary warehousing of every kind for Broadacre City — to these warehouses direct access is had from the truck roadways on either side.

But hazards in motor car traffic are largely a matter of crossing, of turns. New types of road crossings by underpass and overpass eliminate the dangers of cross traffic, and intermediate level does likewise for turns. Bridges thus become a conspicuous feature of the countryside.

Broadacre's bridges are varied, but have a common characteristic, an architectural quality relating their purpose to the form they take. This form, because of long spans necessitated by easy grades, is a suspension, using steel in tension, its economical way. The flat catenary of the cable, repeating the rise of the roadway opposite, finds its anchor in broad concrete piers, or pylons. These pylons, their mass fulcruming about a point at the toe resisting the tremendous pull of the cables, perfectly express the reaction that is their function. This feeling is continued by the slant of the slings, until, at the bridge's center, the lightness of this system of construction is completely expressed. What a profile — what a feeling of a harmonious whole, of a perfect balance between action and reaction — is presented to the motor-car approaching on the roadway below.

The thoughtful engineer finds much to appreciate in the design of these bridges. Just as the composer emphasizes one theme and subdues another, just as the painter intensifies a feeling by intensifying a color, so the architect in these bridges, giving perfect expression to the reaction of the piers by their shape, accents this reaction by slanting the usual vertical slings. And in further fulfillment of his function as an artist, though engineer, too, the architect, near the bottom of the slings, places a subsidiary tension member at an angle, thus reducing the span of the bridge floor between slings — repeating this pattern at the point where the sling joins the main cable to improve the connection!

An interesting variation of the general type is found in the tree-section suspension bridge near the county building in Broadacre City. Here the problem is that of spanning a river and a road, separated by an arena too short to permit spanning each by an individual bridge. Such a situation is common, but the solution in this case is not common.

In this main bridge, each span is made half the usual suspension bridge, with the two spans separated by a flat central section. This central section takes a form similar to a large concrete vase, great in width as compared with its height. The mass of this concrete section receives the pull of the cables of each span, adjusting itself to minor variations in tension in each by balancing on a bearing at what is the narrow section of the vase-form. Here the lightness of steel-in-tension, the perfect balance between the pull of the cables and the reaction of the anchorage, is expressed even more completely perhaps than in the more simple bridges.

Opportunity for sculpture, or an abstract design or in relief as integral ornament, is afforded by the faces of the concrete pylons. This, and the cobweb-like patterns contributed by steel-in-tension, give great individuality and true distinction to structures which commonly are cold and lifeless forms at best. In the bridges of Broadacre City, as in the buildings within it, is found that sense of sound organic planning that will make for a better living in America.

DONALD THOMPSON

AT TALIESIN
March 11, 1935

There is something that is best in us which lies latent when we are in the cities. It is a delight to see it shine forth to be ourselves, by way of change, here in the desert. We lose ourselves in the beauty of nature; walk and forget we are tired; sing spontaneously for we have no audience but the saguaro; kneel to pick up a transparent stone, a perfect abstraction of semi-spheres of onyx.

We come in a group—but we see the mountains, each with a yearning spirit, and we are a group no longer. Each step reveals a magnificent architectural pattern made by the hand of master more than human. This group of stones, this cholla must be studied. Sometimes it is, but there are peaks in the distance which are our goals—desert galore on all sides. We perspire, but that is physical. The fifth "C" of Arizona is exemplified on the desert; Palo Verde twisting at our sides; grease bush displaying yellow blossoms; a staghorn cactus defying everyone and everything. Each has a character of its own. A lizard slips across our path and clings to a stone in blazing light. Lichen of every color form pleasant patterns on the rocks of the desert floor, our pavement.

We look back to see how far we have gone. But our sense of scale does not apply here. A shrub on the mountain may appear to be a tall tree; or a tall tree, a small shrub. We usually underestimate all distances and heights. We look upward to the San Tan peaks and are afraid to judge their height. They seem easy to conquer until we try. They recede and enlarge. Dark holes in the cliffs spot the sheer drops. We find them to be huge natural caves and an eagle nestles his young in one and perhaps the owls are nesting in the one over there.

We find a nook in the mountainside, warm, protected from the wind. We will stop here, we think, but we are impelled to climb on and up. Our true nature is singing—at one with the surroundings. We use a boulder as a footstool. It slips and rolls down the mountainside. We glance down and smile and think of the *Blue Light* we saw on the screen at the Playhouse at Taliesin. The world becomes larger as we rise. Shadows, like monsters, creep up the mountain sides and stealthily glide down to rise again on a neighboring peak. The cumulus strata are not far above our heads. The rocks, secure and insecure, are "multicolored multiforms." We reach the top, stand upon a rocky and weathered crag and shriek like the eagle whose perch we occupy. Echoes resound from the mountains far and near until the last distant scream is swallowed in silence. We sit upon the weathered crag, and gaze in all directions—exult or meditate.

We are aware of something awakened within us which lies latent when we are in the cities. It is a delight to feel it shining forth and a joy to use to be ourselves by way of the change that is here in the desert and comes over us.

Jens Jensen, a true friend of the Fellowship, surprised us with his unexpected visit Tuesday night. We climbed a San Tan peak together and listened to his inspirational words. Jensen and the saguaro, their strength and character, the principle of their structure gave us cause to think, the desert breeze sweeping across our faces. He left us against our will Thursday morning and disappeared in the cottonwoods on his way to Los Angeles. The desert—each flower, each plant—will always bring him back to us.

BENNY DOMBAR

AT TALIESIN
March 22, 1935

[With the exception of only a few more recent constructed works, the Wright-designed structures viewed by the Fellowship during their short respite in Los Angeles, described in this column, were his most recent cache of constructed buildings (even though most were over ten years old).]

One midnight last week the Fellowship's Hacienda was astir with commotion, then, soon all lights out, the big front gates closed and the Taliesin caravan again took to the open road. This time westward down through the desert and the mountains, across the Colorado and the Imperial Valley and on to California's grandiose Los Angeles. This was not a pleasure jaunt to see the sights of this money-mad paradise of the Pacific coast but it was an architectural pilgrimage to the concrete residences already world famous that have emanated from Taliesin's studio.

Concrete as a building material has always been associated with the gutter, of sidewalks, of garages and bridges. Its presumed crudeness has been a counter action for its great structural strength and plasticity of form that are its most valuable characteristics. Its beauty has always been a negatible quality remaining dormant or covered up because of the failure of human imagination to conceive and recognize its true character. Out here in the west it is an ideal building material, the earthquake alone being one item to insure its use as well as its favorable disposition to the climate.

These concrete houses that are scattered among the Hollywood hills are constructed very simply by means of standardized block forms that are made on the site by the same workmen who set them up. These forms varied in profile yet always standardized to give for many different designs and patterns that take concrete from its gutter and give it a quality and richness of texture unknown to any building material. Concrete is dependent upon its molder and its beauty of form comes from the genius of this human contact. Its beauty in these houses gives them just this quality that have made them world famous, that of form coming directly from the nature of the material.

La Minatura, the most famous of the block houses, in Pasadena, placed in its small ravine and dwarfed by the eucalyptus is the example of concrete used with such delicacy of scale and pattern that its beauty is that of gem-quality. The effect of nature and building being of one quality, of a perfect blending together of the two so that the swaying lacy eucalyptus are as much a part of La Minatura and it of them as they are of Pasadena.

Because of a collection of rare volumes from ancient times up through the ages, of Durer and William Blake, Mrs. George Madison Millard has made herself almost as well known as her house.

From the smallest to the largest we went. Olive Hill whose promontory position in the center of the movie capital is probably the largest and most valuable parcel of property in Hollywood. Hollyhock House, the former home of Aline Barnsdall is sequestered among its thick olive trees on its top. Concrete here has been used not in the block form but in large wall masses, as supports for long arcades and wide openings. Hollyhock House is large and of great breadth yet it is always the house in scale with the human and its beauty of concrete, glass and wood forms offered unlimited thrills to us who have previously been thrilled at its photographs but from them can never be judged the mastery of scale and finesse of the real. Then the Freeman House whose corner windows have stirred the so-called modernists to copy them the world over but without success for their real purpose has not been understood and consequently exploited. The Ennis House, the Storrer House, the work of Lloyd Wright who is the most noteworthy of the few carrying out this father's principles, of Schindler, the most well known of Taliesin's apprentices were part of a grand architectural tour of the Los Angeles territory.

These houses are not prominent. Unlike their neighbors they do not stand out as features of the landscape, instead they are part of their respective hills. Their richness comes from their natural form and their beauty from the natural use of their materials. They are surrounded, sometimes crowded by their opposites, the typical Hollywood villa which is today what the old Victorian mansion was to the nineties. They are the stylized Spanish, Colonial, Arabian, and every known type of picture-architecture from every part of the globe. Hollywood is the center of superficialities and the cache of Hollywood culture depends on how many more fake towers and artificial balconies and how high on the mountain side the Hollywooder can build above his neighbor. The picture-artist seems to have run dry, he can't hold up much longer to the whims and fancies for the exotic nor can the hills forever supply the sites.

In Hollywood one wonders where California is, it can't be seen. All that was California is obliterated with architectural monstrosities. However the blue sky is still overhead, the snow-capped mountains further away and the ocean out yonder, all three quite untouched.

AT TALIESIN

March 27, 1935

A few days ago, while we were all working on the Broadacre City model, Mr. Wright walked out into the patio with a letter in his hand that he wished to read us. Most often, these letters are from curious people, or people curiously interested in architecture. However, all these letters are interesting and informing to us, since we are in voluntary exile from "civilization" and "the Public" in the interest of both. The letter was from a Madison citizen asking architectural advice. That was curious. Madison, with a master at close range, hardly makes use of his services. But this Madison citizen wanted to know which side of the City Hall tearing-down question Mr. Wright would be on. It seems as if Madison wants to show some progress, and presumably the quickest way to show American progress is to tear down landmarks.

We asked Mr. Wright what he thought of ripping down the dignified little sandstone building. Naturally, Mr. Wright's answer was vigorous not to say rigorous. He thinks Madison should keep it, and tear down most of the other buildings of which it is more proud. The City Hall, uninspiring as it may be, is a straight-forward simple, dignified stone structure. It makes a period in our culture and not a disgraceful one. Its lean Gothic tracery, tall windows and high ceilings are an honest type of good stone work and so, distinguished. That some of the stone was set up on edge and flakes off, doesn't hurt the appearance of the structure as a landmark in this matter of our culture. There is a spirit of repose in its native stone. The building does not force itself upon the "eye of the box populi" or try to be anything that it isn't. One only needs to look across the street at the pretentious falsity of the Capitol building, to see why the City Hall should stand, if many of the newer buildings are to stand. And I guess they are.

One could feel at home in the City Hall as he is dressed, but he would have to wear a Roman Toga and smoke a big black "seegar" at the bragadocio angle, to be similar in effect at the Capitol building. There are few sincere-decent buildings done by popular eclectics. Now Madison has a chance to keep one, even though its face no longer shines so brightly as it once did. If a building is to be torn down, how about the Roman Baths and Temples with which our dear neighbor has latterly adorned herself?

EDGAR TAFEL

[The Madison City Hall, built in 1858, survived this referenced threat. Unfortunately, it eventually met with the wrecking ball in 1954.]

AT TALIESIN
April 18, 1935

Writing for the papers was far from our minds during the past weeks in Arizona. All time was used in finishing minute details on Broadacre's model, proclaimed complete on the last day of March. The truck was loaded on April 1st and, carrying "all our eggs in its basket," was sent to New York City.

Five carloads of us were left to finish up other work for a few days. The sun was getting hotter and we were looking forward to spring and summer. Mr. and Mrs. Wright and Iovanna left for the east by train but not until after the five cars departed from the Hacienda on Saturday leaving the patio and the familiar courtyard deserted.

One by one we left Arizona and one by one the cars that had resigned Taliesin to its snow storms last January came up the hill to greet it in April sunshine. During the days of the long journey across the dust swept country each car was an entity in itself. No one group saw another for almost six days. And at the end each had a better tale of woe and excitement.

The Ford was the first to pull into the courtyard at Taliesin: Indians and rugs and bartering for baskets with nickels and an alarm clock; so much dust that those sleeping on the ground were completely covered ("and we slept out every night") "one morning we woke up to see a band of Indians on horseback standing over us startled to find us alive."

The next evening—Thursday—brought Jim and his new roadster: "better baskets, lower prices; worst dust, worst places to sleep."

Friday very late the Cord roared up the hill, its horns blowing and tooting victoriously: glorious trip; thirty-five miles for a mechanic—five hours on the heights of the Apache Trail under the hot sun; cowboy races and cowboy horseplay on Tonto Basin's "main" street; the cliff dwellings of Monte Zuma—architecture; fifteen miles for mechanics — three hours in the shade of the Oak Creek Canyon; asleep on the brink of the Grand Canyon and showers of rain in the very early morning — sun later and look — below us! the painted desert at sundown; muddy roads; dust swept roads; icy roads; pink and green tourist cabins and just cabins with wood stoves that wouldn't work and finally from out of the chaos onto the Lincoln Highway homeward.

Bud and Betty and "Bodago and Eric" arrived early Saturday: two whole days stalled in blizzards at Sidney, Nebraska; "Bodago and Eric" are doing nicely, thank you.

The last to arrive on Monday were Marybud and John and Peter and Chub ("Chubby"): mountains, snow; stuck.

And thus finishes the epic three months in the life of the Taliesin Fellowship.

News of Broadacre City's triumph comes to us from New York. After it tours through the country it will take its place with collateral models as a permanent exhibit in the Fellowship buildings giving Sunday visitors enough to see for many a summer and winter.

The Playhouse will be opened once more for its regular programs on May 5. Activity in Taliesin's studios and farm has resumed. Plows, plans and pianos sing "Joy in Work is Man's Desiring."

EUGENE MASSELINK

[The Broadacre City models were exhibited for the Industrial Arts Exposition in the Rockefeller Center Forum in New York City from April 15 through May 15. The models then traveled to Madison, Wisconsin, where they were displayed in the State Historical Society Gallery from June 5 through June 14. Four days later, on June 18, the models were being exhibited in the Auditorium of Kaufmann's Department Store in Pittsburgh through June 28. From July 2 until July 21 the Corcoran Gallery in Washington, D.C., held the models for exhibit. The Fellowship then took back possession of the exhibit, installing it in Hillside's unfinished drafting room and then finally in the Fellowship's living room (after a short display at the Mineral Point/Iowa County Fair from September 7 through September 10).]

AT TALIESIN

May 4, 1935

An Ode to Manure

Every poet has written an ode to spring. Some have written an ode to sheep and chickens and horses. Mr. Wright in his Autobiography has written a beautiful ode to the cow. But no one has ever written an ode to manure, except Walt Whitman's Compost.

Now that spring is here and all the lovely flowers are sending off their celestial aromas and the tiny shoots of oats are seeking the light, and we might as well mention the singing of the birds—I sing an ode to manure.

Few people seem to know that the heavy odor given off by manure is healthful. There is an ammonia gas that when inhaled clears the nose and head and is a tonic to the lungs.

You city folks, when you see the odious cow-flop, you quickly hold your nose and jump or step gingerly aside. Perhaps I used to do the same—but now I proudly stand on a six foot pile of it and pitch it into the spreader as if it were gold I was loading and then I drive the team over the fields and watch the stuff fly off the back on to the hungry ground. I sit high as a king riding over his domain and view manure with deep satisfaction. The landscape looks twice as grand when viewed from the seat of a manure-spreader because you mean something vital to it.

Manure is an essential link in the great cycle of life. It is spread on the fields to enrich the soil to help the grain-germs find life. This new life is born of the decay that is death. The manure is plowed under in the fields and then the grain planted, becomes full grown, and is gathered from the fields by men and the horses, like trees of the forest decaying to give new leaf to other trees. This is immortality.

It is fundamental to all past civilizations. They have all been based on it. Perhaps the advent of the tractor on the farms will be a contributing cause of the decay of our modern civilization for when manure shall have vanished from the face of the earth you can be sure that the end of man's existence is not far behind, and neither castor oil nor machine oil can save it.

ABROM DOMBAR

The Taliesin Playhouse, having been closed while the Fellowship was in Arizona, opens once more on this coming Sunday — May 5th, at 3 P.M. As usual there will be coffee and cookies served by the fireplace. Since you have last seen the Playhouse it has been changed slightly and the new arrangement of the seats make for a much more pleasant association with your neighbors, with the fireplace and with the screen.

The picture that celebrates the opening of the Playhouse is *Man of Aran.* It is a stark simple chronicle of stark simple lives made by Robert Flaherty on the Aran Islands off the west coast of Ireland. He spent two years on the islands making his pictures; and there it is a naturally authentic ring about everything in it. This picture which won, last year, the first prize at the International Film exposition in Venice, has been highly praised by critics. It is stirring natural drama, and it has been superbly photographed.

AT TALIESIN

May 22, 1935

[The architectural school that apprentice Cornelia Brierly refers to in this column was Carnegie Tech in Pittsburgh, where she attended from 1932 to 1934.]

I have just returned from a visit to an architectural school in the east where I was enrolled as a student before entering the Taliesin Fellowship. A discouraging visit. Discouraging, not only because of the cramped concepts of the so-called "crits" and students, but because of the principles which established the entire architectural school system under the stagnation of Beaux Arts competition.

Try to conceive the group of young people in the United States who enter this system each year. These young people who enter don't come to flounder through a college course with the hope of hitting upon some work that interests them sufficiently to make it their vocation. Rather, they have within them some creative urge that inclines them toward a profession as difficult and as extraordinary in its attainment as architecture. Their minds are growing, receptive, plastic. These are the qualities with which they enter only to be subjected to a system of superficial paper architecture which cramps their imagination because copying and even "calcing" of documents receives the laudation of crit of such pallid resources that few of them have even had the opportunity of experiencing the growth of a single building under the direction of their own creative energy.

Naturally they are unable to teach from experience and lean instead on shelved reviews of foreign architecture that belongs, not in the soil of America, but in Normandy, England, Spain, and Italy, where it was developed. How much better it would be if those students were to be taught to reason out, as Mr. Wright suggests, the harmonious relationship a building has with its site when it grows from the soil and fits with the character of the people who live there. And how much more valuable a crit would be who, instead of helping his students make meaningless renderings for Beaux Arts awards could show the value of the space enclosed by a building or point out the romance of using materials according to their nature—stone as stone, wood as wood. These are principles that present an outlet to the creative student mind that under the present system wants to be original but has no basic knowledge on which to build new forms.

During my visit these are the things I discussed with the head of the architectural department and here is the substance of his answer:

"In every age there are leaders like Mr. Wright who surge ahead until they have left the scope of the average mentality of the mass. These leaders have their followers, even as the apprentices of Mr. Wright. But it is the duty of the architectural schools to educate their students only to the level of the mass mind so that their architectural knowledge serves the mass in the thing it wants and can comprehend."

I maintain this view to be a stupid outlook or goal for any educational institution for, it seems to me, that it is the duty as well as privilege for an educated person to give to the inexperienced mass something that it has been unable to attain for itself. A fruitless argument. For when I left the office of that great high chief of the architectural department he placed upon me the stamp of "young reformer." But perhaps since it is a slight distinction from the mass, the title is not to be scoffed at.

L. CORNELIA BRIERLY

AT TALIESIN

May 24, 1935

We—the members of this Fellowship group—are too prone to look upon ourselves with self-approval and not often enough with self-disapproval. We are too ready to use brilliant generalities to make a broad, sweeping, only semi-true statement about ourselves. We talk and we write too often about what we would like to be and we forget what within ourselves we are.

We are apprenticed to the ideal and to the purpose which Frank Lloyd Wright, our master, is. It took many years of one of the greatest life-times the world has seen to make him as we know. Can we expect by simply asserting we do believe in this organic way of life and of architecture that automatically we are a part of his architecture and his philosophy concerning his architecture? No!

It is a long struggle of becoming that we have started upon. The only credit that we can take upon ourselves is that we have seen the real truth of this organic life in the face of the eclecticisms and untruths of the life we have grown up in, and have come voluntarily to work in it and for it. This much we can say for ourselves and no more. We cannot point at the great buildings that have come out of Taliesin's creative spirit and say "ours." We can say "his," and be proud in the realization that we have an inner sense of this building as architecture that few people are capable of having today. And not until we—the members of this Fellowship—come to this greater sense of our relationship to Taliesin will we grow into or be fit for the heritage that is being presented to us.

To read some of the written statements that we make about ourselves one might think that angels and archangels treading the heavens were no less perfect. One of the principles for which we are striving is to live a more genuinely human life. And in some of the generalities we carelessly throw away our life is represented as the "dream" that we always resent its being called. We—as a group—are not articulate. Constantly we shall need all the power within us to present forcibly, clearly, and honestly the principle upon which our lives and our creative work is based and from which it springs. We must talk clearly. We must write concisely. We do neither really well. We allow Mr. Wright to talk for us and write for us and think that as long as we go on working it is enough.

Our weekly chapel services which we conduct—preaching, talking, reading and singing ourselves—is a step in the direction to make us utter what we have to say. The articles we write weekly should bring about a clear expression of the same thing.

Mr. Wright is building with us perhaps the greatest edifice he has erected. He sees with clear vision the structure in its perfection and beauty—in its organic completeness. We are his material—not stone, wood, steel or glass—but human. We cannot see as clearly as he the noble thing that is being formed, but when it is finished we will be as important a part of it as it is a whole. We will make it possible for the structure to bring forth an architecture worthy of its heritage. But to be worthy human material we must grow WITH the building—not seeing ourselves as already perfected little units but as a part of the whole growing into it. We must have this proper sense of ourselves until life as architecture is fulfilled within us and ready for expression.

EUGENE MASSELINK

The brilliant and famous international film *M,* will be seen at the Taliesin Playhouse on Sunday, May 26. A huge success in Berlin, Paris, London and New York, it has not, however, been shown extensively in the Middle West. We are the first to have the opportunity of presenting one other of the great historic events of the screen in our part of the world. Peter Lorre gives a powerful and intelligent portrayal of a pathological character, the leading figure in the story—a madman. And under the remarkable direction of Fritz Lang the imagination of the audience is brought into play so that details are suggested more often than they are shown. *M,* they say, "is a tribute to the art of the

Fellowship in Front of Parsons & Hocking Meat Market, Dodgeville, WI, Enroute to Arizona, Wednesday, January 23, 1935. *Left to right kneeling:* Bennie Dombar, Iovanna Wright, Jim Thomson; *first row:* Etta Parsons, Etta's mother, Mr. Parsons, Bob Mosher, Mrs. Wright, Hulda Drake, Alfie Bush; *next row:* Mabel Morgan, Bill Bernoudy, John Howe, Mr. Wright, Betty Barnsdall; *top row:* Cornelia Brierly, Bud Shaw, Fred Langhorst, Abe Dombar, Bill Schwanke with cap, Bob Bishop; *between* Schwanke and Bishop: Burt Goodrich; *behind* Wright: Blaine Drake and Edgar Tafel. Photo courtesy of the Frank Lloyd Wright Foundation.

"In the courtyard of our Hacienda the master and his apprentices are working on the model of Broadacre City" (Cornelia Brierly, "At Taliesin," February 24, 1935). *Apprentices Working in La Hacienda Courtyard* (photo taken ca. early 1935 in the La Hacienda courtyard, Chandler, AZ). Photo courtesy of the Frank Lloyd Wright Foundation.

Apprentice Frederick Langhorst Working on Broadacre City Model, Section B (photo ca. 1935; taken in the La Hacienda courtyard, Chandler, AZ). Photo courtesy of the Frank Lloyd Wright Foundation.

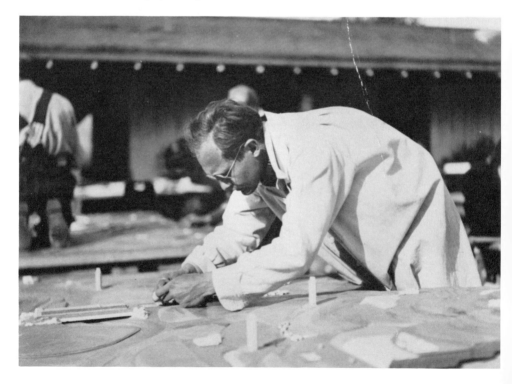

"Jensen and the saguaro, their strength and character, the
principle of their structure gave us cause to think. . . ."
(Benny Dombar, "At Taliesin," March 11, 1935). *Jens Jensen in
Arizona* (photo ca. March 1935). Photo courtesy of the Frank
Lloyd Wright Foundation (Cornelia Brierly Collection).

"Its lean Gothic tracery, tall windows and high ceilings are an honest type of good stone work and so, distinguished" (Edgar Tafel, "At Taliesin," March 27, 1935). *Madison City Hall* (photo ca. 1938). Photo by Harold Hone; courtesy of the State Historical Society of Wisconsin.

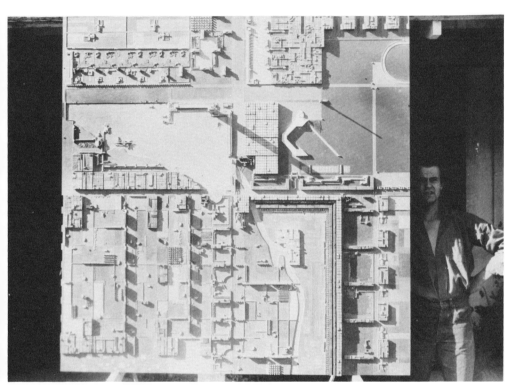

Broadacre City Model, Section A (photo ca. March 1935; apprentice John Howe proudly beside a finished section of the four-part, twelve-foot-square model; La Hacienda courtyard, Chandler, AZ). Photo courtesy of John H. Howe, Architect.

"I sing an ode to manure" (Abrom Dombar, "At Taliesin," May 4, 1935). *Taliesin Fields and Cows* (photo ca. late 1930s). Photo courtesy of Pedro E. Guerrero.

"Richardson's buildings are noble because he was noble himself" (Frank Lloyd Wright, "At Taliesin," August 9, 1935). *Allegheny County Courthouse and Jail,* 1888 (photo ca. 1930; view of jail). Photo courtesy of the Carnegie Library of Pittsburgh.

Broadacre City Model Exhibit Installed in Hillside Fellowship Living Room (ca 1935). Photo courtesy of the Frank Lloyd Wright Foundation.

Dam and Pump House at Taliesin (postcard). Photo courtesy of the Kenneth Spencer Research Library, University of Kansas, "Taliesin Collection."

motion picture, a monument to intelligent direction and sincere, capable performs."

AT TALIESIN

June 1, 1935

The Design for Broadacre City—A New Reality

The truck is packed securely with the biggest single object that is part of Mr. Wright's life experience as an architect and the result of five months effort on our part. The 12' x 12' model in four sections and all the larger scale auxiliary models made during the past five years and plywood sheets of explanation and information are ready for the trek back and forth across the country and on to European capitals. The model, however, expects to be in Madison on June 5th to stay 10 days at the State Historical Library. The exhibit opens Wednesday noon and will continue for ten days. As yet I have failed to comprehend the entirety of the display in one exhibition. Seeing the House on the Mesa, St. Marks, the gas station and theater and all the homes and the big model and plywood panels altogether is too much for me to see. Photographs will be the only way I will see the setup, I suppose, until I see it in Madison. Since it is impossible to get the real essence of Mr. Wright's work with photographs, I will probably lose the opportunity unless I pick it up there.

In the middle of December, Mr. Kaufmann of Pittsburgh started the ball rolling by offering to pay the costs of the big model for the exhibition—National Alliance of Arts and Industries in the Forum of Rockefeller Center, New York City. One month later found the Fellowship on its way to Arizona. At this news the New York exhibition officials presumed we had abandoned the idea. It was a clever move, however, and the climate and change of scene were vital necessities to the accomplishment you may see. We wonder now how we could have finished the model in Wisconsin.

When leaving Taliesin the model had blue acre lines across the plywood expanse, the highways and the tourist cabins plus several buildings such as the county building, the small factories, etc. When I think back to helping Jack rule the acre lines and think of the lapse of time I wonder where all the work came from.

The detail on the model is carried out to quite a remarkable degree. We might work on such a model for another six months but it must be out and we are all sorry and glad to see it go.

The immediate impression of the model is its delightful color scheme with sunlight in every color. The details of the workmanship are exact and clearly cut. The model is an organic whole and reaches an abstract perfection in the slightest detail as well as in the whole plan. No effort was made to reproduce nature in the reality. Symbols were used: trees, bushes, and grass were expressed in abstract patterns so as to form the essence of the particular thing. Distinction between the buildings and the acre tree blocks were secured by painting the foliage a dark green, whereas the buildings were in white and copper green and other colors which would not confuse them with the trees.

A leisurely stream winds down from the hill, through pine forests and levels out to form a peaceful lake. Commodious dwellings and diverse types of large homes are planted on the advantageous sites of the hill section. At one corner of the lake rises the county building, 50 stories, our tallest building and the only skyscrapers are the five standing glass and steel apartment towers in the foothills. In the county building are the county authorities and business offices. Its starry beacon is the sky mark for aerotors which drop vertically into their hexacombs at the post office, near the county building, and the aerial for official broadcasting.

One quarter of the model—in the center—is devoted entirely to small homes, medium and minimum houses. Each home has one, two, or three acres of land which is cultivated or green with grass. The number of acres is adjusted by the requirements of the particular family. Since no traffic enters this section, school children encounter no difficulties at crossings as they go to the center. Two lower-grade schools and a high school are at play with brilliantly colored gardens, small museums, auditoriums, two rectangular lakes, and playgrounds. On these lakes, as well as the large lake at the county seat, are colorful barges for gaiety and music, all easily constructed and appearing natural to their function and position.

Running east and west along one edge of the model is the super-highway that used to be the railway. It now has broad levels for monorail at the center, high-speed touring cars at sides, trucking on lower levels, etc. The complete width of the whole main arterial is about 400 feet. The roadways are of stained concrete to stop the sun glare. The usual lamp posts disappear to make place for the unusual two feet high search-lights which spread diverging rays across the road. The lights occur alternately so that the entire roadway is flooded with lights. Automobile headlights and street lights are thus useless. The concave road slopes in the center 1 to 30, having a continuous drain at the center with electricity, gas, or water lines laid in below a perfling along both sides of the road. The perfling protects water from being struck by passing cars. Where one road crosses another, through traffic is uninterrupted, either on grade or dropping down one level. All turns occur on the level above grade and only left turns will cross lanes at exact center. Since the percentage of left turners is only ten percent the number of left turners from different directions at the same time is about one tenth of one percent. This small percentage and the obviousness of the crossing lanes makes this intersection just as practical as any four level one could be or a "clover leaf." Underpasses and overpasses occur frequently to allow undisturbed and safe driving. Where bridges are necessary, steel in tension is used, anchored in concrete pylons to form a graceful architectural result.

On the lower part of the hill section is the university, zoo, arboretum, and the aquarium. They form a prominent row which terminates in the circular stadium. The university will serve mainly as a place for scientific and agricultural research. The stadium will serve as a place for convocation for the Broadacre citizens as well as pageantry and for games. Athletics are further provided for at the polo field, baseball park and numerous tennis courts sprinkled over the model. The larger homes such as the House on the Mesa and the Conventional House will be equipped with swimming pools. Small farms with modern farm buildings all in one form rows near the model's edge. Using steel and concrete as materials the farm model has a maximum of comforts and modern conveniences. All homes are also of various standardized materials, their differences lying in the extent to which they are carried and the means by which they are carried out.

To get all the ideas involved in the whole plan one has to study carefully because so few people are accustomed to seeing anything not a realistic picture. But there is much in it all for everyone although all may not grasp the significance of everything.

BENNY DOMBAR

AT TALIESIN
July 4, 1935

At last we are happy to announce the arrival of a trio at Taliesin: Anton Rovinsky, pianist; Edgar Neukrug, violinist; Youry Bilstin, cellist — all of New York City. Mr. Rovinsky, well known as soloist, in orchestras in many large cities will take charge of our musical activities during the summer. He is bringing some ancient instruments such as the spinet and gamba d' amour, which will be used at our programs at the Playhouse each Sunday.

The Broadacre City model is now set up in Washington's best exhibit hall, the Corcoran Galleries. Mr. Wright and Blaine Drake drove to Pittsburgh, picked the model up there after its visit had been extended from one to two weeks and took it to Washington. Cornelia will be charge of the model in Washington for the next ten days.

Harold Wescott of Milwaukee, a painter and teacher at the State Teacher's College, has joined the Fellowship for the summer. Jim Thomson has returned from his home in Farmington, Connecticut, after visiting there and attending his sister's wedding. Jim has the rare distinction of driving his car from Arizona to Connecticut without any license plates. He says he had trouble only once, in Pueblo, when the entire city's police and detective force swooped down on him with guns and demanded to know if he were Public Enemy No. One, the noted Karpis. After extended questioning and long distance telephoning, the police department decided that Jim wasn't much of an outlaw, anyway, and let him go. But on his way out Jim picked up the chief-of-police's gloves instead of his own, and again the harsh words of Pueblo's law were on our Jim.

Fortunately, Taliesin is in an ever state of change. Walls are being extended and new floors are being laid to accommodate our musical friends. We are trying out the new concrete mixer—which marks a new day in our building activities.

Last Sunday we returned again to the Chapel in the valley. Uncle Enos, Richard and Mary Lloyd Jones, Mr. and Mrs. Porter and Charlie Curtis were our special guests. Don Thompson took charge of the service and delivered a pertinent talk on "Relaxation." Don's conception of relaxation may be condensed into three words: "change of work." To relax from one labor, try another and another. If tired, if the body is drained of its resources, then rest—stretch out and relax completely. Sleep if necessary. But never sit, just for the sake of sitting.

News from Bar Harbor, Maine, tells of Marybud and her chow dog flying in a big transport plane along the coast: "Chub-chub" is now big enough to fly alone but his master won't let him.

EDGAR TAFEL

Excellent entertainment at the Playhouse next Sunday, July 7th. A French comedy, *Prenez Garde a la Peinture,* which has been a very great success in the east, will be shown. It makes full use of the latent possibilities of the screen and more than justifies its right to be seen on the screen. With this feature will be show a charming French travelogue: *Cotes Normandie.*

AT TALIESIN
July 6, 1935

Eating at Taliesin

Meals at Taliesin are a three-a-day delight, which repetition never seems to dull. Eating, of course, for people in good health is always a pleasure, and open-air living and open-air work certainly do not detract from this pleasant state. Four hours of ploughing, of shoveling sand, or swinging a hammer, create a vacancy that welcomes even the plainest food well-prepared. And it is well-prepared—our two cook-apprentices, stimulated by the comments and criticisms of the eaters, are continually in friendly rivalry seeking to present old familiar dishes in new and pleasurable forms.

Surprise thus becomes an element contributing to the delights of eating at Taliesin—for one never knows when the old familiar hamburger, perhaps, will turn up inside a roll of flaky pie crust, or the even more familiar potato present itself as a succulent morsel baked in wine. The oldest food of all appears in a variety of ways, not only at white wheat bread, but—much more the favorite, this—as the brown loaf baked of those darker flours so mysterious to the uninitiated, a rich crusty slice suggesting that molasses, perhaps, adds its bit, too. Nothing is more pleasant to contemplate than bread baking at Taliesin, the tray full of loaves, hot from the ovens, round brown, crusts swelling over the tasty sweetness within, butter-brushed shining curves of that comfortable contour peculiar only to loaves of bread.

The uncertainties of forage are sometimes experienced at meal times, to contribute their touch of despair or delight to gustatory feelings. Particularly is this true of breakfast, when a minute may mean the difference between starting the day off well with a three-course meal from fruit to coffee, or four hours of labor on an empty stomach. Breakfast at Taliesin is served from 7 to 7:30, a precise half hour as determined by the kitchen clock. Unfortunately the kitchen clock, like humans, is prone to err, and unhappy is he who lies abed till 7:25, to discover that his watch and the kitchen clock cannot agree on the hour. He enters the dining room, he approaches the serving window, confident in the thought that in a moment he will be a part of his happy throng, eating breakfast—peeling an orange, choosing his cereal, being served his bacon and eggs and toast, drinking milk or coffee or even both. His appetite mounts with his anticipations, his nostrils scent frying bacon, his mouth waters, his hollow belly cries silently for food. Then, and not until then, does he discover that the kitchen clock and his watch differ by two minutes, the 7:31 of the kitchen clock calling his 7:28 a liar, and he is dashed, at the very peak of gustatory anticipation, to the depths of famished despair.

But the deadline-pusher is typically American in that he will take a chance on anything, and losing, accepts the fact in philosophical resignation. As a matter of routine, he registers with the cook a formal protest at the inaccuracy of the kitchen clock and its consequent unfairness to himself, but realizes from long experience the futility of this as a practical means of getting food. He may have an apple in his room, he may pull a radish or two from the garden, but mainly he passes the morning with quaking vitals, and tight-pulled belt, definitely resolved to rise early the next morning and get breakfast at any cost.

The next morning, missing the 7 o'clock bell as usual, he rise by his watch, at 10 minutes after seven. Leisurely he dresses, brushes his teeth, washes his face, and leisurely proceeds to the dining room, secure in the thought that an ample breakfast is his this morning beyond any possibility of doubt. He enters the dining room and is surprised to find no one there. He has sudden sickening suspicion. He feels faint at the pit of his stomach: did he misread his watch? . . . can it be past 8 o'clock? Then, spying someone building a fire in the kitchen stove he is reassured — but chagrined to find that the kitchen clock announces the time as ten minutes to seven! A quarter of an hour later, as he sits eating his breakfast and paternally greeting newcomers to the dining room, he is a mild sensation at being the first one in to breakfast.

Thus, breakfast at Taliesin can be more tangy than fried ham alone can make it, when the pleasure of the chase are in a measure added to it. This slight uncertainty as to the outcome of one's efforts to eat extends itself at times to other meals too, so that the entire schedule of eating is lifted out of the realm of routine into a state more continually interesting. As a matter of practical cooking, for example, it is impossible to estimate exactly the number of especially tasty oatmeal rolls thirty apprentices can eat. If his cooking bear ever so much toward that peak of culinary perfection all good cooks strive for — then there is bound to be tremendous demand for those royal rolls, these magnificent muffins, and the institution known as "Seconds" will do a thriving business and be sold out in no time. Then, if the hungry apprentice has the ill-luck to be half a mile away across the farm when the dinner bell rings, unhappy is he again, for he will in all probability get only one muffin. As so it goes. To compensate, that same night at dinner Fate may seat him next an absentee, and so put him in an excellent position to garner the absentee's dessert.

We are all pigs at meal times, the more so because our appetites naturally got by naturally balanced activity are naturally sharpened by

Nature herself, to whom our living at Taliesin is close. We pull radishes from our garden and eat them, washing them off, to be sure, but certainly with less relish and no less eagerness than our porkers go after their food in their pen a hundred and twenty feet from our dining room. When we line up at the serving window for lunch we are thirty strong young animals who push a little less, possibly, than our fat four-footed friends at their trough. But perhaps that is one of the more readily apparent of our desirable characteristics, this quality of being natural, of a natural living expressed simply in natural functions such as our eating that is the fundamental aspect of our life close to the soil here at Taliesin.

DONALD THOMPSON

AT TALIESIN

July 25, 1935

On Thursday last, each apprentice took a bath, shaved and rushed around Taliesin as if his head were cut off, and tried to find the place scheduled for himself in an automobile. The Fellowship was going to Janesville to visit with Mr. and Mrs. George S. Parker. The trip was also the christening of the new station wagon. The day was hot, and for the first time in its life the Fellowship was out en mass on a new type of activity. It was being entertained. Instead of receiving week-enders it was itself a week-ender. Upon arriving in Janesville, Mr. Parker had a grand dinner spread over the lawn of his country home—Stonehenge, and we divided our time between eating and feeding the Parker's pet monkey, Benito. We made our home at a new camp of Mr. Parker's, about a half mile from Stonehenge. It was a new type of vacation (any "vacation" is new for us except the one we are in every day in nearly every way but this new way). Bunched together in "Camp Cherrio," with our activities reduced to reading magazines seated in soft lounge chairs, the Fellowship grumbled and quarreled. This being together, indulging in several hours of non-activity was a new one on us.

However, I guess it was fun—observing ourselves and others whiling away time reading magazines and sitting—just as we might be in a score of years from now, and then instead of quarreling with the fellows it'll be with our wives—maybe.

The next morning after breakfast we were shown through the Parker Pen Company's factory. We followed the operations of the manufacture of the pen through its five thousand stages. The Ford assembly idea is used in assembling the pen. They start the barrel moving along the assembly line, and each worker adds a part, fitting and polishing all the while, until the pen reaches its final glory labeled, recorded, tested, packed—it's all done but the selling. Even the selling is accounted for in the recording office, where each retailer has a card, duly punched and kept on file, telling of the quantity and types of pens in his stock. If one found a pen and wanted to trace its owner, it could easily be done by sending the pen number to the factory. Within a half hour the dealer who sold the pen could be sifted from any one of the many dealers, there being thousands spread through sixty-eight countries. The peculiar part of the merchandising of the Parker pen is that half of them are exported. We then went back to dinner and, ready to go home, fizzed out trying to sing our chorale without an accompaniment. We hope the Parkers had a good time, but we don't know.

Don and Mary Thompson left for Washington on the large truck to pick up the Broadacre City models and Cornelia Brierly. Cornelia has been away over a month, in charge of the models in Pittsburgh and Washington. Soon after the return of the models we will set them up at Hillside for exhibition before it goes on tour again. It is estimated that over 125,000 people have seen Broadacres so far, while it has been shown in three major cities, not to mention our own minor Madison. The reaction is almost unlimited in its diversity. Broadacres has been called every name, and classified under every theory of government. Yet, its principle is quite simple—both in words and in model form.

Among our visitors very soon we expect Karl Jensen, Mr. Wright's former secretary. Karl is working in land rehabilitation surveys, and is being sent to various parts of the country to study and tabulate conditions.

EDGAR TAFEL

Youry Bilstin, Russian and a musical genius distinguished in European concert circles, a true master of the cello and viola da gamba, will play with the ensemble for the first time on the Playhouse program next Sunday, July 28th. The three artists, Rovinsky, Bilstin, and Neukrug are working almost constantly on a group of programs of rare music by the great masters. They are making wonderful music afternoons for the public beginning sharp at three o'clock Sunday afternoons.

At three forty-five entertainment a la mode begins. *Escape Me Never,* the English film, starring Elizabeth Bergner, will be shown following the recess after the music program. Elizabeth Bergner is one of the greatest of actresses, we said when we saw her in *Catherine the Great.* We are looking forward now with high anticipation to seeing her next Sunday in this, her latest film.

AT TALIESIN

July 28, 1935

A Bowl of Jello and Me

The preparation of Sunday night buffet supper in the house is anticipated by the apprentices with no small amount of anxiety and perhaps fear, but when the moment arrives, that is, when it becomes the turn of the two apprentices to perform — efficiency and correlation of all latent faculties (including cooking) takes place of prevailing fears and doubts.

It was with this feeling that Edgar and I began our supper. We had what we thought was a splendid menu. The dessert (because we both like desserts) was planned as "top" for the program and we began making it early in the morning before the usual Sunday noon picnic. Cool, brilliant crimson Jello with all varieties and assortments of rare fruits sliced into it. It was to be molded into a great architectural mold and we were going to carry it triumphantly through the phalanxes of guests into the climax of the evening.

So, to town we went after the fruits and only after great trouble (and no little expense to ourselves) did we get what we wanted. After a futile search for a large enough platter, we decided to serve it in a large bowl with the fruit cut into interesting abstracted patterns over the top. And the bowl we chose was the Fellowship treasure: one of the beautiful rich Indian-red pieces of Catalina ware — circular, about two feet in diameter.

It was a warm day and it took until four in the afternoon for the Jello to "jell" sufficiently for the fruit to be added. First we put it on the porch — no result. Then we put it into the milk room — still no results. After about an hour in the refrigerator it finally began to "jell" so we took it out, added the fruit (mixed with ripened bananas) and part of it into the great bowl. Then we put the bowl in a dish pan of ice in the storeroom, but it refused to "jell" any further.

I have been accused by my chief of being a "putterer," but after the Fellowship and the guests had finished the surprisingly successful supper (the previous cooking experience of both of us hadn't extended much beyond the boiling of an egg in water) time came for dessert and all were waiting. It seemed to me that all eyes were on the buffet kitchen door (ice cream had been served the week before).

Meanwhile I was hastily bringing down the jello from the kitchen on the hill where we made the supper.

When — suddenly — where was the jello?

I — sprawling on the pavement — no longer had anything in my hands.

In a moment of anguish — I saw it all over the pavement in the court, as a varied colored mosaic, but no longer beautiful (I thought of my moment of anguish). No longer beautiful to me for a great part of the color mosaic — now an unsightly smear on the stones — was supplied by the brilliantly gleaming tiny pieces of the rich Indian-red Catalina ware treasure bowl.

Now — all this efficiency and correlation of faculties at the mercy of a stubbed toe was replaced by the feeling one has when his heart sinks to all his toes and they all feel like two big ones.

Prosaic canned apples replaced the artistic jello.

The bowl — not so easy. I have thought of taking up a collection. But another bowl is still somewhere else.

Gentle readers of this sad tale — if all of you who read this would enclose 10 cents in stamps and send the stamps to me I am sure the beautiful bowl would come back. Yours,

JACK HOWE

AT TALIESIN
August 4, 1935

I Have a Little List

". . . assorted dried cereal, meat, prunes, chips, toilet paper, and ham," I shouted over the rural phone emphatically and desperately to Etta at our general store in Dodgeville—16 miles away—through a wired maze of farmer's wives, daughters, sons, and farmers themselves passing the weather at any time of day or night.

Breathless, I paused after this frantic résumé of our next week's-to-be menus-in-the-raw to look up and see Hans the cabinet maker with a small screw in one hand and the demand that we need "vun udder chust like this vun—only vun size bigger." Obediently went the order under Bill the chef's request for five pounds of butter: Housemother Mary's threat—No. 50, black silk, two spools: Utility Jack's coal: and General Alfie's perpetual "pig feed, egg mash, chick growing mash and chick scratch grain." It seems that the Farm Bureau will have to go down under Alfie's raids on "mash."

Well—I furtively hid the growing list and furtively pecked out an address on the typewriter.

Then in strode a battling Alfie (the fifth time that day) with a threat that if no chick-growing-mash were forthcoming, the little chicks would straightway not only stop growing but—worse, the big ones would stop laying!

"Hurrah," I thought savagely but only smiled and underscored once more that familiar items on the bedraggled list.

Have I a little list? Koko was only an amateur with his.

Lists—lists everywhere and lists for everything. Large important Madison lists on large white paper. Spring Green lists on any old paper. Dodgeville grocery and butcher lists on ruled notepads from the kitchen. Lists typewritten and lists handwritten in every kind of pen and or pencil within reach. Lists lost and half remembered—they flutter about me dominating my kingdom of letters and articles and filing cards and endless odds and ends of what is bravely called "business." The word should be spelled busy-ness, or why not busy-mess. But the list is only embryo compared with the listers actually getting what the list lists. There are so few who will stand to wait longer than three days for what they've listed and at the end of that time a package of cigarettes or "Plowboy" or "Red Man" or one spool of thread or a pound of 6-penny casing nails will assume terrific proportions. Not my peach only but my life is continually jeopardized by little lists.

Running this way and that to collar any car leaving for town is a matter of strategy and tact and frequently a matter of running madly halfway down the hill road. Every car whizzing past my studio window is evidence of either my ignominious defeat or some supreme triumph, depending whether by means of either charm or threat I have been able to cajole that car to return with two rolls of No. 120 film, Verichrome, bread for tea, some green peppers, or a pitch fork.

Sometimes in desperation, I admit I betray my fellows by asking that if only the mail is mailed—nothing else in the world matters: the mail that only makes more "little lists" from day to day.

But I will say for my year and a half experience of "listing," covering the four miles of road to and from town for those who have to trust in my ability to somehow get them what they want, that it has been rare indeed that I have suffered the indignity of having to go to town myself to dutifully return with egg mash for tea and bread for the chickens or gamboge for the tractor and litharge for the roof. The three-fold way of life requires little lists more varied than any "from a pin to an elephant" that used to be the standard department store boast.

Yes—and I find that it is just another—"little list."

EUGENE MASSELINK

AT TALIESIN

August 9, 1935

[Wright's involvement with his client Edgar Kaufmann, Sr., brought him to Pittsburgh many times, beginning in December 1934. Kaufmann's showing of the Broadacre City model exhibit in Pittsburgh in June 1935 began an undercurrent of controversy between Frank Lloyd

Wright and the city of Pittsburgh, with Pittsburgh's mayor condemn-
ing the Wright's city as socialistic ("You can't tell people how many
babies they're allowed to have"). Apprentice Edgar Tafel hurled a
response to the mayor's criticisms, as reported in the *Wisconsin State
Journal* on June 27, "Let's not go into the conditions that cities like
Pittsburgh have imposed upon the 'average man' or upon 'average
families.' The by-products are new tenements, the dole, the pauper-
ism, and the outlook generally hopeless. . . . Broadacres is not
socialism. . . . Broadacres is freedom conscious." Wright visited
Pittsburgh and toured the city on June 29, during which it was
reported that he made his now (in)famous statement about Pittsburgh,
"It would be cheaper to abandon it." Shortly after his return to Spring
Green he felt the necessity to write a letter to the Pittsburgh press
(dated July 16, 1935) with "Frank Lloyd Wright to Pittsburgh." In it
he retorts, "My criticisms of Pittsburgh, given in the short hand of
epigrammatic humor, were nevertheless the sound sense of an architect
extended in a friendly way to a friend. The architect seeing what the
friend—Pittsburgh—could not see for lack of perspective, for one
thing, and, for another, the lack of knowledge of the nature of
architecture." This column is certainly a continuation of Wright's
outspoken position as well as a brief tribute to an architect whose work
he greatly respected—H. H. Richardson.]

Something told me in Pittsburgh showed the citizens far ahead of
their benefactors in point of culture; "the citizens had refused to allow
their courthouse and jail to be ruined by the addition of more stories."
In their jail and courthouse Pittsburghers own a masterpiece of
architecture. A great American architect H. H. Richardson of Boston
built the building. He was a big man in every way and his bigness was
of a kind that not only marks a distinct epoch in American architecture
but commands the respect of the civilized world. Everyone of his
buildings is on record as of value. Even the minor ones, like the big
little Protestant Episcopal church on the North Side, built by him, are
of such caliber. Even in that little straightforward honest church
structure you may see something of the qualities that make a building
or a great man—simplicity of character, straight-forward purpose and
mastery of the uses of materials, generous in scale.

Richardson's buildings are noble because he was noble himself even though he did die owing the butcher, baker, and candlestick maker over $60,000. A major Chicago architect of my acquaintance cherishes a $15 check given him by Richardson. Rather than take the money he preferred to keep the signature.

By noble I mean the reverse of ordinary and mean because of creative vision. He handled the stone he loved in a better way than was characteristic of most of the noble old Romanesque buildings that were his inspiration. No such masonry existed in the Romanesque era. His mastery of the medium in which he chose to work stands out from the crowd of architects who followed him as starlight stands above electric light and Pittsburghers must have felt something of this in his work when they refused to let Pittsburgh opulence or cupidity, or was it just plain stupidity, ruin their gift from so great an American.

The courthouse and jail in point of American culture is worth all the other buildings of Pittsburgh put together. The courthouse and jail is "Romanesque" in style only to the point where it becomes Richardsonian. Therein the building transcends the other eclecticisms that might seem, as such, to have justification for their existence. In the courthouse and jail the man was bigger than the style. The only instance of the kind on record.

What might Richardson not have done for America had he grown entirely beyond the style as he was surely doing when the excesses of his impulsive big nature ended his usefulness to the American people?

Pittsburgh should tear away the buildings that crowd upon the great building and surround it with a park.

FRANK LLOYD WRIGHT

We are happy to announce the extraordinary program to be presented at the Playhouse this Sunday, Aug. 11.

Four films, of such importance and such different character, will form one of the most significant and delightful performances ever presented at the Playhouse.

Le Million, one of the best films by the greatest French director, Rene Clair—no film made, unless it be another by this same director, has integrated sound and movement more beautifully;

A Dog's Life, an early and rare film, one of the few remaining made by Charlie Chaplin;

Orphan's Benefit, the funniest of all the 30 or more Disneys we have seen;

Czar Duranday, a wonderfully made Russian cartoon of a famous Russian fairy story.

Three of these films have been chosen from the finest we have seen during the past two years at the Playhouse. Don't miss this "picnic" next Sunday at three if you want to enjoy a hilariously entertaining afternoon.

AT TALIESIN

August 16, 1935

The Box Man

[This column is an apprentice-written, Fellowship-inspired fable ("to be continued" according to the original manuscript contained within the Frank Lloyd Wright Archives).]

Once upon a time there was a country—great lands that spread between two oceans—spaciousness that knew the rain and wind over the earth. With the earth and by way of the earth there lived a people who knew a simple life. Fruit of agriculture, industry, art. Unto this people it was given that their homes were out of the earth. Their wigwams sloped as the pines of the earth's forests. Their desert homes embraced the cliffs. A white man came and told them that with his coming their homes were in a new world called America. Later the country came to be called the United States. The white man stayed but the life he brought with him was not out of the new earth. Earth's spaciousness frightened the white man and he said to himself and to all the other white men, "Such vastness is not for the white man for we have come from towns and villages where there is space only for thought. We do not move over the earth like the wild people of the wigwam or the people of the cliff. Our homes we build in safe groups for we are civilized. We remember the homes of our forefathers."

And even as the white man remembered, he built his home on the top of the earth as a close box close to his neighbor's box and next to his neighbor's neighbor's box. He cut holes in his close box so that when he looked out he could smile indulgently at the ephemeral wigwam that had now to return to the earth from which it had sprung.

Other neighbors seeing the white man's superior smile, joined him until his box was surrounded by other boxes. As the space around him became less and less as his neighbors, still wishing to be as close as possible, adopted a way of building box upon box until the pile of boxes became so flatteringly high that the man and all the neighbors (overcome with the glory of their accomplishment) observed the stacks of boxes and whispered in self-esteeming awe, "We have built on top of the ground boxes of greater proximity and height than our forefathers. Thus we have developed America! These boxes we've heaped into piles form the great cities of the great United States!"

But the closer the white man built his boxes the less safe he new felt. His box was so confined and he became so dependent upon the people in similarly closed boxes that he could no longer find food and clothing. When he went into the street to walk between the rows of neighbor boxes to find these necessities one of his stronger neighbors — the boarder — (who had said to himself, "God intended me as this box-man's landlord") took the white man's box. Took his shelter, you see because it was built on boxes and not on its own ground. The poor Box Man wandered up and down the streets until he was lost among the maze of boxes whose building he had planned himself. He couldn't go back to the wigwam because the Great Spirit had taken it back into the ground and with it all knowledge of their three fold way of life combining the arts, industry, and agriculture.

True that the Box Man did know industry — hadn't he worked all his life handling white hot ingots in a great steel mill? But the pursuit of agriculture was a foreign occupation — the dull way of livelihood from which his box-city purposely held itself aloof. As a matter of fact he had once, in an attitude of great good humor taken his children into the park to see the grass and once in the country they saw a cow.

The children — rolled in the grass when they were taken to the park but were puzzled because they couldn't understand how grass came to be. And among themselves concluded that the thick green carpet must have been made in a strange factory but working like their father's. They wanted to take the green carpet with them but when they tried to life it they found it securely fastened in the dark earth. They had discovered something — discovered that the grass came by way of the life of earth. But the man paid no attention to the children. He sat near them on a bench and saw only a printed page that he had brought with him from his box. When it became so dark that he could read only the large headline — "Stock Report" he went to the children. "Come," Man said, "We will go back to our box." But the children drew back and pleaded, "Let us stay, Father, for we are building on the green carpet — building with sticks that we pulled out of black earth." The Box Man gathered them with a contemptuous gesture, "At night time your green carpet is not so safe as our box."

This had happened years before the stronger neighbor — the boarder — took the white man's box — before the white man lost himself in the streets. As he wandered through the city he passed a gate on which was written a powerful name, a name that he remembered seeing in the printed papers. So that he knew that in the box behind the gate there lived the President of the country who was, of course, president of all boxes. The man went to the President passing on his way 365 secretaries — one for each day in the year all working every day and all of whom asked his name and why he had come. To all he replied, "I am the Box Man. 'They' have taken my divine box away. I am naked. I am hungry."

Now all the 365 secretaries were in the good humor of early afternoon because they had just feasted in celebration of the first secretary's birthday. Seeing the hungry Box Man they simply made notations on their desk pads and quickly passed him from one to another until by the first evening he reached the first secretary. There the man waited until the President disposed of the conferences then in session. When the Box Man saw the President, the man addressed him saying, "Oh generous protector and servant of your people, help me! The strong neighbor has taken away my box. I have no food, no clothes!" The President was not surprised for he had seen many Box Men idle in the streets. He looked at him kindly and said, "All your life you and your people have lived smugly in your boxes, you have made the streets of your life narrower by making them higher as you lived. This specialization you boosted of as civilization. You have brooded over industry placing money value on all things for the benefit of the hoarder. You scoffed at the farmer who raised your food and material

for your clothes. The farmer scoffed at man who made his plows and
served up his garments. You Box Men have developed great machines
among you but you haven't learned to use them to make your lives
more complete. For a long while I have seen this plight of our vast
country and have tried to use my power to save it from destruction. I
have tried to stabilize the wealth of the country by a National Recovery
Act that threw capitalism into jail, then by taking money from the
country's capitalists I have planned extensive relief agencies and built
some new communities intending to help the country's workers. But I
see now that none of these can solve our country's problem. I appeal to
you, Box Man. Go among the people in multi-boxes and find suggestions for a new way of life in America. Bring your suggestions to me for
I will hear them and I will know if they are good." And so the Box Man
went out again into the streets among the boxes. By chance he entered
a very grand box not far from the President's own box. This grand box
was used as an art gallery and in it he found a display which he was
puzzled by, because it was entitled "Broadacre City: a New Freedom
for Living in America." The Box Man saw it, as from afar — and asked
help to see it nearer. Finally he saw it as a great spaciousness where each
person lived on an acre or more of land instead of living in boxes two by
two. There were no boxes anywhere or even piles of boxes except where
boxes were useful as boxes. Each family lived in a home that grew out
of the earth because of the earth. The people of the earth homes all had
free right to a medium of exchange instead of money. Their lives were
complete and developed because they had learned to build their homes
with a feeling for the land and learned how to use both to best
advantage. They had developed their home industries in small workshops in human scale where they could enjoy putting their own
thought and feeling into them. They had planted their lands with
fruits and vegetables and flowers and beautiful lawns and useful trees.
Their streets were broad and devoid of wires, telephone poles, and
glaring lights. Their roads were great lighted ribbons along which
they motored in safety and could go in either direction without
crossing traffic or stopping at crossing.

The Box Man visited Broadacre City day after day and each time he
found crowds of other men diligently studying and admiring the
completeness of its conception as a fruitful way of life for America.

When he had learned to grasp some of its significance he went away humbly to take to the President that which he had learned. The secretaries were no longer in a good humor but he managed to pass all 365 with only minor bruises. When he arrived before the President he explained the idea that some great man had given to the country by way of an exhibition at the art gallery.

But the President with a weary gesture brushed him aside. "Not now Box Man, my time is valuable, my busyness is great, and even now Congress has placed before me another Bill that demands my consideration."

The Box Man left the President's box by way of the gate where the great name was written to wander among the boxes and ponder upon what he had seen.

CORNELIA BRIERLY

The Playhouse presents on Sunday, Aug. 17, another of the ensemble. This trio has already become famous during its short span of life at Taliesin for the splendid playing of great music. The opportunity of hearing them will soon be over and Madisonians and people in this region about us are warned not to miss the rare privilege.

"Entertainment a la mode" on this Sunday will be *The Unfinished Symphony,* an English picture made of the life of the German composer Franz Schubert.

AT TALIESIN
August 23, 1935

The Fellowship has, more than ever, been hearing great music this summer, not only in concert in the living room at Taliesin and in the Playhouse, but in rehearsal when music comes up from beneath the eaves or through the vines and walls that enclose it within the spaces of Taliesin. Music makes the life within those spaces more completely an enriched unity and Taliesin plans to continue and develop its relation to the finest chamber of music by its own performances.

The life expressed by music has a depth of form and line and even-patterned surface by way of the movement that the walls and roofs of Taliesin make with the hill and the buildings at Hillside as well upon their gentler slope. Music in graphic terms is made also by way of the many plans and the drawings and models of executed buildings and building being designed in the studio. Taliesin life had a depth of thought by way of writing, speaking, discussing. Now it better knows the depths and significances of sound as the great masters felt them.

Taliesin's walls sing. They speak naturally. Great music belongs to them as organically and intrinsically as the more humble materials of which they are built.

The life in the Fellowship is becoming more familiar with another sense of the same rhythms and patterns and forms that we see about us in buildings, painting, sculpture, and in the earth: forms, rhythms, and patterns conceived by Bach, Brahms, Beethoven, Schubert and the earlier ones by Tartini and Loeillet and other 16th and 17th century composers that began the later patterns on the ancient instruments the Taliesin Trio brought with them.

Anton Rovinsky, pianist, bringing his spinet came with Eddie Neukrug, violinist, bringing his viola d'amore and later Youry Bilstin, cellist, bringing his viola da gamba joined them. Slowly at first, feeling their way perhaps, they gradually opened up to us the full power of their thorough training, their native talent, and their amazing repetoire. Little by little — as things go at Taliesin — their work is being built into the life of the Fellowship. This was accompanied by the "Maestro Suite," three rooms made over for them, and the arrangement at the Playhouse which brings them into a more complete relation with the room — both from the point of design, of sound, and of audience. They are made an integral part of the color, pattern, and acoustical structure of the Playhouse. Wherever they play the same thing happens to them. They have made themselves of the environment, not "on it" as some excrescence. An experience somewhat new to them but natural enough.

The "Maestro Suite" was finished by knocking new windows into walls, rhythmically relating walls and ceilings to each other by contrasting white with brilliant color — arranging groups of Japanese prints and old Chinese paintings upon the surfaces with a few pieces of simply improvised furniture and a characteristic flower arrangement. All turned by Mr. Wright into a simple flowering of the thing organic architecture stands for: the rhythms they understand in music turned in upon their daily lives as "environment."

Artist—fellow workers, one of the hardest things the musicians had to learn at Taliesin this summer was to get up at 6:30 in the morning and do their own "service." Taliesin reversed New York habits and New York hours but the musicians are more Bohemian than most New Yorkers.

During the two months they have been here, they have brought us—and those of the public who have joined us on Sunday afternoons ancient music on ancient instruments: spinet, viola d'amore, viola da gamba—hauntingly beautiful primitive music a quality of tone in the ensemble more unified ever than those of the modern instruments. Such early music as they play is of fine simplicity. We have been hearing compositions that are rarely played anywhere—early works by great masters, among them a naive composition without opera number by Schubert when he was 15. And we have heard many of the great classic compositions that are played only by the great virtuosi in grandiloquent circumstances.

To celebrate the trio's sojourn at Taliesin, this weekend is planned as a gala event. There will be two full length feature concerts: Saturday evening, Aug. 24, beginning sharp at seven o'clock, and Sunday afternoon, Aug. 25, beginning at three.

The programs for these two concerts will be:

AUG. 24 - SATURDAY

Ancient Instrument Group

Bach . . . Aria From Cantata
Viola da Gamba and Spinet

Tartini . . . Trio Sonata
Viola da Gamba, Viola D'amore, Spinet

Modern Instrument Group

Beethoven . . . Trio in B Flat Major

Grieg . . . Sonata
Cello and piano

Brahms . . . Trio in E Flat Major

AUG. 25 - SUNDAY

Loeillet . . . Trio in B Major

Modern Instrument Group
  Beethoven . . . Sonata in C Minor
    Piano and violin
  Tchaikovsky . . . Trio in A Minor

The admission fee for each occasion is 50 cents. Kindly telephone your friends and ask them to telephone their friends provided they love the best in music played as music is seldom played in our country.

AT TALIESIN
September 12, 1935

Broadacres has returned from the Mineral Point County Fair where it stood on sawdust floor under a rough white-washed board roof—in an ear shot of prize chickens and huge hogs. Many of the country folk who saw it there grasped its ideas and its significance in relation to their own lives far better than the New Yorkers because these country people are living out on the very ground for which Broadacre City is planned. While Broadacres plans for the betterment of living conditions, socially and economically, for both New Yorker and Wisconsin farmer—for both city and country folk—it is the farmer who has not the smoke of the city slum in his eyes but the clean, fresh country air and who can see what such a plan will do for him and his family and his family's family.

EUGENE MASSELINK

[The *Iowa County Democrat* (Mineral Point, Wisconsin) reported on September 12, 1935, "The fair house was filled with a great assortment of home and garden exhibits and one wing of the building was devoted to 'Broadacres'. . . . the visionary and future city of the nation." N. S. Boardman, president of the Southwestern Wisconsin Fair Association, announced in a letter to Wright, written after the close of the fair, that "Broadacres" was the outstanding attraction of the Fair and credited it as having "saved our Fair from folding up."]
  The Taliesin Playhouse on Sunday the 15th of September, at three in the afternoon, will present an outstanding Russian film, *The Czar*

Wants to Sleep. This film is built upon the story by Tynianov and based upon historical events during the reign of Paul the first, the made Czar. It was directed by Feinzimmer and the music is by one of the greatest of modern composers, Prokofief.

AT TALIESIN

September 19, 1935

These are busy days at Taliesin. In the valley the boys are working with Mr. Wright to rebuild the dam. Some of them work with the tractor and scoop, redistributing the black muck of the basin, in order to change the water level of the pond. Others lay stone to change and build the spillway, or mix and pour the concrete that seals the joints. Perhaps the work will be completed today. We invite our Spring Green friends to come and see it, for a good looking dam it is.

At the house, we are equally busy. The girls have been re-upholstering the chairs of the living room and loggia by using old remnants of theatrical gauze and curtains that were no longer useful.

It is canning season in the kitchen and the shelves are lined with many two-quart jars of tomatoes, preserves, pickles and apple butter. Frances Fritz is our star apple butter maker. Frances sat for days by the fire in the court yard, while she stirred the spicy butter, and sometimes when we passed by she would give us hot sticks of cinnamon covered with steaming apple butter. But Frances has gone back to Madison.

Our secretary, Gene, is at home in Grand Rapids, Michigan, for a short vacation, and the office isn't nearly so cheerful, even though Gwen is very conscientious about keeping the typewriter in practice. Alfy left, too. Much against his will, his father decreed that young Alfy must return to Brooklyn to attend for the winter the Polytechnic Institute. Just before spring, Alfie will return to Taliesin.

We have an apprentice, a young architect, from Michigan — Karl Monrad — who seems to have been here longer than a week, and at present is working with the squad down at the dam. Just before Alfy left, a new apprentice came to Taliesin from Beloit. Her name is Cornelia Schneider, but since we already have one Cornelia, we have adopted her as "Kay."

Do you think Ivy Olson has returned to Spring Green? Taliesin misses hearing her friendly voice in the courtyard. I, also, have a hunch that many apprentices have great stacks of laundry waiting for Ivy's return.

CORNELIA BRIERLY

The Taliesin Playhouse is going to present on Sunday, September twenty-second, one of the most ingratiating pictures of the month.

It is the British *It Happened One Night* and just as good entertainment. Starting off with a smash, *The 39 Steps* gathers dash and speed, and suspense until it has you jittery; and you won't be disappointed with the ending — a rare occurrence.

Trust Robert Donat, the *Monte Cristo* hero, and Miss Madeline Caroll, beautiful star of *I Was a Spy,* and *The Loves of a Dictator,* to hold you enthralled.

The *39 Steps* is a tale of international intrigue that will fascinate every lover of mystery stories.

The *39 Steps* is directed by Alfred Hitchcock, whose uncanny gift for cold chills and suspenseful thrills made *The Man Who Knew Too Much,* a sensationally successful thriller.

Theater time — 3:00 P.M.

AT TALIESIN

September 26, 1935

[This column was written by Eugene Masselink upon his return from vacationing at the Bluffs on Garthies Farm, Northport, Michigan.]

I stood upon the hill where four years before I had first stood and saw far beyond me and below me the endless blue depths of water made patterns upon the undulating strips of land. The depth of that blue — blue green to blue purple — flattened the rolling country — land that was knife edged by the unending narrow strip of hard, white sand and cut into rhythmical shapes, bounded by the blues of Lake Michigan and the numberless bays and inlets and lakes. It was a land dotted with cherry orchards and peopled with happy, hardworking, singing Norwegians — sturdy Lutherans.

I saw all of this, just as others who had stood on this highest hill must have seen before me. But I saw more. I was seeing in perspective — as it were — the movement of my life before, during, and after the two summers I spent among these low hills, bounded by these spaces of water.

In perspective I saw clearer than I had ever seen before how the parts of my thinking and working and dreaming were at that time as separated from the whole of my life as the buildings of that small farm below are separated from each other. Just as meaningless a pattern as that barn, pigsty, chickenhouse, silo, and farmhouse make in scattered confusion on the hill slope, so meaningless were my painting and drawing and working now and then, scattered in confusion through a year of my life. Life wasn't then thought of as being creative or even an entity. It simply went on, working toward no really great purpose. If, every now and then, something by accident happened that might be called, at best, inventive, why so much the better. But it was a happy life and among honest people who were living a naturally progressive life — serenely amongst the cherry orchards and wheat fields of their land life edged against the repose of the endless blue which seemed to condition the repose of their own lives. At least, that much I saw and appreciated and in a measure understood; the goodness of this life in the low hills of the country — far away from the nervous noise of any city.

In my thinking upon the hilltop, time drew in closer about me and I remembered how, just two years ago on this same hill I had received the message which brought me into another country with greater hills — into a life which was as completely one creative unit as the buildings of Taliesin are themselves. I saw that life at Taliesin, too, in perspective. It was even more perfectly one great movement toward the flowering of a great purpose and ideal than I had known — working hard within it. And the many minor struggles caused by dogged determination to free work from the routine of regimentation and to form within young men and women by this freedom greater initiative and strong individual beauty of the life.

Americans have too long considered architecture, art, music and any creative expression separate from daily living. These expressions, in reality, are the truest and most integral part of human life — the life that is now crushed and killed by the working to earn money to buy bread to eat to work to earn money — money that conditions all life for mere maintenance in America today.

I stood upon the hill with all the blue of the world in my eyes and longed to immediately rejoin that endless work for organic creative life at Taliesin.

EUGENE MASSELINK

AT TALIESIN

November 15, 1935

The Scullerite

Mention of the word "scullery" causes my nose to crinkle and my thoughts to dwell on murky things. But recalling my year of work in the kitchen, I think the word is a perfect onomatopoeic description of the work itself. Scraping burnt macaroni from a dutch oven, or making a roaster secure from any vestige of caramel sauce in which ham was baked, deserves no very pleasant sounding name. Any mixing pan covered with dough offers quite a trial to the innocent dishwasher, especially if the cook forgot to soak the pan after using it as cooks do. In such a case, a small copper "chore-girl," or chore-boy either, is of negligible aid. A meat cleaver would be more practical in such cases.

The successive dishwashers in the kitchen have had particular dislikes concerning pots and pans especially difficult to clean. Thus Blaine detested the orange squeezer and Jim's greatest enemy was the burnt oatmeal pan after breakfast. The pie tins caused high blood pressure on my part but the regard of their contents was ample compensation for me. One can see that considerable fortitude is required of a cook to declare, "We are having muffins for lunch," in the presence of the apprentice who is on an equal footing with him and whose pet aversion is muffin tins.

When the sparkling, soapy dishwater casts off its alluring iridescence and assumes a grey, even duller and more disheartening than the grey clouds before the storm, then a touch of color in the water performs wonders to the sinking apprentice-spirit. Elderberry juice was most often found there (since few apprentices were fond of it) and it caused a most curious and rare shade of blue, whereas cherry juice or wine were effective too. One day, searching for some elderberry juice, I found a small plateful of elderberry sauce left over, used the juice for coloring matter but threw out the berries, which I soon found out was precious "caviar," a recent gift to Mr. and Mrs. Wright from a Russian friend.

It is interesting to note that each apprentice during his two weeks of scullery work, finds attachment for some particular work which seems to him to be neglected. Just as, for instance, John started scraping the woodwork and Edgar polished everything in sight that was polishable.

All the kitchen workers, however, are unanimous on one issue, that they would rather dig trenches, mix concrete or saw wood than labor with the dishes and pans.

Just the same, there is a feeling of accomplishment connected with this kitchen function: to be surrounded by piles of pots and piles of pans, colanders, strainers and measuring cups, Mexican and Catalina pottery and Leerdam glassware at every step, knives and meat boards and salad bowls—all seemingly as dirty as one cook could possibly make them; and then, even if it be only an hour or more, to see the happy pots swinging immaculate on their hooks, the floor clean, all the table tops with reflecting surfaces, bread, butter, milk and eggs back to their appointed places. This, so it seems, is the reward! But if this be accomplishment, then the evening meal is the most satisfying accomplishment to dishwashers because there is no cook to take the egg beater, just now washed, and beat up a mixture in which I knew there would be sorghum, eggs, and sour milk. After supper the kitchen will be clean at least for 10 hours after the evening cleanup.

But if, perchance, anyone happens into the kitchen in the late evening and several pans, with mouths turned down, lie soaking, he will know that the dishwashers have had a hard day and that the pans are there to cheer up the scullery boys when they start their day anew in the kitchen. The trouble with work in the kitchen is—that, like farm work, it is never really finished.

BENNIE DOMBAR

There will be the usual program at the Taliesin Playhouse beginning at 3 in the afternoon on Sunday, Nov. 17. We are showing a Russian short, *South in Tambov,* and also two sound films from Japan, *Cormorant Fishing* and *Bamboo.* The feature picture will be the famous American film *The Informer.*

The program coming from Russia, Japan and America promises to be excellent and enlightening entertainment.

AT TALIESIN
November 21, 1935

The other day several of us were loading buckwheat hay into the truck driving up and down the field where it was raked into rows. The cows had been turned into the field for the past couple of days and were either very much interested in what we were doing or resented our taking the hay which had provided them with easily obtained meals because two or three of them followed along behind us and several gathered into a group ahead of the truck and had to be driven along before the truck could go ahead. This strange retinue accompanied us up and down a couple of rows when we reached the bottom of the field and the Irish setter Duschka came bounding into the field with a graceful, effortless spring. She pranced up to us happily wagging her beautiful red tail. The cows fell noticeably to the rear as she joined our procession but they continued to follow at a respectful distance.

Soon Duschka found a field mouse tunnel and started digging. We paused a moment to urge her on and then left her busily at work making the dirt fly, snorting, burying her nose in the tunnel and then digging again with renewed vigor as she struck terror into the heart of some grain field dweller. We went on with our work and had driven the truck ahead a hundred yards or so when someone glanced back to see where the dog was.

Duschka was still busily at work but by no means alone for the cows who had heretofore watched our activities with what mixed emotions we'll never know gave up to sheer curiosity and started gathering round the dark red-brown individual busily at work with her home wrecking.

We too stopped our activities to watch this strange actress and audience. One by one the cows drew closer until 8 or 10 of these tawny beasts formed a complete circle around the dog. Some stared curiously directly at the work in hand (or should I say paw?) while others peered with great, serious eyes over her shoulder as Duschka continued to dig in a splendid frenzy entirely oblivious of her audience.

Suddenly, however, she must have felt the pressure of so many eyes trained on her for she ceased digging and looked up with a start.

Now Duschka is usually supremely indifferent to cows, considering them stupid and beyond notice, but to be confronted and unexpectedly by several cow faces at such close range would give anyone a turn and the poor dog cowered, wheeled, and started off in the opposite direction only to be faced by more large tawny countenances with staring saucer eyes.

This so unnerved her that she broke into a fit of hysterical barking and yelping and wheeled once more about her circle of inquisitives, snarling menacingly. Now was the cows' turn to be alarmed and they, to express their affright, turned away in all directions as hurriedly as they were able, running a few steps in mild dismay.

Meanwhile Duschka made her escape between the legs of a couple of them and came scurrying up to the truck with her ears back and tail at half mast, only to find us in such fits of laughter at her plight as to be no comfort to her at all.

As we regained our composure at length and Duschka hoisted her tail once more to its usual arrogant pitch we looked again to the scene of this little drama and found the cows gathered in a knot at the bottom of the hill staring back at us with a look of bewildered disgust.

NOVERRE MUSSON

Transatlantic Tunnel, an English picture just finishing a long run in New York, will be shown at the Playhouse on Sunday, Nov. 24, at 3 P.M. The picture with a notable cast, including every one from George Arliss and Walter Houston to Richard Dix, is a dramatization of the construction of a tunnel between London and New York—all taking place many years in the future. With the feature picture will be the usual introduction by a member of the Taliesin Fellowship and coffee and cakes will be served.

AT TALIESIN
December 5, 1935

The New Tenements

[In 1935, the Museum of Modern Art invited the French architect and founder of the modern international style, Le Corbusier to the United States to present 23 public lectures in various cities on architecture and urban planning. On November 26, he presented a lecture entitled "Modern Architecture" in the University of Wisconsin (Madison) Memorial Union Great Hall. Also accompanying Le Corbusier on his U.S. tour was an exhibit of photographs, models, and drawings of his work; this was installed in the Memorial Union Gallery through December 6, 1935. In a letter dated August 21, 1935, to Tom Maloney, Wright responded to an earlier inquiry regarding Le Corbusier's tour, "I scarcely feel much reaction. . . . Our people, including our architects, are very ignorant of Architecture and Le Corbusier may be good kindergarten for them. As usual, they will take from "abroad" what they neglect at home." Contrary to local newspaper reports, Le Corbusier did not stay with Wright while in Madison. They did not actually meet face-to-face until June 1937 when they both were at a dinner in Paris honoring Wright and August Perret. Wright was en route to Moscow, Russia, then to attend and participate in the First International Congress of Soviet Architects.]

At the Memorial Union Tuesday, Madison had the opportunity of hearing one who is called "A Prophet of Modern Architecture," Le Corbusier. For many years Corbusier has propagandized that "the house is a machine to live in" and that cities should be planned with future development in view. In his lecture here, these points were carried to a more definite clarity with the aid of drawings, lantern slides and moving pictures, to the extent that there is no doubt in anyone's mind what Corbusier's ideal is.

Corbusier outlined his future city, or "La Ville Radieuse," as a community where 88 percent of the ground area would be "play" space. The other 12 percent would consist of buildings and highways, both elevated, to ensure additional play areas. Probably 5 percent of the ground would be left open, the rest free for this space called "play area." All windows would face the sun, all buildings would be hermetically sealed, and air conditioning would have to be used extensively if not entirely. Corbusier said there was no reason why Madison should not be as large as Chicago some day, therefore should prepare for better physical conditions than Chicago has now.

At this time there is no one who doesn't believe in city planning, or one who objects to having sunlight, cleanliness and play areas. And it is easily seen that our cities are in most every way inhuman, and if we had the chance we would move out into the country. We have also noticed that architect's plans are carried out into city planning and, that there is one fundamental that must be overcome before planning on a large scale can become a reality. We simply haven't a form of government for it. And if we did, we would not find Corbusier's ideal much better than our hit-and-miss improvements. Where Corbusier falls is chiefly at the start. His words and works show that the ground is only "an evil" to get away from. That "La Ville Radieuse" is merely one cell stacked on another cell, and that man's contact with the ground as a man is intolerable. Corbusier only points to standardization that is basically bad and structurally poor. Madison has no basis for ever becoming as monstrous as Chicago. It hasn't the physical elements.

Corbusier wants centralization, a beehive home life, where the only difference between one beehive and another is a hundred meters distance. He showed no place for the farm, our basic industry. Apparently the farmer would live in his "cell" and drive to the farm in a fast car on a viaduct. It would be a horrible moment when the farmer set his foot on Mother Earth and found that his barn had to be on the ground. It would be another horrible moment when the citizen realized that he had become more the machine than the machine itself and that in "La Ville Radieuse."

Mr. Citizen must forget those simple ways of life where his garden was on the ground, he a part of the house, where his architecture was in human scale, and where every wall wasn't a white wall, and where all furniture wasn't made with polished gas pipe. The new citizen would have to expect this new architectural sense: that the house was a cardboard box on stilts, with holes punched in at points where light should enter. His new house wouldn't have natural breezes running through it, natural ventilation would be supplanted with canned air. All of which sounds homey.

It is clear that Corbusier is not designing for the heterogeneous America and does not use the basic wealth, and capacity to produce of this country or any other, as a standing point in his planning. Beginning his career as a "functionalist," and now seeing its inhuman harness, Corbusier turns to "Radiant Joy!" His last house, with its meaningless barrel vaults, glass walls, all growing out of designing in elevation, shows that he is concerned only with surface, instead of space and materials. In this surface decoration Corbusier lives in this house of unreality with the Picassos, Gertrude Steins, and Debussys, all on stilts. It is also clear that this "La Ville Radieuse" regimentation can only be realized through fascism or some perverted form of socialism.

EDGAR ALLEN TAFEL

1 9 3 6

Taliesin seems to be getting a chance now.

—Frank Lloyd Wright, letter to William Bernoudy, September 3, 1936

INTRODUCTION

While the major focus of the headlines in early 1936 was the trial, conviction, and execution of Bruno Hauptmann for the kidnapping of the Charles and Anne Lindberg baby, it was good news all year for Frank Lloyd Wright and the Taliesin Fellowship, who were at last active with outside (and significant) architectural commissions.

In 1936, plans were completed and construction was under way on "Fallingwater"; the Johnson Wax administration building (Racine, Wisconsin) commission was secured, and design drawings were prepared during the summer for a September construction start. Five houses in various states were being designed in 1936 by Wright; each early examples of his Usonian House concepts. As Wright put it to Abrom Dombar in a letter dated January 10, 1936, "We are going into the small house business as a Fellowship next Spring in earnest, meaning to build them for our neighboring cities in large numbers." Writing to William Bernoudy on April 14, Wright again stated, "We are now building houses in eight states and I believe everyone of them is going to be a credit to our ideal. At any rate we will have a fair chance to do our best to make them so." Jacobs House in Wisconsin, Hanna House in California, Roberts House in Michigan, Hoult House in Kansas (acknowledged to be the first Usonian House), and Lusk House in South Dakota were all at Taliesin, in various stages of design and development, in 1936. Construction of the Jacobs, Hanna and Roberts houses was completed during the following year (the Hoult and the Lusk designs remained unbuilt).

Wright and the Fellowship also took their second excursion to Chandler, Arizona. While there, they made an effort to experiment in the design of economic and functional furniture prototypes for use in the homes conceptualized by Broadacre City. The "At Taliesin" columns from Arizona in 1936 reflect a much more relaxed atmosphere at La Hacienda. Back in Wisconsin late spring, the Fellowship continued to modify, under Wright's direction, Taliesin (laundry, kitchen, and increasing the size of Wright's bedroom and terrace) and Hillside (major modifications to the Playhouse interior), as well as continuing the usual work on the grounds and in the buildings. The Fellowship also worked on plans for an entrance to Hillside off the highway (complete with a footbridge, parking area, and gatekeeper's structure), which unfortunately never progressed beyond the design stage.

Frank Lloyd Wright lectured less but wrote more in 1936. He produced at least eight of the fifty-one "At Taliesin" columns printed, and he wrote several important articles for magazines. He also entered into a contract with Professor Baker Brownell of Northwestern University to co-author a book that was written and published in 1937 as *Architecture and Modern Life*. In a letter to Brownell, dated October 10, 1936, Wright wrote, "I've signed the contract — therefore "my neck is out." Of course your name comes first. Were a building in question your name would come next but, a book! I am only a dub-writer."

The "At Taliesin" columns written in 1936 were much more varied and much less intense than the previous two years. Curiously, with the exception of the Jacobs opus, very little was written in the 1936 "At Taliesin" columns of the new architectural commissions. Again, they mostly wrote of the variety of Fellowship experiences at Taliesin, with topics on furniture design, flower arranging, the "cultured man," kitchen work, the American Southwest and the Russian "red menace" and Japanese "yellow peril" scares. The first "At Taliesin" book review was written (Churchward's *Children of Mu* by Cornelia Brierly, May 1, 1936), and the apprentice "sermonettes" continued as did reports and impressions on Broadacre City.

AT TALIESIN
January 3, 1936

Crises or Emergencies

I believe if I were ever to write the story of our Fellowship I would choose "The Crisis" for the title first, because the Fellowship was born due to a crisis, and secondly, because ever since it was born its existence has been a series of crisis. Needless to say here that these facts account for the fresh, radical (of the root), pioneering group that we are. Without the continual crisis or emergencies we might become merely academic and, therefore, just another educational institution.

The crisis that caused our being was America's crying need for indigenous culture; the youth of America are beginning to realize that culture comes first by way of the natural scheme of things and that otherwise we are merely automatons, machines or encyclopedias. Growth is happiness and, like the Dutchman's delphinium, we need culture for growth, not "education" which is seldom culture. America is growing tired of staying adolescent in her scientific era and wants to grow up. She (those of her who can realize anything) realizes that science without culture is rather futile and that now, with all her scientific advancement she has a true basis for culture and it will be a culture of the machine age but also of the ground.

So, that is how we came to Taliesin and why we're here. This crisis has brought disillusioned university students (most of their brothers are still under the spell, not suspecting that the diploma is no longer the magic wand it was in their father's day) from all over the United States to Taliesin—to work with the architect of the machine age where architecture has a new and broader meaning, and we speak of "architecture" as of life itself.

The emergencies in our life here which are probably most obvious but least important are such things as pushing cars up the icy front drive, pulling wells, hauling wood, draining radiators, cooking and catching chickens. We are our own heating and lighting system, transportation system, water and sewer system, church, theater and entertainment. There is always a need for wood, coal, kerosene, gasoline; for painting, staining, roofing, waxing, washing, sweeping, firing, plowing, cutting, cooking, cleaning, hauling, and pumping — always pumping.

But these are not the important crises. Most of them are tolerated as necessary maintenances, though of course we benefit by the doing of them; and no one knows better than we do that maintenance is an infinite occupation and to spend too much of one's life maintaining oneself is the height of futility. Unless one's life is truly creative it is nothing but mere maintenance: "the upkeep of the carcass."

Most people think of maintenance (the ordinary "job" is merely a maintenance) as they do of money; that is, as an end, rather than as a means to an end.

The really important crisis, and certainly the most interesting, are such things as: finishing the theater in time for the first performance (though in a sense nothing is really ever finished at Taliesin if a better way of doing the thing turns up); quickly building interesting rooms to house the new apprentices who are to come in a few days; spring plowing and planting; perpetual anti-weed wars; building the new spillway and repairing the dam, washed out last spring (a real engineering job); staying up nights to finish house plans for a frantic client; and last but not least came the big emergency for 1935 — building Broadacre City for the Industrial Art Exposition in New York City. On all of these emergencies we concentrate all of our effort as a kind of symphony orchestra, with Mr. Wright at the helm (or as conductor, if we must have complete parallel).

In short, everything that catapults us out of the ever-present menace of routine, keeping our minds alert and fresh and ready to tackle each new situation clearly — this is the crisis welcomed to Taliesin.

Here at Taliesin is this urging need for creation that precipitates crisis after crisis and is itself above all the great crisis. Even we ourselves often lose sight of that greater crisis in the morass of everyday maintenance crisis. In this greater field of activity (this effort in the realm of an integral culture for America) the designing of better buildings and better furniture (that is, the architectural office) acts as center line or in other words, "constant crisis" number one. Another such "constant crisis" is the writing of articles such as this one to be hastily written before a newspaper deadline—always Wednesdays (often called "blue Wednesday").

Other "constant crises" are the Sunday event when some one Fellowship is the rector; the Playhouse programs where we try to show the best the world produces in the way of films (experimenting with making films ourselves); the publishing of the delayed Taliesin monograph; the crafts for which we need tools and materials, that is, rug weaving, pottery, metal work and leather work. Perhaps painting and sculpture are in front this week. And there is always a crying need at Taliesin for music, better music—great music; though our theater sound system and rapidly growing collection of fine records makes for a marvelous musical instrument independently of any musician's personality.

JOHN HENRY HOWE, III

Sunday, January 5, is the last Sunday that the Fellowship will present its regular weekly program to the public at the Taliesin Playhouse until we return from Arizona next April.

In order to make this occasion an eventful one we are presenting *Maria Chapdelaine,* one of the recent great pictures from France, coming directly to us from its New York premiere.

Maria Chapdelaine won the Grand Prix du Cinema Français. It is a stirring, full blooded and tremendously beautiful screen edition of Louis Hemon's now classic novel of French Canadian life. It presents the Gallic cinema at the top of its achievement. The photoplay captures the soul of that strong, simple race which has clung bitterly to its heritage and guarded its identity during 300 years in the New World. *Maria Chapdelaine* preserves the integrity of the Hemon work with a skill that gives the film the nobility of an epic poem.

This again is an opportunity to see the latest in World Cinema at the Taliesin Playhouse. We cordially invite you to witness with us another great example of the art of the screen. The program begins at 3 in the afternoon and coffee and cakes will be served as usual.

AT TALIESIN
January 10, 1936

In the Projection Booth

The reproducer turnstiles turn and trumpets blow with all the vehemence and fervor of which they are capable. The Prokofiev concerto, the stage curtains, the playful lights, the crackling fire, a cup of coffee and a piece of cake are the spirit that prepares the visitors for a magnificent film production. In the projection booth a different spirit prevails, where we are preparing for the show.

Kettle drums add their vibrating powers to the spirited music. A convertor hums above my head. Two projection machines sing the identical and unchanging song. I try to listen to the music and to forget the hum and drumming as I rewind the 10 reels of film. I stop to change the record and adjust the filament control switch to adjust the power. A most pretentious switchboard is arrayed before me. Plate 1— Plate II—Plate Total III and IV—Filament 1 and 2—Mon. Vol. Control—Fil't.

Control—Output—Charge—Operate—each dial has its glass eye with an arrow and a lot of numbers in it. The arrows dance back and forth and need frequent adjustment as machines are turned off and on and off again. I turn around to shut off machine number one. Two glass eyes on the side stared at me. I look to the other machine for consolation. The same two eyes.

The turnstiles now are huge eyes spinning at me. A raucous buzzer connected with the director's seat adds its sound to the conglomeration. I know what it means so I turn off the sound in the booth and lift the receiver. But the convertor still hums and one machine is drumming that same sound. "Play the next record softly for the interpretation." I hurriedly thread the first machine—rolling film from the full reel onto the empty, setting the empty in the right groove and proceeding to wind the film over and under wheels and through bars, fitting the film always onto the sprockets.

The reel is just framed as the record ends. Off go the house lights and the music continues in quiet chords. Peeking through my little window I see Gene, below, stepping onto the platform with a sheet of paper in his hand. A single light carries the attention to the interpretation. A clear voice subordinates the music and acquaints the audience with the film of the week, tells what the Fellowship thinks about it and what its reputation has carried with it. A beautiful Japanese mask hangs on the glowing light and holds the eyes of the audience. When I see the light turned off, I shoot the film onto the screen and pray that everything is all right in the machine.

From then on the reels are threaded in their proper order, and the film switches from one machine to the other to keep the film one continuous stretch. The change from one machine to another is brought about when the que marks are seen in the upper right-hand corner of the screen. The change over is made at the sight of the 2nd que mark which follows 10 seconds after the warning que mark.

"Carey," the Texas apprentice, is the other projectionists. We alternate.

After projecting for a long time one gets to feel a slight measure of repose in the booth. Now I can stare harder at the glass eyes than they can at me.

BENNIE DOMBAR

The French film *Maria Chapdelaine* which we showed Sunday is the last film of the season. For in a few days the Fellowship will skid out of the snow covered valley onto the Dodgeville road and make haste for the brilliant desert of Arizona.

AT TALIESIN

January 24, 1936

The Taliesin Fellowship has completed the second long trek across the country from their Wisconsin River valley in the north to the Salt River valley in Arizona. Twenty-five in all, we traveled in caravan cars with sleeping bags, and the truck carrying all necessary to our living and working in the desert.

We started at 4 in the morning, instead of at high noon as we did last year; we drove the 2,200 miles in four days instead of the six and a half it took us before; I can tell you the story of this journey in two pages instead of the six it used up last time.

It was a very dark and cold 4 in the morning of Jan. 11 when we started—each car lined behind the other on the crest of the hill: three Indian red, one tan, another black—the truck in advance four hours. And it was not until we had left the Mississippi behind that the sun finally discovered the caravan winding through the low hills of Iowa. We left snow and ice lit by a purple dawn through which a huge red sun shone on Iowa and came through good clean roads in Missouri. That night—in Lawrence, Kansas, after dinner with George and Helen Beal, fellow apprentices, the boys of the Fellowship measured 16 crosswise side by side, by 6 feet wide, the length of a sleeping bag, laid out on the floor of the architect's office just big enough to lay us out.

Nights, however, were the least of our difficulties. We arrived in the night and were on the way each day long before dawn. So still in the night we left Kansas' college town, Lawrence, and the affectionate Beals regretfully behind and the sun chased us far south into Kansas, Oklahoma, and it was another night at Wichita Falls as we came into Texas.

The road lay black before the path of the car I was driving when suddenly there loomed directly ahead—a cow. First one cow and then, unexpectedly, behind the first, another and others. There was hardly enough time to slam on all brakes available, turn to one side to just gently tap the retreating rump of the dismayed cow who never guessed how closely she came to turning from cow to beef on the spot and what our fate would have been?

Next day, all day, we drove through the billowing prairies, the rising and falling seemingly endless plains of Texas and as last year, toward nightfall in a lingering sunset we climbed the low foothills of the Sierras and stopped at Texas' resort town—El Paso.

Up again before sunrise and speeding along, the sun on the final day of the drive threw long undulating car shadows alongside the roads to mingle with shadows of giant cacti and the lordly shadows of the approaching mountains. We were well on the way from El Paso to Lordsburg and then on through the mountains to the Arizona desert. Car tops down now, faces burning in the warm wind and hot sun; spirits singing with the rhythms of the winding twisting ribbon of road and finally, as gradually as we had risen, we settled down again to the reposed plain of desert decorated to left and to right with the familiarly unfamiliar desert plants—home once more to this other winter-summer world we have made for ourselves in Arizona. A change of scene and way of life for what it may all be worth to us.

Home again in La Hacienda where we have a full schedule of work ahead. Under Mr. Wright's direction the Fellowship will design and construct the models of a complete line of furniture to furnish a modern home. Two issues of the monograph will be assembled and published while we are here and there is other work in progress and in prospect. Details of this activity will be written and published in this column from week to week as we settle down after four days of cross country driving averaging 550 miles per day, without mishap.

EUGENE MASSELINK

AT TALIESIN

February 7, 1936

Why are we in Arizona?

Last year the Taliesin Fellowship came to Arizona from its home in Wisconsin, for a specific purpose. This year we are here again, and for a purpose, similarly specific, and closely related to last year's. During the past year, the product of our three months effort has been viewed by 175,000 people and had travelled 10,000 miles. Broadacre City was our pride! It is a group of models which forms a display 40 feet by 40 feet, and presents as its theme what the city of the future will embody as its theme. We are 27, not too spoiled, fellows (boys and girls) to carry out the ideas and principles of our master, Frank Lloyd Wright, under his leadership.

In Broadacre City, we think, every care and necessity of life in the future is properly taken care of to make it a better way of life than now exists. And the detail to which it is carried is as far as any radical, i.e., basic, scheme on a large scale should be carried.

The next and logical step, we are here in Arizona, our winter quarters, to work upon. We expect to show in detail by actual working models of furniture what the interiors of houses on Broadacre City would be like: what the people would live with, sit in, lie on, walk upon. Of course any particular house should have particular furniture to emphasize its features and take advantage of its characteristics. Nevertheless, there is a quality and a practicability that knows no division or classification. Repose has no categories nor good sense rival! We are working upon a type of furniture that is not a thing in itself only. One couch has its form, its height, its material, its grammar in sympathy with the furniture about it, all of a light, movable nature, capable of being moved easily and rearranged often. In all furniture, the closest to the plane of the floor that is capable of being comfortably used is from our viewpoint, best. All upholstery should be easily detached and sent to the cleaners. When imagination enters an untrod field, results are infinite!

First, we are selecting plywood as our experimental material. We will make enough plywood furniture to demonstrate its capacities, its advantages, and its beauties. Then we will work on stick-furniture, bringing out corresponding qualities in that case. The peculiar properties of either material are, of course, the means to bring out the charm. We won't try to "shoot a peculiar note from our right eyebrow." Simple metal edges or bindings might be used to strengthen and beautify the plywood furniture. Why are we in a machine age if it carries with it no advantages? At present thin sheets of strong plywood are made cheaply and thin sheets of strong metals are manufactured easily. It is time for the $400 living room set with its flowery wood frames and its uncleanable and just as flowery upholstery, and its 400 percent profit to the furniture dealer, to be put into the attic to make place for an exceedingly better set of integral furniture at an astonishing low-cost, especially as such standardization as we are planning enters.

BENNIE DOMBAR

[This early exploration into the design of furniture by the Fellowship, especially using plywood as their experimental material, did not come to the expected fruition. In fact, in his "At Taliesin" contribution of March 27, 1936, Burt Goodrich states, "In spite of all the beautiful things we have said about the desert and its helpful and beneficial effects it has upon us as men and women and artists, I must honestly conclude that as far as furniture is concerned the effect has been undesirable. Being sensitive people and absorbing the spirit of the desert and also being artists we express what we absorb and we find our furniture taking on the spirit of the desert. In spite of all efforts chair after chair turns out and flowers with that spirit, that same come closer, inviting, intimate air so familiar and famous of the cactus family. To come to some sensible conclusion and an understanding of the difficulty involved, I maintain that it is not the fault of environment, construction methods, approach or the artist himself but rather of mankind alone. I suggest the easiest way out is to be that man, give up the idea of having chairs, tables, beds, etc., and take life standing up. Only in extreme cases be he allowed to sit or lie down, and then if it becomes absolutely necessary let him sit or lie on the original seat — and bed — a log and — Mother Earth." Certainly it can be seen that this early exercise preceded the typical furniture designed and incorporated in the many later Usonian homes.]

AT TALIESIN

February 14, 1936

Ten of us awoke last Sunday morning at the foot of Superstition Mountain but only four of us climbed to the top.

It was a cold windy morning and we knew by a watch that somehow got into the party that the sun had already risen unannounced. We separated into two parties after breakfast — which like all breakfasts in such circumstances was too good to be true. Six followed some Mexican gold paners in search for gold and four — Marya, Noverre, Jack, and myself set out to conquer the mountain.

We were an extremely unconventional and unconvincing mountaineering party: Marya in spotted slacks, linen coat, something scarlet bound her hair; Noverre suited out in black; Jack in shorts; me in "ski-pants."

Marya — with a notable mountain climbing record to her credit in Poland — strode forward, scarlet blowing in the wind, gaily singing

Polish ballads. We followed. And gradually we wound up an indecisive cow path which finally disappeared and left us on our own.

Marya's wide blowing slacks attracted all cactus and suddenly she stopped short—cursing (in Polish) at a great "century plant"—she called it (it was cholla) clinging to her ankle. After that she came along in the rear—gingerly—limping for a time and softly singing some lullaby.

We had slowly climbed along a saddle to a foot-hill directly below the actual mountain.

I looked down to where Marya was gently—and expertly—extracting the fourth "cactus" (cholla). After the rains of the previous week all the desert plants seemed about to burst into bloom. They filled every cranny and crevice with their strange forms. Each rock was minutely decorated with orange and yellow-green lichens. Columbines added their color and grace to the intricate beauty of the mosaic in which we were walking.

The sky was filled with great clouds and the sun scattered their shadows far and wide over the desert floor already far below us.

We were climbing up the north side of Superstition. Jack (the Howe) visibly (but secretly) shivered. Suddenly our path stopped short before a huge cliff. Our adventures seemed doomed. We skirted the precipice for several hundred feet until we came to a slightly less high but no less hazardous and dangerous ascent. Determined, we pushed and we pulled; we encouraged and we threatened. Finally we sank exhausted at the top and looked about us over an upper plateau—the top of famed Superstition Mountain now much nearer.

Elated at the thought of setting the first foot upon such impassible land we stride eagerly forward. But we hadn't advanced five minutes when directly before us we saw—we dared not overlook—painfully unmistakable signs of . . . cows. Momentarily crushed—but undaunted—on up we went. Each new height led on to another. We were continually reaching the "top" only to discover another "top" above us.

The sun made things warmer. Jack spoke proudly of his shorts. I shed my jacket. Noverre and Marya discovered water cupped in the cool depths of a wide tropical leaf and we divided the third of the four grapefruit we had brought along.

We were afraid to listen to shouts from the other division of our party—afraid that we would see them on up ahead of us somewhere but a spot of color located them far down on a lower plateau and that was the last we saw of them.

Together we mounted onto a great saddle which led straight to the very top. We were amidst the rock pinnacles guarding the heights of Superstition and we climbed through them to the highest rock of all.

The pallisaded rock masses standing hundreds of feet up into the blue surrounded us in the wind and sun. Through the vertical sentinels we saw far down and beyond the horizontal stretches of desert. All of our part of Arizona: its varying forms—its serene level desert—its mosaiced mountains—was at our feet. The cloud shadows raced with the wind and sun—twisting and turning everything into dazzling pattern.

We stood up straight on the highest rock and shouted—one great long shout.

And then—we divided the last grapefruit and a Heaven-sent orange (Noverre's left over from supper); Marya from a capacious pocket supplied each of us with a blessed square of chocolate and we were ready to start down.

It took four hours to reach the top. It took two and a half to get back to the car. And it was another half hour before we finally convinced the rest of the party of us of our bravery and heroism.

Then—exhausted—we slept.

EUGENE MASSELINK

AT TALIESIN

March 6, 1936

[The house model that apprentice John Lautner describes in the following column was unidentified. It more than likely was a model that was part of the Broadacre City exhibit. Even though this column predated the design of the Jacobs House in Westmoreland (Madison), Wisconsin, one could certainly use it as an example for Lautner's treatise.]

I didn't believe it — but I guess there still are two kinds of people — the cave man and the nomad. Even today one man wants to be cooped up in a den and the other to be out in the sunshine. I showed a house with windows from floor to ceiling across the entire living room — this house was on exhibition and thousands of people saw it — some were delighted (the nomad), others glowered and tried to find something wrong because it wasn't just like every other house. Still others would approach and say, "My boy, have you studied the conductivity of glass?" "How much more coal do you burn?", etc., etc.

Actually, the house had no more glass than others but it was sensibly placed — giving a spacious feeling to the inside and making a beautiful bright, light, living circumstance. I felt like telling the man he was just an old traditional cave dweller. One of this group who are "dead at 30 and buried at 60," who shut everything up tight, can't stand a breath of fresh air — in fact the people who build as cheap as possible — who build dark stingy little apartments. Why should we be enslaved to buildings, or machines, or to cities?

There is no law against building a building to suit its purpose and to shelter its inhabitants in a healthy, natural, sensible, light and beautiful way. Nature is plastic. She molds herself to fit her own peculiar circumstances — and she does it in an infinite number of ways — there is not only one way — there are millions. Why not build naturally organically — why not make the house another form of nature by way of man.

But there are too many cave dwellers — they will build you into a little apartment or suburb — tell you it's the thing, the latest, etc. and there you are in a stuffy little place just like every other.

This house I showed was plastic (another form of nature). It was formed by its limitations (or its site, material, use and extent). It fit perfectly — it looked at the view, it grew out of the site, it was spacious yet small enough for the two people who live in it.

Yet it had glass all the way across the living room — think of the conductivity of glass, or, would you rather think of what a beautiful house in which to live!

JOHN E. LAUTNER

AT TALIESIN

March 6, 1936

Reflections on Owing Money (Reflections Which Reflect Upon Us)
[Needless to say, Frank Lloyd Wright's reputation and attitude toward money was, and still is, legendary. Still within the taught grip of the depression, he offered this column.]

Our guilt pursues us. Secret black marks accumulate against our "character" in spite of efforts to be good, true and beautiful in money-ways when, God knows, there is no such thing possible to anyone now if ever such a thing was possible "once upon a time."

We, the Taliesin Fellowship, are young — in swaddling clothes really — needing everything in the way of materials and equipment so badly that we are willing to mortgage our future to any extent hoping to be allowed to work believing that we can sometime pay back any reasonable sum — and at the most any sum that we could put to work would be a reasonable sum.

We work hard and think pretty straight. We want the best for everyone and in spite of handicaps get some of it, often. But we want it to happen oftener by making the basis for the happening more sensible. We want to extend our usefulness to work in general to make it a little better worth doing than it is now: get a better, finer human content back into work again.

Middlemen can't help us. They hang by their eyebrows from sky hooks, that is to say they live on margins added to margins by margins.

If you don't happen to be cut on the small-town model — and we are not — God help your "character." Character in our town is mostly a matter of paying your bills promptly.

And, speaking of character, I wonder why it is that the most agreeable, generously useful and inspiring men we know can seldom pay their bills promptly and are therefore bad "characters" — and the meanest and strongest passers of the "buck" that we know do pay promptly and are therefore good "characters?" Why?

It goes to show, I think, that the standards of character are pretty badly twisted and twisted just for commercial purposes.

If you do pay promptly you may be guilty of any meanness or downright rascality and yet have high rating as to character. The worst cheats and most skillful exploiters—those who would take candy out of a baby's mouth do pay their bills regularly. Why? Why because they know it is the basis of their own game, that's why. I suppose this money-matter is the backbone and ribs of what they call civilization in the U.S.A. Really when they speak of civilization now it is only commercialization they mean. Therefore your character and mine is largely this matter of paying your bills promptly if the civilization (commercialization) is to continue to be as it is.

Lately in our town—a grocer (to whom I've paid considerable sums of money and whom I began owing in the debacle of 1929 and to whom I still owe about a hundred dollars) came out of the postoffice holding a letter in his hand. He jerked his head over toward the corner in a furtive way signifying to me that he would like to speak to me there. So I went on over to the corner. "Say," said he just above a whisper. "I got a letter here from one of them there secret-service credit companies askin' me in confidence about you—they want to know what kind of a character you got."

"Character?" I said. "Hell—man, tell the back-stair men that all you can ever know about my character is that I've paid you a lot of money but have owed you some for years or more and that as things are going I don't know when I can pay you if ever. Thats really what they mean by my 'character' and, I guess, all that you are qualified to say," and I walked away.

His grocership looked puzzled and for the ninth time, I guess, I became a bad "character" in the accustomed manner in the U.S.A.

Now I don't know how bad of character I have but of course, during this heaven-sent "depression"—(for which I thank God)—I've had enough occasion to believe that the "listing" must be pretty vicious and my own conscience tells me that I must deserve it from the standpoint of any "secret" or back-stair interest whatsoever.

Yes and fair enough—I say—if only the term "character" were to be disassociated from their merchantable secrets and from a-la-mode finance in general. But there you are. If you can pay your bills your character is A-1 but if something happens to you and you can't, your character is bad and that's final. After that happens to you you are at the mercy of all that is sordid and mean in human existence. And there is a lot of it, I can tell you.

All right, let's admit that you are bad for their "set-up," certainly. But so many things enter into even their own shameless little money-equation that even though you might be years behind with your bills you might meantime be the most useful member of your community even bringing all manner of benefits to your own community, to your state, and to your country. And yet just because of that innate character that made you able to be beneficial to them all you would soon become, by way of their "secret-service" (which is a back-stair assassination of course) no longer useful. Not even useful anymore to the sordid interest itself because of its own stupidity. Which all goes to show that money-minded is monkey-minded and that we are living in a trades-man's paradise in a tradesman's way.

But I know well that no argument whatever could possibly cover that side of the case. I should be taken out and shot at sunrise if the secret service had its way and the facts are . . .

Well, I have been taken out and shot at sunrise any number of times where they are concerned.

But — strangely — I still have left to be my "character." Somehow they can't take it away from me nor dispose of it as they try to do. So something in character must function above and beyond these conve-niently narrow standards of theirs which were made to fit the purpose in our town which after all, like any other town, is there solely for the purpose of making money. There would be little point in all this if the tradesmen themselves did not do more harm to their own cause by way of their secret service than their secret service can do them good. I've seen it happen a number of times that the most useful members of a community are unable to bring their benefits immediate or in future society because of this back-yard-stick by which the money-maker impertinently assumes to measure "character."

They say that if any upright householder were to listen in back-stairs most any evening he would want to close his house and end his days elsewhere — somewhere — anywhere where he could stay away from servants. And, as a matter of course this "secret-service" is only the servant-mind in this omniscient matter of money-making.

Now, I wish "character" were so simple as this "secret-service" to petty tradesmen makes it out to be.

Unfortunately it is not so simple.

For instance, I should say any service of this secret sort really had a bad "character," however useful to the husky town-money-makers it might be and showed a bad trait in their "characters."

I submit that this back-yard-stick may measure only one feature of character, no infallible measure even at that.

And that no one can estimate the loss to society by the curtailing of the usefulness of its most productive men and women just because the servant-mind black-marks as character what in any honest analysis often has little to do with great even "good" character.

FRANK LLOYD WRIGHT

AT TALIESIN
March 20, 1936

Taliesin to Arizona

Hans Koch arrived at Taliesin early last summer master carpenter in the Fellowship. Hans is German, a builder, a poet, philosopher. With flowing white hair, bristling eyebrows, sharp eyes, he is sturdy, stocky and has the infectious hearty laughter of the Saint Nicholas he somewhat resembles. Faithful vegetarian.

We all contributed something of our own to a book of individual work presented to Mr. Wright on Christmas Day. Hans made the plywood cover and laced it with leather thonging but he also wrote and contributed a vigorous work song in German — an epic of his life, the anvil and the forge.

He is in charge of Taliesin while we are in Arizona and many of us have come to know Hans better by way of his vivid letters telling of the winter storming about the life and the structure upon that low hill near the Wisconsin River.

This letter to Jack, Taliesin to Arizona:

Dear Jack: You must be a lucky bunch down there. Not only because you have it sunny and warm — this we will get in time here too . . . and enjoy the colorful desert — color is richly around here too . . . but because you are able to do the things you like to do, and for this I could envy you. I myself, I look now every morning, though a little late, up to the sky. If there is a bit of sparkling light, then I feel alright; if not, I will turn around once more and lay another hour right flat on my face. For it is the sun I want to see when a new day is here. Its brilliance edifies me. Its warmth regales me. It lights the inner sun which is potentially in man. So empowered, the shadows of everyday become only little episodes without any further significance — Glory to the sun!

To this bright orb go all my thanks. He breaks this terrific cold that nearly crushed me. He soothes the pain in my bones which nearly froze out of joint. It does not matter much that Taliesin is an ice field in the forenoon and a big river in the afternoon, with many cataracts the noise of which shoots and splashes through the walls. The sun will bring Taliesin to its normal state too, I am sure, and you will find it as fine and lovely as ever, crowning the Hill and rising upward — Glory to the sun!

I am a sun worshipper, Jack. He is not a god to me, but he is the Sun. If not for him, there would be nothing: and, for this, an axiom upon which it is impossible to pin any "you never can tell" . . . I adore the Sun . . .

HANS KOCH

AT TALIESIN

April 3, 1936

Many heard a particular concert given last summer at the Taliesin Playhouse in which Tchaikovsky's Trio in A-Minor formed the second half of the program. This work, dedicated by the composer to the death of a great artist, is a powerful unfolding of a theme, simple in itself, but covering a great breadth of thought and emotion in its sweep.

Last Sunday over the radio from the stage of Radio City's Music Hall to us here in the desert came the same Tchaikovsky's Trio; no trio this time, but fully orchestrated to the demands of all the instruments of the orchestra. The three stringed instruments gave way to three times ten instruments. The results naturally were not good. At best some powerful effects were obtained but obtained only because of the tumultuous combination of instruments. The original balance and brilliance, the clear tone quality of violin, cello, and piano was drowned in the tumult of orchestration. The charming variations on the theme in the second movement became forced solos for fancy instruments.

It was simply another great work mutilated and its master exploited by a discipline rampant. It was similar to the act of taking one of our colored pencil drawings made often here in the studio for clients in which three colored pencils had held the scale of color throughout the sketch and with twenty four colors instead of three try to arrive at the same brilliance and simplicity that characterized the original three. Too many colors superimposed usually results in dullness—the equivalent of mud.

Or similar to the act of taking the plans of a house in which three materials, say brick, wood and glass dominate the form and determine the scale, and adding a dozen other building materials all unnecessary to the structure and making superfluous additions, just to use the other materials. Construct the building all out of scale a number of times over on a site and in climates unfitted to its purpose and the simile would be complete. Comparable to the triumphant disciples, mutilation of a great piece of music is the lack of thought given to any simple form of architecture on all sides of us.

Out here in Arizona the simple house form we see all around us is the same as in Kansas or Iowa. There seems to be no thought of the climate, no protection from the heat here as differing from the protection of the cold of a northern house. The little windows are apparent as holes in the walls and the walls are the walls of a box, an expression of simple construction, thoughts of open screens, for comfort and economy is in disfavor for it isn't Spanish, Mission or just plain Sears-Roebuck. To copy, to make over what has been done and that done here badly seems to be the criteria of today's vain boast of progress.

Tchaikovsky's transcription bore tremendous applause but Tchaikovsky's turnings in his grave were many if he heard the transposing conductor's Wagnerian training running away continuously with the original Tchaikovsky's passages.

So too in the architectural profession when any true thought is given to the subject it is easily grabbed by the bystanders, changing a bit to enable the pilferer not to suffer too much guilty conscience, when he calls it his own. Soon you find in concrete and steel your own conception of what was true to wood and stone, but surely unfit for concrete and steel.

So Conductor Rappee simply had to add to keep on good terms with himself the great bong of a cathedral gong as original finale after Tchaikovsky's funeral march reached its climax. A indierous anticlimax but enough.

ROBERT K. MOSHER

AT TALIESIN

April 22, 1936

The Postmistress of Tuweep

On the map was a blank space. On the blank space was a single dot and one taught wavering line joined the dot with many other bigger dots and more important lines spelling civilization.

By the dot was the word "Tuweep."

We had traveled four days and many more miles than crows would fly in that time to reach the same places, to find ourselves on the edge of that civilization bordering a barren space about the Grand Canyon in which somewhere was this place called Tuweep. All natives but one said, "Tuweep?" and laughed, shaking their heads: trail impassable. But the one, a ranger picked up by Mr. Wright, Bud Kent said . . . "the road?" . . . well, the scene incomparable; the north rim of the Grand Canyon and he drew a crude map to show how to reach the place.

Following the fascination of the name: Tuweep, and the ranger's rough sketch, five of our cars turned away from tourists roads to Zion Canyon. I was detailed to follow the truck fifteen miles to a junction where it was to be left over night and pick up the drivers to go with us. We started back to follow the others—an hour or so behind them.

We had hoped to overtake them before dark but the sun was already sinking when we met a man high on a kind of hay-cart who replied, "Have I seen'em—Say young feller . . . the whole of the East is bumpin' along ahead of you down this yere trail."

Short Creek, a last outpost of Mormonism, was also the last indication of human occupation. There we filled up with gas and were wise enough to take on an extra five gallons for good measure. Night came suddenly as it does in the mountainous region.

Snow capped peaks all about the horizon and we were left alone with a rising moon and a pair of timid uncertain tracks called a road, winding through the sage of the high plateau, sometimes diverging when we would have to go off in one direction only to come back again to the same road or bump about through deeply rutted holes. Sometimes octopus-like bypaths started out in every direction and we would get down on all fours searching for the trail—the trail our cars had left behind. A recent rain had blotted out all the others. Finally one "freshest" trail ended up the side of a mountain.

The last light we had seen was miles back so we retraced our own tracks to a tiny pair of crude wooden houses near a stockade. I went to the one with a light and a pleasant-faced young women answered my knock.

"I am the Postmistress of Tuweep," she said in answer to my question, "and THIS is Tuweep."

I looked in at the immaculate wooden shanty—three small children asleep and the postmistress smiled. "Tomorrow is our red-letter day," she said, "Tuesday, when the mail comes through—once a week."

And she made us coffee with water they have to carry twenty miles. A fire ruined their home three years ago. All the curly headed pretty children came since that time. No jobs out here at the end of the world except one "postmistress."

The "postmistress" made our visit so agreeable that we lingered and finally tore ourselves away. Now the trail seemed easier and somehow—never ask us how—we did discover after another hour and about two o'clock in the morning the light of our Taliesin camp.

No sound. All were asleep in their sleeping bags on the flat rock top of a great plateau around a fire of cedar logs.

To find a place to sleep, we walked over the flat lichened rocks among hardy dwarfed pines and cacti, never seen before until . . . the world stopped: a sheer rock cliff dropped three thousand feet to where the Colorado distantly roared below.

The plateau in one sweeping horizontal extended for miles. Other lower plateaus jutted into it. They formed a series of flat planes one against the other in rhythmical fashion; noble silhouette against the sky. To accentuate and to contrast the serenity and repose of this eternal building, the nature-architect cut the mighty chasm and with rock, nature's material, formed fantastic colorful shapes or decoration. The canyon may be seen here for 67 miles in one grand vista.

Death Valley, with its rounded sand-cut mystical forms with color poured over them, Mr. Wright called painting. Zion Canyon, bas-reliefed cliffs, was unmistakably, as he said, "Sculpture."

But this, Tuweep, was the noble "Architecture" we were searching for. Inspiration for an organic architecture and a tremendous lesson for us all.

And we thought we understood when we drove back through the purple green sage of the sweeping valley of the plateau which gives Tuweep its name (the Indian word for "good ground") why the Postmistress of Tuweep in her growing home was happy so far away from the things that usually make most women happy.

EUGENE MASSELINK

AT TALIESIN
May 13, 1936

Changes in Taliesin

Today, as I stood for a moment on the studio roof, I looked around me and saw the variegated roofs of Taliesin and I realized more fully than ever what a natural growth on this Wisconsin hill Taliesin was. Here was the best example of the organic architecture that is our gospel and of which we have written so much.

Why the best? Because it is the architect's own home and has grown with the architect during all the years it has been his habitation.

Originally built as a small summer home and studio with long, overhanging, simple hip roof, circumstance and imagination have pushed long low stone walls along the hillsides as a vine sends out new shoots and have pushed up the roofs into the variegated roof planes that we now see, as a flower sends up new shoots and blossoms.

This may sound like just so much romancing but it's a true parallel, for our word "organic" means the essentially natural in this sense. Here in the native material, wood as wood, stone as stone, rough from the hillside quarry, erected by native workmen at the home and workshop of a great native who is proud of his heritage and so builds out of it.

So it is interesting to see how Taliesin has grown from the original small cottage to the present edifice, for such it is. One is intrigued by occasionally seeing where a wall or roof formerly terminated and how it was later extended for more accommodation.

One may see how the low roof of the original narrow studio was pushed up to the north to roof an enlarged studio and make for a new, large two-story window to the north, now after two fires the main house was each time changed and enlarged considerable though much of the old construction was used (the roof even being pushed up to make for an upper floor and overhead windows in the lower floor). Often new chimneys were built when required. One may see how the old carriage house, stables, and granary were converted into apprentices' rooms, new farm buildings and garages being added beyond; how the old water tower was enlarged and converted into a beautiful trio of apprentices' rooms; how the dining rooms have been enlarged, the gardens extended and the driveway changed from above the buildings on the hill, to below the buildings on the hillside. Such is the natural growth of Taliesin (shining brow).

The buildings at Hillside have also experienced a similar growth. The Lloyd Jones grandfather built on the site when he first settled in the valley, always known as the Lloyd Jones valley because it was peopled by the sons and daughters of this hardy pioneer. Two of the daughters became school teachers and the homestead was converted into the Hillside Home School, the old farmhouse was moved up a hillside to be used as a dormitory and a school building was built over the old foundation by the young nephew, Frank Lloyd Wright. It was about 1883, I believe, and the daring new windmill was built on the hilltop about the same time. Later came the laundry building, the greenhouse and a gymnasium. Then in 1903 Frank Lloyd Wright built the new school building containing a new gymnasium, twelve classrooms, workshops, art hall, science room, and a large assembly room with library. All this of native sandstone laid by native craftsmen (it is probably the best example of stonework in Wisconsin) and native oak sawed into large beams.

Now after 15 years of disuse, the Home School buildings are coming into their own again in a new way. Four years ago the Fellowship began adapting them to its own uses. The gymnasium was converted into a theater, the art and science halls into galleries, the assembly hall into a living room for parties and entertainment. We built on the site of the old gymnasium a large drafting room, flanked by apprentices' rooms along either side, and we started a new dining hall building alongside it. The old Home School music cottage we are converting into a house for the resident leader—the first school building can't be recognized in its new birth, made now to belong to the group as a generous dormitory. The old greenhouse, barns, and laundry buildings will be a pile of firewood before the month is up (for isn't pruning necessary to growth?).

Spasmodically the place hums with activity; Hillside seems to grow by jerks from emergency to emergency but always finer and more consistent as a great whole.

Now the place is humming again and the theater we once thought completed is undergoing a major operation. Such is the growth of an "organic" building under the creative hand.

JACK HOWE

Sunday, May 17, at 3 P.M. —*Madame Bovary* by Flaubert. Coffee and cakes in the entrance. Enjoy the fireside hour at Taliesin.

AT TALIESIN

May 22, 1936

The Taliesin Playhouse floor stood on edge a few weeks ago. On a Tuesday, sharp saws ripped the floor into sections. Excavations allowed the stage to drop. The old floor level shifted to new levels to form a more intimate and dramatic little theater. On Sunday of that week was the opening of the season and that meant work all day and as nearly as possible — all night.

As we worked inside, on the lawn outside the girls worked on the theater curtains, changing them for the new circumstance and, as we worked, our food was brought to the lawn under the trees outside or to the fireplace inside.

In the distance the tractor's steady firing meant that Carey still plowed, as the last of our acres were turned over. Now all the available tillable soil on the 200 acre farm is not only plowed but planted: five fields of oats, one clover and oats, two corn-fields, and one clover field from last year.

The garden was planted early. We have planted practically everything but peanuts and pop-corn. Eating our onions and radishes already and have had rhubarb and asparagus for two weeks. Sweet corn is up while squash is 9 or 10 inches high. Hotcaps were a great boon to the garden this year and turned the field into a veritable army encampment.

From the garden we hear hammers pounding at Taliesin. One week of carpentry by Blaine and Noverre and Albert make the new laundry about complete. Bert is making new cases for the kitchen. Ready to put in. The girls are gathering dandelion for next year's wine. The click of the typewriters goes on in the studio office.

The first swim of the season! The Wisconsin River has fallen to allow safe swimming.

Riding horses have had good workouts lately.

Our two-and-a-half-year-old colt no longer has complete freedom. Earl and Carey started breaking him on soft plowed ground. The saddle on his back was distasteful to him and his rider promptly hit the ground after mounting. The colt was finally ridden in circles at the end of a long rope which two apprentices held. Another day we led the colt, riderless, his halter tied to the horn of my saddle as I rode "Satin." The colt stubbornly stopped, two straps broke, and I hit the ground with the saddle over me.

Two weeks ago: the sixth Fellowship wedding — Blain and Hulda were married Sunday night in the Taliesin living room by Rev.

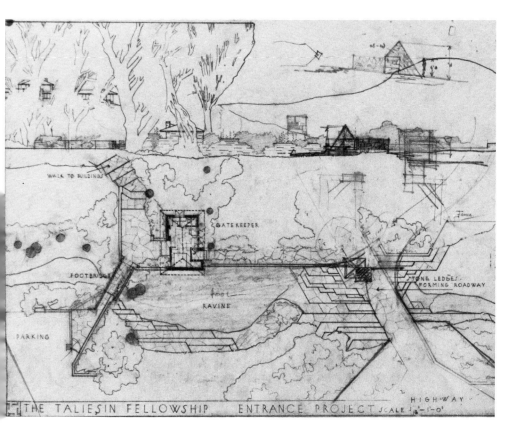

The Taliesin Fellowship Entrance Project, 1936. Drawing courtesy of the Frank Lloyd Wright Foundation.

Taliesin Playhouse at Hillside, 1933 (photo ca. October 1933; note projection booth *upper left*). Photo courtesy of the *Capital Times.*

Apprentices at La Hacienda (photo ca. 1936; apprentices *left to right:* Kay Schneider, Noverre Musson, Bennie Dombar, John Howe). Photo courtesy of the Frank Lloyd Wright Foundation (Cornelia Brierly Collection).

Apprentice John Lautner with His Sister Cathleen (photo ca. 1934;
Lautner designed and constructed furniture at Lautner's home in
Marquette, MI). Photo courtesy of the Frank Lloyd Wright
Foundation (Henry Schubart Collection).

"Last summer saw quite a bit of this seasonal growth. . . . a
sunny new bedroom, also developed from an old one, for Mr.
Wright" (Noverre Musson, "At Taliesin," March 12, 1937)
Taliesin (enlarging Frank Lloyd Wright's bedroom in 1936;
apprentices Blaine Drake and Jim Thomson). Photo courtesy of
John H. Howe, Architect.

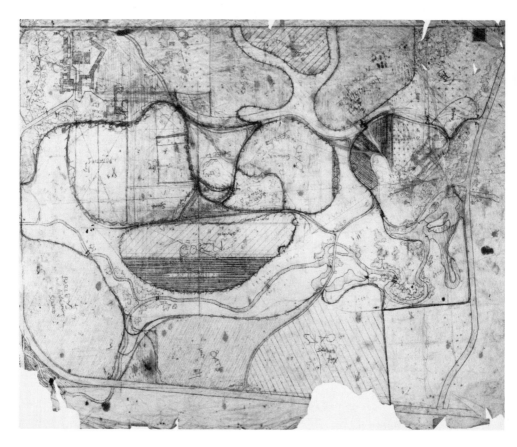

"Garden planning at Taliesin is done in the same way as building planning. Using a large map of the farm and a box of colored pencils, the entire garden layout is planted" ("At Taliesin March 15, 1934). *Planting Plan of Taliesin Farmland,* 1934 (Taliesin *middle right,* Hillside *upper left corner*). Drawing courtesy of the Frank Lloyd Wright Foundation.

"Please don't be misled, it is only a semi-circle. But, nevertheless, the tea circle is symbolically placed in the general plan of Taliesin" (Everett Burgess, "At Taliesin," May 26, 1936). *Taliesin Tea Circle* (photo ca. 1930s; apprentice Kay Schneider *lower left*). Photo courtesy of the Frank Lloyd Wright Foundation.

Apprentices Edgar Kaufmann, Jr., and Bill Bernoudy with Frank Lloyd Wright Inspecting the Prefab Farm Unit Model (photo ca. 1935; La Hacienda courtyard). Photo courtesy of the Frank Lloyd Wright Foundation.

"The kitchen, strange as it may seem, is not only one of the most active but one of the most interesting places at Taliesin" (Mabel Morgan, "At Taliesin," September 12, 1936). *Taliesin Fellowship Kitchen, Hilltower Wing* (photo ca. 1930s; Mabel Morgan at stove). Photo courtesy of the Frank Lloyd Wright Foundation.

"There used to be a ragged wall in the Dana Gallery" (Eugene Masselink, "At Taliesin," December 11, 1936). *Apprentice Benjamin Dombar's Completed Fireplace, Dana Gallery* (photo ca. late 1930s). Photo courtesy of the Frank Lloyd Wright Foundation.

Holloway. Simple but charming. The Fellowship worksong was the wedding-march.

Work on the planning of new houses goes on after tea far into the night. Piano practice and singing voices are overheard from several directions.

What more except the element of tragedy would you suggest to fill out a complete weekly cycle of a constructive creative life? And even tragedy looked in on the scene when Sascha, one of Mrs. Wright's tall Borzoi, was shot for raiding a nearby farmyard.

Visitors continually.

BENNY DOMBAR

Following the suggestion of Madison friends, we are changing the hour of starting our Sunday afternoon programs from 3 o'clock to 4 o'clock in the afternoon. The change will occur for the first time on Sunday.

We are presenting on this Sunday the romantic and picturesque English film *Rhodes the Empire Builder,* starring Walter Huston. Coffee and cakes will be served with good music as usual. Please remember to tell your friends "4 o'clock."

AT TALIESIN

May 26, 1936

[Not included in this volume is an earlier "At Taliesin" column by apprentice Charles Edman (February 16, 1934) crediting Japan and the Orient with being the influence that created "Teaism at Taliesin. From Japan the cult of Teaism has spread its function if not its ceremonial beauty and significance to nearly every part of the world. And as a social function it remains with only the hospitality of the hostess and the philosophic resignation of the guest to suggest the existence of the Oriental culture. Such a cult founded on the adoration of the beautiful among the sordid facts of life cannot be lost to apprentices of beauty in life and art, the real appreciation of which exists as the tea-masters knew it should exist, as a living influence. So Teaism lives and grows at

Taliesin and begins to breathe its faith once again." The practice of
4:00 P.M. tea and conversation at Taliesin continues still to this day.]

There is an old English custom — or is it "fashion" over Europe — I
speak of "Afternoon Tea." Tea time at Taliesin comes like most well
ordered teas, at about four o'clock. Most of the time, tea time is on
time. However, if tea isn't on time, it is quite naturally after time, but
it really doesn't matter because we continue our work until the tea bell
rings, that is, unless we have a watch. The tea bell by the way, is the
rising, breakfast, dinner, and supper bell merely rung at tea time.
This bell besides calling us together for social and bodily sustenance
has another deeper and more profound significance; it marks the close
of the manual labor day and the commencement of the studio period
during which the "higher" arts are pursued. However, if we eliminate
the days in Spring at Taliesin when emergency work confronts the
Fellowship (at which time the hours of physical labor sometimes
continue far into the night or at least until supper time), and we
eliminate the several who have special chores, and also those few who
are waiting for the spirit to move them, one can readily see that the
rush for the studio drafting tables is seldom as upsetting as it might
be.

At the sound of the tea bell, all drop their work whether out in the
field, up in the kitchen, over at Hillside, down in the office, back in
their rooms, and attired just as they are, head in toward the tea circle.
Please don't be misled, it is only a semi-circle. But, nevertheless, the
tea circle is symbolically placed in the general plan of Taliesin; it is just
half way between everywhere even meals. Blocks of stone, set in
concrete, form the seat which encircles a large oak tree making stone
terrace garden, with a small pool of water at the center. To prevent
absent-minded or too casual apprentices from stepping into the pool, a
wooden tea table is set across it upon which are placed all the tea
goodies. Tea setting rotates from member to member and so the nature
of the tea goodies varies according to the imaginative resources and
practical capabilities of the tea-getter, also the condition of the tea
time money fund. Yes! Ah, me. Alas! We are subject to false economy
programs too. I have seen periods when tea was discontinued entirely.
Lest some misunderstand let me add, that it is considered the lowest
possible tea form at Taliesin to buy in town any of the tea goodies.

Architecture even in food and ingredients is encouraged at Taliesin. Those architects who are dull, that is to say without skill, imagination and patience (or perhaps time) fall back upon the old reliable tea with toast and jam. Other more daring will tackle delicacies ranging from oatmeal cookies to cream puffs, strawberry indented with a sprig of mint in the tea. The tea goodies, which of late have been in charge of one particular apprentice, have been most excellent. And our tea things are getting more appropriate little by little as we give more teaish in appreciation.

I suppose you are wondering now what we do upon arriving at the tea circle? The first five minutes need hardly be explained. Some apprentices are actually hungry. A few just victims of the tea habit. Into small brown tea cups we pour from larger brown tea pots a shot of steeped tea, which is followed by a rush of hot water, a thin slice of lemon, a dash of sugar and then a swish—all this done in sweeping manner—no carpet beneath the soil. The first sip of tea is always a pleasant surprise, the cups, you will remember, are pottery and brown and we don't remember always whether we have hot water or just straight tea. But after getting hold of our tea cup and a nibble, we retire to the stone seat. Some of us climb upon it and sit on the upper level with our feet on the lower level, ordinarily the seat where ordinary people would sit. When sitting thus—upper and lower level—in a semi-circle, all naturally face the tea table in the center; which automatically acts as a check on how much the others are eating, it also makes it rather difficult for one to get away with more than his share without publicity.

What do we talk about? The range is wide open to everything from roots to Roosevelt, carriages to marriages, Moses to noses, actors to tractors, means to ends, miles to styles, artics to architects, friends to trends. In fact there is nothing we do not talk about. Sometimes, however, we prefer to just sit and say nothing.

EVERETT BURGESS

Sunday, May 31: *Crime et Chatiment.* A French screen version of Dostoyevski's *Crime and Punishment.* This picture won the Mussolini prize at Venice in 1935.

AT TALIESIN

June 5, 1936

My first introduction to Ivy Olson was somewhat of a shock to me. I went in to see her in Spring Green with Edgar who was bringing her some laundry. She came out to greet us. Jolly booming voice, flushed laughing face, large and strong. "Hello Ivy," Edgar shouted, "How many babies this week?"

"Two healthy ones," she sang out — "expecting another next week."

I gasped inwardly. No one had told me that doing all the washing for 21 Taliesin apprentices was only a hobby for her and that her proud occupation was "midwife."

For the first three years of the Fellowship on regular days each week come the familiar puffing of Ivy's little Ford coupe up the hill — and then Ivy herself, strong arms laden with laundry bundles — going from room to room — laughing and talking all the while — about the babies mostly. Everyone looked forward to her visit. She might caution one fellow about his room — praise another. Generally she was full of praise and always eager to help — sometimes pitching in with a little scrubbing here and there.

We are just now completing the laundry unit at Taliesin and are equipped to do all our own washing and ironing — and even mending, though never the way Ivy used to mend. And although Ivy doesn't come out as often as before, her interest in the Taliesin apprentices never ceases. She is motherly and kindly and is always full of questions about the work we're doing and eager for news about those who have come or have gone.

And, of course, we must go in to see the latest baby.

Lon Snyder, the blacksmith in the village of Spring Green, has welded, mended, straightened, bent, and sharpened everything from plows to pump dogs that the Fellowship has dragged down to his shop. Besides making the iron forks and grilles we designed to take with us on picnics, he has constructed several fireplace grilles and the big crane in the fireplace at the Playhouse out of simple iron bars — carrying out our designs with real craftsmanship: the same artistry with which he plays his violin — and several instruments in the Spring Green band.

Now that we are getting the better of the equipment we use, there is not so much work for Lon to do to put the tools into shape, but we have heard of his fond wish to get a group of the men in the community together and come out to spend a whole day with us working in the fields and on the buildings—and have a feast together out in the open in the evening. So far his plan has not gone through—but we hope it will some day be successful.

Up in Dodgeville, 16 miles away, is the Parsons and Hocking meat market, managed by Etta Hocking. Each week we send a long complicated order of groceries and meat supplies over the phone to her and we drive up to find half the floor space in her store covered with our supplies.

No one is more genuinely interested in the welfare of our work than Etta. She is always cheerful and always encouraging. Two years ago when we went to Arizona she prepared a tremendous lunch for us. We stopped enroute and all 30 if us gathered about her big round table groaning with enough food to last us for half the way across the country.

Etta is interested in every new design produced by us. She gives us advice—expert, believe me—about the garden and the flowers. She is greatly interested in all the phases of the government and her store carries pamphlets of the people she implicitly believes in. For her convictions are strong and not to be trifled with.

When there was a big celebration in Dodgeville two years ago each merchant was asked to have a special exhibition in his store window. In the window of Parsons and Hocking meat market was placed the model of the farm unit of Broadacre City, one of the most important buildings in the plan designed by Mr. Wright.

Said Etta proudly, "There were more people by our window than any other in town. Had to chase people away to get into the store."

EUGENE MASSELINK

The film we are to show at the Playhouse on Sunday is hailed as a deeply human drama—a picture flourishing with humor and charm. It is the latest film produced by the Soviet: *Three Women.* It is a tragically human account of the part three women played in the dark days, when civil war ravaged the country in 1919.

In contrast with the power of this Russian drama we will show — one of the best Disney cartoons — *The Hare and the Tortise.* Coffee and cake as usual, and remember 4 o'clock.

AT TALIESIN

June 12, 1936

That the apprentices, regardless of years, should have the spirit of youth is a cardinal qualification of membership in the Fellowship. Nothing has brought that quality to the surface more than the "treasure-hunt" we held on the occasion of Mr. Wright's birthday. While the treasure hunt lasted we were all children very young in spirit. Don't laugh at us for being childish until you have tried the hunt yourself. You will find that you will leave most of your dignity and all of your reserve at home or lose it on the road.

Early evening — our five cars lined up in the court ready to go — we receive from the first glass jar our first clue:

> Go where that comes from,
> Which was separated and soured,
> 'Tis made golden and mellow,
> By a "picturesque" fellow.

A scramble of cars followed but we thought — "That could be no other place but the milk room. Sure. Butter! that's it, and look — no one else has thought of that — they're all rushing off pell mell."

But, we were wrong we finally decided it must be the cheese factory where a tattooed cheese-maker made the cheese, everyone was ahead of us. We arrived just in time to see and benefit by an undignified scramble over the jar containing the clues — someone else's discovery of the next clue:

> As the spokes were attached to the wheel,
> So is a container marked F. Ll. Wright.
> Finding this quest will, we hope,
> Bring you delight.

The mail box of course. But just try to get out of the jam of five cars all trying to turn around in the same place at the same time. Here the dexterity of the driver counted for more than the ability to discover the clues quickly.

The treasure hunt became a battle of wits at the jar containing the fourth clue:

> Man built,
> Planned for conversion,
> 'Twas last summer's diversion.

This tricky one split the scurrying groups into two schools of opinion.

"To the Chapel," said those who were always looking for the obvious.

"To the dam," cried those who looked for hidden meanings. As both solutions seemed to fit the clue perfectly, those who talked the loudest won. The spillway the Fellowship made last summer was right as we learned after an unsuccessful trip to the Chapel. "Conversion" meant water into electricity.

The next clue, with a hint of "greens" and "hole one" led us to the golf course in town. Here the hunt became a test of endurance. I think we made the 300 yards down the fairway in about 35 seconds.

That clue when found led to the Midway barn where "by way of scent" we found clue seven:

> An iron gate, a pine tree walk,
> Here after meeting, the flock would talk.

"This time it is the chapel" — we would bet a nickel. It was. The clue found there began: "Lovers renowned . . . " Just one glimpse at that; we didn't need to read more. We knew that meant "Romeo and Juliet," the windmill tower at Hillside.

The next port was obviously enough. Pope's restaurant in Spring Green. The cars were quite separated now. We, in the station wagon, were in the middle. Jim's group was so far ahead that we had almost conceded the victory to them. Gene and his group were also ahead.

On this clue:

> New life has come forth in this place
> There may be a wash out, but you may not find a trace.

The first group — being idealists — slipped up on "new life" and "wash out" and went all the way back to Taliesin to look for flowers in the garden and a washout—or something like that.

But we considered more sensibly and decided it would lead us to Ivy Olson's, she who took care of new babies and used to hang out the Fellowship laundry on her clothesline. We were right but we soon discovered that Gene's group had reasoned rightly too. A little difficulty in finding the hiding place for the clue—startling the residents—put us in the lead, however, with Gene on our heels. The clues eventually led us to the shot tower at Tower Hill where we guessed correctly that the clue would be found at the bottom entrance while the other group groped about with flashlights in the deepening darkness at the top of the shaft. Now safely in the lead, we breathed more easily. The last clue we found in one of the two big boilers at Hillside:

> Hurry back!
> But if "where" you ask?
> The Treasure is in the Loggia
> And to find it is your task.

So we did hurry back only to find Mr. Wright there waiting for us. It seems that by some skillful deduction he had divined the location of the treasure and, feeling sure, he had left in the midst of our wild chase and gone directly to the end. In the darkened house he found, sitting snugly near the warm glow of the loggia fireplace—a live Turkey Gobbler. But the prize was ours just the same for all the clues were required and he did not have them.

The following morning we enjoyed a more characteristic celebration. An earlier than usual breakfast with Mr. and Mrs. Wright presiding over a huge bowl of strawberries, pitchers of cream—and enough otherwise to call it a good dinner. Then keeping up with the spirit of the occasion we had a review of the Sunday Playhouse program—one of the best we've ever had in our Playhouse. The feature film was tremendously powerful: the Russian *Three Women*—the depth of our emotion confirming our belief that Russian pictures reserve the most important place in world cinema today. We always come away from the Russian effort with renewed energy for our own struggle. A more dignified idea of the beauty and meaning of work.

EARL FRIAR

On this coming Sunday we are presenting two important films: *Modern Times,* the latest great Chaplin film, and *The Plow That Broke the Plains.*

Nothing we could tell you about the first should have to convince you that no matter how many times that you were to see *Modern Times* there would always be a fresh slant to the genuine humor of the great American actor — Charlie Chaplin.

The Plow That Broke the Plains — an American documentary film — is being distributed by the Resettlement Administration in Washington. Great interest has been aroused throughout the country in this very recent film for its splendid photography and we are pleased to be one of the first to show it to the public.

AT TALIESIN
July 5, 1936

Has it ever occurred to you how far behind one's actual thoughts and feelings one's own expression is? That is, the expression of an amateur such as myself. (An amateur, of course, is anyone whose love for his work has not suffered sordid degradation.) I find myself trying to express my thoughts of today with my expression of yesterday. If only I could have expressed myself even that well yesterday, but alas, I was then expressing myself in the expressions of the day before — etc., etc. The time lag, I suppose.

It has been said that people write or talk most when they are not at peace with themselves. Trying to express new expressions is like trying to put new wine into old bottles? Only, thank God, vinegar isn't necessarily the result of the first. The wine may still be good wine.

But, thoughts and feelings have such a forward jump on expression that expression would be discouraged were there not a chance of improving thereby, that is, improve by expressing oneself. It is because of this that the Fellowship persists in writing these amateur articles, some quite good? and some not so good. But all in one direction. And we do "kill several birds with one pebble," for, by the pebbles we throw from time to time — we ourselves grow and our neighbors are made acquainted with what we are, what we are doing, and what we intend to do and you who read them are seeing something grow up out of our own soil—as someday belonging to you. That day will be when culture is indigenous and belonging to you.

JACK HOWE

Frontier is a new Soviet masterpiece directed by one of the great Russian directors, Dovjenko recently awarded the Order of Lenin. *Frontier* is a screen poem on the subject of patriotism and an artistic document of great power and conviction.

The film will be shown at the Playhouse Sunday at 4 P.M.

AT TALIESIN

July 9, 1936

Some people regard Taliesin and its Fellowship as an establishment. As time goes on, the tendency grows to regard Taliesin as less and less the home of a creative architect and more and more some kind of educational institution.

Really it is no more like an institution than it was like one when Frank Lloyd Wright built it as a place in which to live and work. The apprenticeship then was never more than 10. Even with enlarged facilities at present apprenticeship will never be more than 30. At one time the danger of institution loomed ahead. That was in the days when the first Taliesin prospectus was issued.

But the danger soon became apparent and the plans of that date were discarded. Others were made, intended to preserve individuality, flexibility, and original integrity, or, let us say, the integrity of originality that primarily characterized Taliesin.

Taliesin will never be "established" nor will it ever be an institution. Nor will it become a popular success in anyway while Frank Lloyd Wright lives. It will remain as it is—a slowly growing propaganda for creative work—its founder and owner on "one end of the log," whatever group may gather there on the other end in conference. But more especially it is a place in which to work together with him. Nevertheless Taliesin has a tradition, perhaps the only cultural tradition America can call its own. That tradition is the birth and growth on American soil of the philosophy and ideals of an organic architecture.

To live this is to live completely but dangerously enough and, as things are, more or less at the mercy of misunderstanding and prejudice which must have its "social rebels."

Nor is the Taliesin Fellowship in any danger of becoming a mere cult. Its leader despises "cults" too much for that to happen.

So to regard Taliesin as an individual attempt to grow the creative artists America so sorely needs, a need developed rather than satisfied by her academic systems is to get Taliesin properly into focus and be able to understand its aims and the essential simplicity that characterizes them and the life lived there.

Taliesin is so American in spirit as to be un-American in method and where technique is concerned it is already making a new technique. One it can call its own.

Meantime the place is subject to all the ills that such growth is heir to. Both misunderstanding and prejudice can do things to people and ideas. Taliesin can't escape the doings and has not escaped them, doesn't expect to escape. Friends will be few. Enemies many. The indifferent—most.

It may survive them all, because its faith and center of gravity are both places where no praise or blame or sedition can reach them. Falsehood may hurt and momentarily harm Taliesin but cannot spoil its purpose nor ever destroy its real character.

FRANK LLOYD WRIGHT

Rebellion, revolution, retribution—and romance come to the Playhouse on Sunday—at 4 P.M. sharp—in the form of a splendid English picture *King of the Damned* starring the great European actor Conrad Veidt.

AT TALIESIN
August 25, 1936

[This column was not found in any newspapers, but its original manuscript is within the Frank Lloyd Wright Archives as an "At Taliesin" column (dated August 25, 1936). In a letter to the editor of the *Grant County Herald* (Lancaster, Wisconsin), dated August 31, 1936, apprentice Eugene Masselink "recalled" a recently submitted column—"Dear Mr. Sherman: The article by Mr. Wright that you received last week was sent in by mistake and should not be printed. We would appreciate your returning it to us." Perhaps there was concern that the satirical nature of the column might be misread and interpreted as high treason? It is now quite harmless.]

Something happened in Washington last week. The Taliesin Fellowship incensed by the little colonial hot boxes the Resettlement Administration has been building regardless in drought districts, west and down south, southeast and southwest, raided the architect's various divisions in the administration building. Dividing into five squads, squad Number One kidnapped Frederick Delano as he was returning from luncheon with his cousin—the President. His whereabouts became known only yesterday. Meantime the boys entered the offices of the principal architects employed by the administration, threw them bodily into the street and sat in their places giving orders to the employees who were only too glad to have something sensible to do.

It was an interesting fact that the employees of the assistants entered into the spirit of the thing heartily, not only not opposing the Taliesin apprentices but giving what little assistance was needed while the eviction was taking place.

The deposed architects, more ashamed than afraid to return, have disappeared for the time being and the boys, with the enthusiastic support of the draughtsmen, are carrying along designs for a more human habitation—before the government money is all spent and the chance to give the United States better housing is lost forever.

Owing to the connivance of the workers under the various government architects, the exploit attracted little attention. The higher officials all being absent on vacation are yet unaware of what has happened.

However, notwithstanding the justice of the eviction and the fact that the rebellion seems justifiable to most everybody concerned (the architects themselves included)—some repercussions are expected soon. Meantime the Taliesin boys are carrying on.

FRANK LLOYD WRIGHT

Taliesin is inaugurating a new series of European films this coming Sunday: we will see cinema from the north in Sweden, the south in Italy and from Russia and Czechoslovakia during the coming four weeks.

On August 30th—at four in the afternoon: *Sangen till Henne* (*The Song to Her*), the really first great Swedish musical production starring the celebrated tenor Martin Ohman. The film is distinguished for its liveliness in action and in music and beautiful photography in the refreshing northern spirit of Sweden.

AT TALIESIN

September 4, 1936

[This column was originally sent to the secretary of the Southwestern Wisconsin State Fair on August 14, 1936, by apprentice Eugene Masselink for their use "as you wish with your publicity." It found its way into the *Capital Times* (Madison) newspaper as an "At Taliesin" column on the opening day of the fair.]

Mineral Point County fair visitors last year saw Broadacre City, the model of the city of the future planned and designed by Frank Lloyd Wright and built by the Taliesin Fellowship. They saw in it a new freedom for living out upon the land that is America. The scheme was rendered obvious enough by way of the big 12-foot-square-model— four square miles of the new city, numerous collateral large scale models, and may lettered panels.

This year at the fair, Sept. 4, 5, and 6; in a portion of the same space there will be an important exhibition of a more concentrated group of useful buildings from the Taliesin studios. These buildings will be of especial interest to all the farmers and townspeople in Wisconsin because they are planned for the use of the ground by the people of moderate means to realize a saner, better life here in the future than is now.

A small-farm unit will be the center piece of this exhibition. Therein you will see how the farmer might come to live in circumstances as fine in quality as his richer neighbors, a better order made possible to him by means of such modern advantage as prefabricated units and appurtenance systems and new applications of factory methods to other structural parts of the buildings.

The farmer is here arranged with his family, his mechanical equipment, his feed and his livestock, and his harvest under one broad protecting fire-proof roof shelter—all in convenient relation to his way of living and to the ground from which his living comes.

Along with this model for little farms will be shown several models for small houses. These houses all have heating and plumbing systems as prefabricated (factory-built) units in a utility stack and have standardized construction, but the houses themselves could vary in appearance and structure, as the ground would change in character from California to New York and from Texas to Minnesota—and as the individual needs of the people might vary without any loss of the new economy.

This farm group and these modest houses were planned as part of this new freedom for living for the people in Mineral Point, in Wisconsin or in all America that is called Broadacre City. All are practical solutions of our present day—every day needs. This exhibit will be an educational feature of the Fair you cannot afford to miss if you are interested in your own future in the future America as an American.

The Taliesin Fellowship will be represented to explain the models to those who are interested.

Sunday, September 6th, at four in the afternoon: *La Marcia Nuziale* (*The Wedding March*) with Tullio Carminati. The first Italian all-talking film based on a famous play, the *Wedding March* by Henri Bataille, acted by a foremost cast and acclaimed by the New York Sun "the best Italian film to date."

AT TALIESIN

September 12, 1936

The kitchen, strange as it may seem, is not only one of the most active but one of the most interesting places at Taliesin. For it is here that each apprentice must spend a two-week period about every 6 months, helping to make the meals for all the other apprentices, and while he is serving this "kitchen duty" he is anxious to concoct new dishes and experiment with the old "tried and true" recipes.

Besides the standard American foods it is often our lot to have delicious Russian foods which always seem more exotic than ours, maybe because they are foreign. But this is beside the point.

From the account, thus far, it would seem that being in the kitchen is just one nice time making good things to eat. There is also the unpleasant side. After each meal the kitchen is piled high all around with dishes and skillets and pots and pans—and it is then that the apprentices have the opportunity to show their speed and skill in changing a most untidy kitchen into a tidy one. Some of the "kitchen duties" are very fast and it is amazing to see how fast the pile of dishes goes down; others dawdle about and think about how nice it would be to be doing something else—and hauling rocks, plastering, or any of those things that are often distasteful, are very inviting at this moment. But whether they like it or not—the meals must be made, and so they are—and with a singularly good-humoredness, at that.

Probably the most difficult of all, especially for the sleepy heads, is the task of getting up early in the morning, for they are the first ones up—to start water boiling and set tables before everyone else starts clamoring for breakfast.

But once one is up, even this is not unpleasant, for Taliesin is more peaceful and perhaps more beautiful in the morning than at any other time. And there is a certain satisfaction in ringing the bell to awaken everyone else who is still sound asleep. (Perhaps I should not say "everyone" because there are always some who find it too much of an effort to get up at six thirty and consequently go without breakfast.)

After everyone has been satisfied with fruits, cereals, bacon and eggs, the kitchen crew start baking and cooking for the rest of the day. This is a process which goes on without end until noon—another meal served and then dishes.

The noon dishes are hardly washed and dried before it is time to start making tea—for 4 o'clock tea is one of the Taliesin traditions.

After tea, it is soon time to think of supper, and so the days pass, each full of excitement to have each meal ready on time and to have all the things in the meal please, which is fairly easy, for most are not too critical.

Last Saturday night at Hillside five fires were made, grates were put over them, each person given a pan, vegetables, and things which when cooked are "Sukiyaki" and each carefully watched his or her own, Mr. Wright adding more soy sauce here, or mushrooms there, then when it was cooked we had to struggle with chop sticks to eat it, and all the while much laughter to see someone almost get something to his mouth only to drop it. Mr. Wright was the only person skilled enough in the art of "chop stick eating" to be at all graceful or at ease; the rest of us managed with fingers and cups and incidentally chop sticks.

Easter is an exceptionally merry time in our kitchen for it is then Mrs. Wright's Baba and Paschal cheese is to be made, something like 140 eggs to be broken, much beating and mixing, then several hours later we watch her taking huge round yellow loaves from the oven, carefully placing them on pillows and rocking them to and fro until cool.

To make delightful dishes from France, Germany, Russia, and Poland such as Brioche, Borscht, Chiarpchichi, Shashlick, Vsvar, Golubisi, Colivo and many others under the personal supervision of Mrs. Wright has been my unique experience at Taliesin.

MABEL MORGAN

Anna, a recent film from the Soviet, will be shown at the Taliesin Playhouse Sunday, Sept. 13 at 4 in the afternoon.

Anna is a great success enhanced by the fact that it was produced without the obvious studious efforts and frills. It is an artistically strong, excellently produced realistic film. A natural document—a piece of Soviet reality—of life itself.

AT TALIESIN
October 16, 1936

Two weeks have passed since the rainy Sunday I arrived at Taliesin. Two weeks of learning about and adopting a mode of living so different from the past three years of life in college that I can think of no adequate comparison.

To use a minor point to illustrate:

Does one make wine in college? I never did and don't believe many colleges endorse wine making as a curricular activity while here it is a mere incident in a continuous round of varied activity.

There is a quality about Taliesin that is inspiring to one recently arrived. Work of intellectual importance and spiritual significance amalgamated with such ordinary prosaic duties as dish washing gives a sense-perspective to life.

Probably the first impression of a material sort that a newcomer receives is unendinglessness of the open hearth. Fireplaces everywhere reach out and desnare with their chill-dispersing glow. Placed so naturally that the realization of their number didn't manifest itself until I started counting. There are 18 of them at Taliesin!

Individualism is encouraged here—but not the "rugged" individualism. It is seemingly subordinated to the spirit of cooperation; perpetuated by the individual pride of group accomplishment and fed by habitual initiative.

The futility of this trivial attempt on my part to characterize it strikes me as I look over at Romeo and Juliet, a culmination of the hill of which it is a part, symbolizing the indefatigable spirit which pervades Taliesin and permeates the Fellowship.

LAWRENCE LOW

Next Sunday afternoon at 4—*The Divine Spark,* a Gaumont-British, being the story of Bellini, the composer. Beautiful setting and fascinating music. Coffee and cakes served in front of open-hearth fire. A picture you will all enjoy. See Taliesin with its October verdure.

AT TALIESIN

October 30, 1936

Sunday, Nov. 1, 1936, is the occasion of the celebration of the third anniversary of the opening of the Taliesin Playhouse.

Let us go back to the first Nov. 1, 1933, when after several months of work transforming the large room which had once been the gymnasium of the former Hillside Home School, the last feverish days of painting and building and lettering came to an end. The motion picture apparatus was moved into the new projection booth, the great Bechstein concert grand took its place near the stage, curtains were hung, lighting features magically hanging pendant, red and yellow oak branches mingling with dark green fir were brought in to fill the room with added color and decoration. The fire in the fireplace roared welcome.

The Taliesin Playhouse was officially opened to the public.

It was the first gesture the Taliesin Fellowship extended to the public as a welcome to all who would come and spend at least one afternoon with us on Sundays in an atmosphere of beauty and harmony and to enjoy with us good music and the best entertainment we could bring from the four corners of the world via the new art of the cinema.

During that first year the programs did not stop because of the winter weather and before the steam heating system was installed tremendous fires were kept going in the fireplace all night long. People began to expect and look forward to these pleasant and eventful afternoons at the Playhouse and during the summer of 1934 and thereafter the crowds increased steadily. The regularity of the programs was only halted twice: during the two winters the Fellowship spent in Arizona.

The films we have shown come principally from France, Germany, Russia, and England as well as from Italy, Sweden, Japan, Ireland, and Czechoslovakia. The colorful peasant life and the drama and vivid movement of these peoples throughout the world portrayed so brilliantly by means of great photography, direction, and music have broadened our point of view and have been a real source of knowledge.

Eisenstein and other powerful directors in Russia, the witty Rene Clair in France, Alexander Korda in England, Carl Dreyer and others in Germany are all familiar directors to us now in the creative world of the motion picture and we find the films from different countrys add a contrasting color to the consecutive line of programs. The intense struggle and the vivid portrayal of life in present day Russia a stunning contrast to the gay musical world of Vienna in the days of Strauss and Inner. Disney and other cartoons from Russia and France have been brilliant sparks of humor and light running through the varying moods of the programs during the past three years.

The Taliesin trio was a feature of our own music during one summer and always there is the music from the sound system in the booth where by way of a large collection of records the musical world is open to us. And always, of course, coffee and something to eat by the fireside to make the afternoon an informal occasion rather than a commercial enterprise, which above everything else, the Taliesin Fellowship is not.

The latest major operation in the Playhouse occurred last spring when the floor was cut into sections and lowered into tiers of varying interesting levels and the Playhouse became in actual form a real little theater.

On this coming Sunday, therefore, in celebration of the anniversary of the past three eventful years, Taliesin announces the 135th program of films at the Taliesin Playhouse as follows:

Things to Come, the English Alexander Korda production of the book by H. G. Wells.

Frankie and Johnny, a burlesque on the famous American ballad performed by Charles Laughton and Elsa Lanchester.

The Grasshopper and the Ants, the Walt Disney Silly Symphony.

Refreshments will be served by the fireplace. We hope to see our friends from Madison, Spring Green, Lancaster, Sauk City, Milwaukee and from all about this region joining with us in participation of this gala occasion.

EUGENE MASSELINK

[An account of the Taliesin Playhouse just before its opening on November 1, 1933, was printed in the *Capital Times* and has been included herein in its entirety (see appendix A).]

AT TALIESIN

November 6, 1936

A women said to me: "Love, happiness, and security are the basis of a home, a real home. It doesn't matter if it is on linoleum floors or what furniture is used—that isn't real—that's just taste."

This is true. I have seen many happy homes made in very ugly buildings or in tents—but these people are either ignorant of culture and beauty or are geniuses and can rise above any circumstance to live and have a happy home.

Sometimes I have been jealous of the happy moron—he goes blissfully on—gets drunk every Saturday night—and life is very simple. But he is ignorant, his life is only as rich and as full as what he can understand and appreciate. He has love, happiness and security. But he is only a janitor or a street cleaner.

However it is a good thing we have these men, they have important work to do and are happy doing it. We can't all be geniuses or have the same degree of culture.

But to genuine culture—the complete living condition, including the floors and furniture is a real part of the home and happiness. Beauty is essential—a very real part of life. Love is beautiful. The beautiful is an expression of love and understanding. It is not a superficial thing labeled taste which can be bought and sold. It is culture—the difference between man and beast. The cultured individual always wishes to go to the most beautiful home—that is where he will have the richest and fullest life.

I cannot agree with the women I quoted.

JOHN LAUTNER

The Private Life of Louis XIV will be presented at the Taliesin Playhouse on this coming Sunday afternoon at 4 P.M.

The film is directed by Carl Froelich, the director of *Maedchen Uniform* with a distinguished cast containing Renate Muller, Dorothea Wieck, and Michael Bohnen. The New York critics are extravagant in their praise of this picture from Germany . . . "A handsomely draped costume drama of the 17th century French court and its spectacular, spendthrift 'Sun King' . . . Lavish, skillful direction and excellent acting by a distinguished cast."

AT TALIESIN
December 4, 1936

A midwestern millionaire after completing his last will and testament had $1,000,000 and in order to help settle the problem of how to dispose of it, he asked readers of a magazine for suggestions: the magazine made it a condition that the million was to benefit the community to which the writer belonged. Hans Koch of New Brunswick, N.J., sent the following letter:

Gentlemen:

If I had a million dollars to leave, I would know how to dispose of it wisely in a time such as ours when all higher human values are giving way to ever-growing cynicism, the sure sign vice, and decay in any society.

But the almsgiver would get no portion of my money: the more money spent through the almsgiving agencies, the worse a society grows. Churches and religious institutions would get no portion of my money: they have not solved the vexing problems of society in the thousands of years in which they have practically been dominant, and they never will do so in the future. The so-called educational institutions likewise would get no portion of my money: the passing of hundreds of thousands of young men and women every year through these institutions emerging "gleichgenhalted" as if run through a button machine, did no good to society as the surrounding evidences clearly show. The maecenas of the arts and their institutions would get no portion of my money: they are as a whole interested in the arts of centuries back, leaving the artist of today to starve. And by no means would I endow libraries where all the best books remain so obviously unread.

Instead, I would spend my millions of dollars, or the income therefrom, for the building and the rebuilding of America.

"You don't say, Mr. Koch! With one little million of dollars to build and rebuild this vast country of ours?"

Exactly, Sir! For I foster the creation of the brains for it, the character and the ability.

My town of 100,000 inhabitants and its immediate surroundings drawn in, just as their money flowed into my town which enabled me to make my little fortune, my town with its surrounding is popping with young persons of both sexes eager to prepare for and take up that great creative work.

By a mere chance my interest has been focused upon a place just suited to meet my best intention: 40 miles west of Madison, near Spring Green, Wis., is a place bearing the strange name "Taliesin." Entering from the road direct from Madison, Wis., the two massive gateway pillars disclose at once some of the originality of the art and the idea of its dwellers.

And looking up the hill we see an extended complex of buildings made of sparking amber-colored limestone, original with large sweeping lines, that girdle the crown of that hill and itself compelling any by-passer to inquire more intimately about the outstanding landmark.

There dwells America's greatest living architect and educator—and possibly he will be regarded as the greatest architect of his time—Frank Lloyd Wright, surrounded by the "Taliesin Fellowship," a school for young architects. At present there are at Taliesin 25 students, boys and girls, from all parts of the country who adore their master.

Before the depression Taliesin drew its "apprentices" from nearly every part of the globe, for the message of the art of the master Frank Lloyd Wright is known far and wide and his great influence in architecture is felt and acknowledged everywhere.

Mr. Wright is the creator of an entirely new architecture, typically American. His buildings grow out of the topographic and geographic surroundings, built from inside out and drawing the outside in, the parts forming a whole: the integral architecture. But the culmination, so far, of Mr. Wright's art is the creation of that remarkable model "Broadacre City," the proposal of a human settlement for a new humanity in a most happy environment.

Life has taught me that money will do me the most good if its expenditure rebounds to the greatest benefit to human society, and the greatest good to human society is done if there can be introduced into society that constructive element so sadly lacking at present: creative young men and women of the noblest of human arts, architecture, who will create the new free dwelling for free America.

I believe the houses we live in are mostly responsible for the misery we live in. There houses stay and we have to look at them as they are soulless, flippant, brutal things, dated backward many centuries even if built yesterday. And we have to live in them, and we have to try to relax in them, in order to gather the physical strength sufficient to stand it another day. There is no need to kill with an axe anymore, a house can do it. The eclecticism of our day is bad air to breathe.

The Taliesin Fellowship could embrace more students. But the eager young men and women who would like to enter have to be turned away for lack of funds with which to pay their tuition. Thirty free scholarships would enable as many young men and women to enter the Taliesin Fellowship and follow their calling, returning eventually as creative forces, as I intended, to build and rebuild America.

My million dollars would have to serve that purpose. I would make it a trust fund by the name of my home town, its income expressly designated for free scholarships to the Taliesin Fellowship, for students chosen preferably from my home town and its vicinity. But if the master there should find from the other side of the globe an outstanding student worthy of a free scholarship, I would rejoice in it.

Thus I would serve my home town best by spending my money for creative life itself: to surround the greatest living typically American architect and educator with young students that he might fulfill his calling on the largest possible plan, and send as many as possible of the creative, efficiently equipped young men and women out into the life of America and the world to give it its true creative meaning.

My money would have to serve where it would do the most good to life itself, for life that starts every day anew and creates anew into the eternal future.

HANS KOCH

Arthur Schnitzler's Viennese romance *Liebelei* will be presented at 3 P.M. Sunday in the Taliesin Playhouse.

AT TALIESIN
December 11, 1936

The Long and the Short of It

The Fellowship giant: Wes, all of six foot four. His hair is down to his forehead in his eyes most of the time and overalls cover the expanses down to his 40-league boots. With swinging arms sawing the air, his ponderous steps rocks the studio and his great shout silences most of what's going on. Towering on the hill, he needs to stoop to miss the ceiling in the dining room.

Several weeks ago, two 50-ton carloads of coke were hauled from the station in town up the hill and distributed among the three boiler rooms at Taliesin to the tune of Wes' shouting, singing, and shoveling in the midst of his coal-black crew. When dusk came, the distinction between Wes, his crew, the coke, and the night itself was negligible.

Halloween night Wes strode amongst the costumed Fellowship: a mighty Caesar from the tip of his plumed helmet to the helm of his toga.

With the broadest grin, he would "sock" the first complaining, the latest one up in the morning, or almost anything hindering the progress of work—be it man, bird or beast—(including a creditor or two).

Wes hails from Indiana and comes unscarred from the portals of the Massachusetts Institute of Technology. Wes with all of his 76 inches is well-driller, mechanic, draughtsman, engineer, carpenter, mason, architect, apprentice in the Taliesin Fellowship.

Benny is little more than half the size. He needs to reach for that which Wes stoops to get under. And he comes straight from Cincinnati.

No more cheerful nor alert worker than Benny.

"Lights:" Benny; "Water:" Benny; "Tools:" Benny; "Wood for fireplaces:" Benny.

He is the senior member of the projectionists and has taught all of the four recruits that have come after him how to put across a smooth (or nearly smooth) performance in the booth at the playhouse.

There used to be a ragged in the wall in the Dana Gallery where Alfie, a former apprentice, started work on a fireplace two years ago. Last summer Mr. Wright commissioned Benny to complete a fireplace in three weeks.

So Benny lugged stone after stone into the Dana Gallery. He worked at it at all hours—you could hear him pounding away long after it was dark outside. The design had been carefully worked out. The lintel was six feet from the floor and the stones were all especially cut to form a pattern on the back of the fireplace. It required skill and some engineering to properly construct the flue. Finally with the help of five others Benny laid the greatest sandstone lintel block. And that night at the celebration in honor of the job, the first fire was built.

Hans, solid German carpenter, declares it would never draw and even as the Fellowship held its breath and as the flames roared up, lighting the room with their best six foot height and the smoke went up the flue out into the moonlit night, Hans still shook his head.

We drank a toast: no one that night prouder or happier than Benny.

EUGENE MASSELINK

Emil und die Detektive will be shown at the Playhouse on Sunday afternoon at 3 P.M. The Museum of Modern Film Library has chosen this film as most representative of the modern film in Germany and will preserve the picture for prosperity.

AT TALIESIN

December 18, 1936

Why should pretentious formalizers worry about the discipline of a "style" for Americans before either they or America yet know style?

The methods, materials and life of our country are common discipline to any right idea of work. Allowed to exercise at our best such whole souled individuality as we may find among us, the common use of the common tools and materials of a common life will so discipline individual effort that centuries forward men will look back and recognize the work of the democratic life of the 20th century as a great, not a dead, style. The honest buildings from which this proposed internationalist style is derived were made that way. We can build many more buildings in that same brave, independent, liberal spirit.

It is true that we understand imperfectly our own ideal of democracy, and so we have shamefully abused it.

We have allowed our ideal to foster offensive privitism that is exaggerated selfishness in the name of individualism. Selfish beyond any monarchy. But do you imagine communism eradicates selfishness? It may suppress it or submerge it.

Nor can socialism eradicate selfishness. It gives it another turn. Democracy cannot eradicate it. No, but democracy alone can turn it into a noble, creative selfhood.

And that is best of all for all.

So out of my own life-experience as an architect, I earnestly say:

What our country needs in order to realize a great architecture for a great life is only to realize and release a high ideal of democracy, the ideal upon which the new life here was founded on new record, and humbly try to learn how to live up to its principles.

I am sure, too, that the work of an organic architecture, for the individual, had gone so far in the work, and the world before this self-seeking propaganda came up, as to enable anyone with ordinary vision to see it coming naturally as our future architecture, propagandists aside. So why, now, as a self-appointed committee on a style, do promoting propagandists imagine they can steal the hide and horns of this living, breathing, healthy young organism and vain-gloriously parade the hide and shake the horns to make Americans think it is the living creature?

Granted they are sincere: having confessed impotence, do they urge others to confess too?

Granted they are ambitious: they wish to be inventors as a eunuch might wish to be a father.

Granted they are impecunious: do they wish to get work to do under false pretenses?

Granted they are aesthetes: they are superficial and ignorant of the depths of nature.

Granted they are as intelligent and hard and scientific as they think they are: they are miscarriage of a machine-age that would sterilize itself, if it could, to avoid continuing to propagate the race.

The letter is more than the spirit only to artists of the second rank.

It is the thing said that is more important, now, than the manner of saying it.

Our pioneer days are not over.

FRANK LLOYD WRIGHT

At the Taliesin Playhouse on Sunday afternoon at 3 P.M. coffee and cakes will be served by the fireside and we will present the American production *Ah, Wilderness!* based on the Eugene O'Neil play by the same name.

1 9 3 7

Why not come up and view the remains?

—Frank Lloyd Wright, letter to Robert Llewlyn Wright, January 23, 1937

INTRODUCTION

All the seemingly unnoticed, varied, and diverse efforts of the previous several years seemed to culminate in 1937 into one large explosion of architectural activity and public awareness of Frank Lloyd Wright. Unfortunately, the end of 1936 found Wright suffering a serious and severe case of pneumonia. By the time he wrote his son of his recovery he had also written the first installment of the "At Taliesin" column series of 1937. His column, entitled "The Country Doctor," was, of course, in praise of his doctor's efforts (the unnamed Spring Green doctor was C. W. Wahl). A weary but recovering Wright, with wife, Olgivanna, and daughter Iovanna, left Taliesin in January for a three-month recuperative vacation (first New York, then California, and finally, for the month of March, the Jokake Inn in Arizona), leaving the Fellowship active in the cold of Wisconsin.

Owing somewhat to Wright's poor health but mostly because the extreme amount of significant architectural work at and around Taliesin required constant attention, the Fellowship did not travel en masse to Arizona in 1937. Later that year, however, Eugene Masselink expressed in a letter, dated October 15, to an incoming apprentice of plans for "driving in caravan to Arizona where we plan to build a desert camp near Phoenix—leaving about the first of December." Unfortunately, that December departure was delayed into the following year, again because of pressing year-end work.

The construction of several Wright projects was underway in 1937 — "Fallingwater"; Kaufmann's Pittsburgh office interior remodeling; the Hanna, Roberts, and Jacobs houses; and the Johnson Wax building all kept Wright and the apprentices busy answering questions and solving field problems arising from the uniqueness of the architecture and thus its unfamiliarity to the construction workers. Wright also was busy designing new projects in 1937 — a house for the president of Johnson Wax ("Wingspread" was designed, drawn, and construction started during the first five months of 1937); the Leo Bramson Dress Shop; the Francis Wright Gift Shop; a detached garage for George Parker; a winter residence for the Rebhuhns (previous clients looking to build a retreat on Estero Island on the Gulf in Florida); and a studio for the Mount Rushmore sculptor, Gutzon Borglum. (Of this latter commission, in a letter to Borglum, dated December 2, 1937, Wright wrote, "I suspect a few of your admonitions in your kind letter were due to your disappointment in the stark reality of the sketches I left with you for the Santa Barbara Studio. Cheer up man — you shall have just what you desire if you will only be frank and fearlessly criticize.") A final and successful effort was also made to complete the large "baronial" Hillside drafting room. Probably owing to the now constant and exciting architectural activity, the apprentices in the early months of 1937 wrote a series of "At Taliesin" columns discussing six of the ongoing and significant architectural commissions — "Fallingwater"; the Hanna, Roberts, Lusk, and Jacobs houses; and the Johnson Wax building.

Wright traveled heavily again in 1937 because of the ongoing work and lecture opportunities. In May, he received an invitation to travel to Moscow, Russia, to attend and participate in the First Congress of Soviet Architects, which he left for in June staying abroad until mid-July. Wright was also extremely prolific, preparing at least seven "At Taliesin" columns (including a three-part installment on a discussion of Broadacre City with the German architect Mies van der Rohe), completing his portion of *Architecture and Modern Life,* and writing five articles for specific magazines.

Financial worries, however, were not over for Wright, as the newspapers reported in March the threat of Wright losing Taliesin for nonpayment of taxes. Wright had petitioned the Iowa County Tax Claims Committee earlier for a tax adjustment on the basis that the property was devoted to educational purposes. Taliesin was assessed by the committee at $15,000, and they denied the exemption request. Wright had until early 1938 to satisfy the delinquent taxes.

Wright's "At Taliesin" columns featured another wide spectrum of topics in 1937—September discussions with the visiting German architect Mies van der Rohe on Broadacre City, an obituary and eulogy for his friend and client George Parker, and criticism of the John Russell Pope-designed Jefferson Memorial. The second book review was featured, this one an appreciative analysis by Benjamin Dombar of Behrendt's *Modern Building.* The series saw its first poem in 1937, written by John Lautner, on a very "muddy" subject. And the summer musicians-in-residence increased to six: the American composer Wesley LaViolette (from DePaul University); an associate and fellow composer and pianist George Perlman; and an entire quartet consisting of the violinists Mark Konratieff and William Faldner, violist Anton Beck, and cellist Sam Sciacchastano.

The end of the year found Wright and the Fellowship deeply involved in the design and publication of an entire issue of the periodical *Architectural Forum* as well as assisting the magazines *Time, Life,* and *Coronet* on major articles regarding Wright's survival and strong reemergence as America's preeminent architectural figurehead. With the majority of work completed, Wright left Wisconsin (under direct doctor's orders as a precautionary measure to avoid a second bout of pneumonia) for Arizona on Christmas Eve. Soon thereafter in the early months of 1938 the Fellowship would join him there and begin building their "permanent" desert camp outside of Phoenix.

AT TALIESIN

January 8, 1937

If I had ever seen a man and had to construct him from what I see of his home: according to that, this would be his description: height six and a half to 7 feet, normally. He gets much taller in crowds or large rooms and often shrinks when moving fast but seldom is at any time smaller than 6 feet. His skin is a white enamel, arms and ears probably green, finish very easy to keep clean if properly washed three times a day. His hair is parted right in the middle and curls in swirling brackets over his brow. He has many eyes making necessary windows of different sizes and various heights from the floor. The arms are hinged fairly low on his body. He can take off his feet out doors and walk inside on an inner sole that gives him equal comfort whether he is walking on marble, oak, flax, or plush.

This is what I have deduced concerning his character as a matter of course: he hates everything new and dreads any change. He would like to be continually reminded favorably of himself in everything about him. He feels safest and happiest when he is confined by his house, when he has the feeling of being shut in. Balance is his favorite occupation in the arrangements of his life as of his house. He is relieved to know that if an effect is achieved on the right side that the same effect can be duplicated on the other side. The fact that any object whatever appears to be as and what it is this man finds very crude indeed especially if the object be anything invented since George III or, with some men, since Louis XIV. Other yearns and prejudices have been formed in him by the type of magnificence in which European royalty once lived. All the different parts that go to make up this — probable man's day — must be carried on in special, separated, small rooms. It is as though his purpose would become befuddled — were he to have the apparatus for more than one part of his day ahead of him at any one time. He is so inconsistent that he will get other men if possible to do the work required to keep him alive while he will make up ways of doing much harder and unnecessary work to call it play.

So, this man's house fails to be a place in which to grow and live. Most of all he seems to think that if a building is built of unusual or costly material and has the latest equipment and the new gadgets tucked in somewhere that his is a home as good as the best architect could give him — it is not. Clothes will not make a man any more as man but they will fool a lot of people. A form that was good for yesterday is not good enough for today and tomorrow. Every man knows it is yesterday — not today or tomorrow — but this evident truth is so simple that it is not given a proper place. Any building that will be in the scale of a man as he actually is: that will let him move over the floors with freedom, that will make something alive and beautiful out of the necessities of his own life is the home that he does not seem to want today.

JAMES MacTHOMSON

Koenigswalzer (*The Royal Waltz*) will be shown at the Taliesin Playhouse on Sunday at 3 P.M. It is a light-hearted romantic picture starring the noted actor Willy Forst and has all the charm and delightful music of the Viennese film.

AT TALIESIN
January 22, 1937

[Edgar Kaufmann, Jr., joined the Fellowship late September 1934, the occurrence of which set into motion a chain of associated events that resulted in the creation of "Fallingwater"—the world's most-recognized residence and perhaps even catapulted Wright back into the business of architecture. The weekend retreat for Edgar's parents in Bear Run, Pennsylvania, is one of Wright's master strokes. The Kaufmann House was being designed mentally by Wright since first visiting the site of the waterfall in mid-December 1934. Its actual birth onto paper occurred with a quick, well-documented effort in September 1935. Construction began the following summer with the Kaufmann's moving into the house during the fall of 1937. The construction process was supervised by several Fellowship apprentices (Abrom Dombar, Robert Mosher, and Edgar Tafel) but mostly by Robert Mosher, the contributor of this column.]

In Bear Run—a picturesque wooded ravine in the Allegheny Mountains of southern Pennsylvania is our newest house built for Edgar J. Kaufmann, merchant prince of Pittsburgh.

The site for the house, overhanging a waterfall in the mountain stream cutting through heavily rhododendroned hills, was chosen by its architect because Mr. Kaufmann wanted to make the most of this charming retreat, 70 miles from the city and where he had been coming for recreation many years past.

The surveyor's plot-plan of this site as it came to the architect's hand showed trees, rocks, boulders jutting out from a rock out-crop or cliff which formed the bank of the stream at this point. The stream had carved out a glen and, dropping over rock ledges, fell in waterfalls to deeper glens as it flowed along. There wasn't much room to build a house as a house usually gets built on a flat piece of ground. This one had to grow up clinging to boulders, making room for trees, letting big boulders into its floor and walls in order to exist at all in this rugged maze.

So the house has grown, as something in nature, a series of low cantilevered concrete shelves projecting out from the cliff-bank and projecting far out over the waterfall itself. Each cantilevered shelf formed a floor which is a livable story with balconies, terraces and arbors. There are three such stories, each story receding back into the rock cliff and each in itself becoming a flat stone-paved terrace. The hard varicolored rock, quarried nearby, laid horizontally in the walls as at Taliesin, formed the walls and piers carrying the concrete slabs and rising through them as tall chimney mass and piers. The length of the house parallel to the stream and the rock cliff makes the main elevation a series of long wide horizontal bands of concrete that appear as balconies. The effect is that each story is clear and open to the exterior, the interiors protected only by the floor slab above and by the continuous glass steel-framed enclosing screens between parapet and ceiling slab.

The living room on the first shelf-level and 12-feet directly above the water is a great open room, walled at the back by exposed stonework and with three sides glassed in giving panoramic views of the glen itself.

This living room space is clear from the back wall of natural rock to the edge of the parapets whose outer lines nearly reach the far bank of the stream.

The top surface of one of the large boulders has been left showing in the floor to be the natural hearth of the great stone fireplace. The fireplace is large enough to walk into, deep in the whole structure. At a point where the living room shelf is directly above mid-stream a glass hatchway opens in the floor directly to a wide stairway descending to the water and to swimming. On each side of every room glass doors give access to terraces. Under the rail of the lower terrace or balcony or "story" the stream drops 30 feet to the ravine below.

The bedrooms above, also closed on the side toward the rock bank, are open, as is the big room, to an upper, the third, roof terrace, as the third-floor, (the third-floor level) rises to the level of the shouldering cliff behind it and an enclosed gallery connects this topmost floor, or enclosed terrace, with the ground level to the rear, and above the outcropping cliff.

To the layman the Kaufmann House must be something strange, because it does not resemble any other kind of house, but like the boulders, streams and trees, the logic behind its conception is its reason for being. The function of the requirements for living that presented themselves to the architect's mind and the carrying out of these conditions to a logical conclusion in masonry, glass and steel is all the basis it has for its form. The site predetermined the form of the whole, the unusual beauty of the site suggested a definite blending with native materials in the form of a dwelling. The use of concrete as of the rock — natural use — as cantilever rises above cantilever enables a sense of openness to characterize the whole and incorporating the beauty of the site into every part of the enclosed space to be lived in and that, in this case, will be called the Kaufmann House.

ROBERT K. MOSHER

On Sunday at 3 P.M., Taliesin again presents what it pictures to be one of the greatest film dramas ever to be made: *Thunderstorm.* The film was made in the Soviet from the famous play by Ostrovsky. We have considered the showing of this picture one of the outstanding events at the Playhouse since its opening and are bringing it back for that reason. Coffee and cakes will be served by the fireside.

AT TALIESIN
January 29, 1937

[The Usonian Hanna House represents a radical departure from the square and rectangular modular grids more commonly used by Wright to-date. In their book, *Frank Lloyd Wright's Hanna House: The Clients' Report,* the Hannas recalled a statement made by Wright in their first meeting ("as fans") in 1931, "his (Wright's) hope someday to abandon box-like, right angle corners and to design and build with the more flexible hexagonal forms of the bee's honeycomb." In June 1935 they approached Wright again, but as clients. In January 1937, at the time that this column was printed, construction had just begun on what was to become another famous (and successful) experiment and architectural milestone of Wright's career. The Hannas moved in eleven months later. Undoubtedly, the contributor of this column, John Howe (Wright's "best hand"), had a great deal of involvement with the development of the design and construction drawings of this house.]

God alone knows why the bees make up their honeycomb on the hexagon, but we do know why the Dr. Hanna House, Leland Stanford University at Palo Alto, is built by Mr. Wright on the hexagonal unit and why any house might well be built on that same hexagonal unit. Anyone can see that to use the hexagon (rather than the right angle or any other angle) in a building would eliminate sharp corners and therefore make for an ease of movement and a spaciousness utterly impossible to achieve with even the most advanced plans of today (or any day) and how much more humane the elimination of sharp angles would be. Here seems to be the culmination of all we strive for in modern architecture (organic architecture). The use of the hexagonal unit gives a new and greater sense of enclosed space (really now not enclosed, since there are only screens instead of walls, and this is a fact, in the Hanna House) also a greater sense of growth: here is a definite step toward real prefabrication, a fabrication which will make the so-called prefabricated house of today, which now comes in two varieties: the little colonial hot box and the little modernistic refrigerator cars, look like the work of a William Morris handicraft society.

The Hanna House is primarily: a concrete mat, laid out with the hexagonal units jointed in the mat with a large brick chimney centrally located, from which gently sloping redwood and copper roofs extend outward, supported at the ends by only those sash (all fenestration is from floor to ceiling) which are fixed and, due to their being set at the 120 degree angle to each other, assume the rigidity of a heavy wall. The kitchen-laundry, now called the laboratory, and the bathrooms extend up through the roof alongside the large chimney, receiving top light and ventilation.

The main object in the construction of Dr. Hanna's house may be said to be the use of the lightest possible rigid wood construction. The whole house may be practically thrown open to the outdoors by pushing aside large screens of the fenestration. The interior is as one room with the sleeping quarters and a sanctum (study) screened off by lightweight redwood board screens, no walls as you now know them. On one side of the house is a large private garden screened in by a four-foot redwood fence. The underside of the roofs are finished with a synthetic ceiling board.

This house will contain (could contain) none of mother's furniture, not even Louis the 14th's. Here the furniture is part of the architecture (and this doesn't mean by any means that all the furniture is "built in" or that it assumes the proportions and weight of a grand piano) but merely that it is digested into the house, becoming a part of it in every sense, the furnishing also following the honeycomb pattern, thus eliminating all sharp corners in the furniture also.

I doubt if anyone of the 10 or so people who read this article will be able to look around the living room, or wherever one sits to read the paper, without feeling how much his surroundings suffer from "indigestion." Of course he may and will comfort himself by saying: "It's comfortable." But he will see also, sooner or later, that we have him there—the Palo Alto Hanna House when finished will not only be the most beautiful house yet, but also the most comfortable: this apprentice is sure of that.

JACK HOWE

On Sunday at 3 P.M. Taliesin presents *We Are From Kronstadt:* a notable addition to the magnificent series of Soviet revolutionary films. Superbly staged and photographed and brilliantly acted, it is not so tautly dramatic as *Potemkin* or *Chapayev,* but it has an irresistible sweep and power that makes it one of the cinema's first-rank achievements.

AT TALIESIN
February 6, 1937

[Three days prior to the printing of this column, Frank Lloyd Wright wrote to John Lautner, the contributor of the following column and apprentice supervisor of the construction of "Deertrack" (Roberts House) in Marquette, Michigan: "Have you found anyone to finish the house? I would like to know in detail what is happening up there. There is much to do down here, you know." John Lautner's association with the Roberts' opus began officially, but indirectly, when he married the then future client's daughter, Marybud, on January 1, 1934. The plans for Roberts House were begun in 1935 with construction beginning the following year.]

The Roberts House at Deertrack, near Marquette, Mich., is nearly finished. Like all of Mr. Wright's houses, it is not a type house, nor a style house, but is an individual house in the country: designed and built for one woman with two servants. There is no house in the world anything like it.

It is not expensive house. The primary aim has not been to see how cheaply the house could be built — but to see what a beautiful living condition could be made for the individual on this particular site. Of course keeping the cost down is a factor continually considered by the architect.

The Roberts House projects itself out of a sand hill, looking over other low hills crowned with cedars to Lake Superior beyond. The house itself is literally looking toward the lake because the living room roof and ceiling pitches up like one's eyelash under a visor to the sky leaving nothing but glass between you and the view — lifts upward and outward toward the sun and sky. At night you see the moon and stars instead of the walls of the room. Or another building. In the morning the sun comes all the way to the heart of the house into wake you. There is a broad terrace protected from the north and east wind where you may conveniently have breakfast outdoors early in the spring before the snow has completely disappeared elsewhere.

The plan is made so that Mrs. Roberts may leave the house — close her quarters and leave a caretaker living in two rooms and the kitchen.

The house is built of brick, plaster and glass. Brick walls, brick inside and out; plaster walls, plaster inside and out.

The house unfolds out of the hills into a rhythmic, light, free space for living. It is on three floor levels, following the natural topography. The ground around has been undisturbed.

No grading or fussy planting to ruin what the wind, sun and rain has formed.

It is organic architecture, growing and living. Not existing in spite of, but because of, a beautiful circumstance to live with a joy giving atmosphere that would enrich anyone's life.

Rhythm is exhilarating — so with organic architecture, where living is concerned.

JOHN LAUTNER

On Sunday at 3 P.M. we are showing *Frasquita,* a new operetta from Vienna — produced with the outstanding talents in the Austrian capital. The music is by Franz Lehár, composer of *The Merry Widow,* sung by Jarmilla Novotna of the Prague Wiener Saengerknaben; orchestra, the Vienna Philharmonic.

AT TALIESIN
February 12, 1937

[In September 1935 Frank Lloyd Wright traveled to the Dakota Badlands, Black Hills, and Spearfish Canyon. In a three-part "At Taliesin" column Wright reprinted a letter, dated September 28, 1935, that he wrote from Spring Green to his trip's host, Robert D. Lusk, the managing editor of the *Evening Huronite* ("The Newspaper for Central South Dakota"). It was obvious from the letter that Wright was very much impressed with the raw beauty of the Dakotas. He left the Dakotas and ended his letter with the final thought regarding this "southwestern treasure house": "I hope the noble inheritance — for that is what it is — won't be exploited and spoiled . . . Nature needs from man not imitation, but interpretation. It is quite another story — as you may learn." The purpose of the visit was to tour Lake Sylvan and discuss a commission (with supporters South Dakota Senator Peter Norbeck and Lusk) to rebuild the recently burned Sylvan Lake Hotel (Wright again in his letter to Lusk, "There was a 'hotel' there once but nature disposed of it in her inscrutable way—for cause"). Unfortunately, the commission could be Wright's only if he prepared "preliminary competitive sketches." In a letter to Wright, dated October 20, 1935, Lusk stated: "Were these latter people to be shown a preliminary drawing of the type of hotel you would build at Sylvan—the conception which you had when you stood on the crags back of the present hotel—I cannot imagine any other result than that they would appreciate the difference between the run-of-the-mine architect and a Frank Lloyd Wright." Evidently, Wright had contemplated verbally on the scheme as "a building to bridge the gap between too large rocks" (letter to George and Helen Beal from William "Beye" Fyfe, dated November 25, 1935). Wright objected to such an arrangement to obtain the opportunity and the commission fell through. However, in the following year Wright did design for Robert Lusk what is thought of as one of the first Usonian homes, which was to have been located in Huron, South Dakota. It too remained an unbuilt project but became, in various modified forms, the genus for the rectangular Usonian House genre. The constructed Jacobs House of 1937 has many similar characteristics to the Lusk design.]

Out of massive cliffs of granite are being chiseled the faces of our nation's strongest: Washington, Jefferson, and Lincoln. Stone, magnificently and impressively formed according to natural law, being softened to the semblance of human flesh. The process robs stone of the very quality that made these men or any men great—the natural outward expression of the strength of innate forces working within. Stone born of fire is formed by the interplay of water, air, earth and more stone while man born imprisoned with inherent senses of right and wrong and a sense of the beautiful, therefore, strives to free himself by carrying into effect these inner human desires and dreams. The sculptured stone is an attempt to express the divine in these men while destroying the expression of the touch of the divine that nature gave the stone.

A seeming artist's indiscretion so it seems to me: but thousands hail this gigantic feat, for such it is, as great and wonderful, which it is.

Even beautiful, which it is not. All this they will feel while the thoughts uppermost and most prevailing will be concerned with the largeness of scale, the tremendous courage of the undertaking, the vast sums spent and the originality of the idea. A few will revolt at the double killing of man and stone.

Underlying all expressions of nature is the existence of this integrity of the inward and the outward. Such individual manifestations as the unscarred Black Hills and the Bad Lands of South Dakota inspire by revealing the unlimited forms evolving from working principles and at the same time also teach us the limitations of materials.

This for preamble to the design of a house for Mr. and Mrs. Robert Lusk of Huron, S.D., because the house is the opposite, related fundamentally to the needs of the client, entirely in the nature of brick, wood, glass, or which materials it is to be built. It will stand as a thing of beauty in its own right, imitating no building or style of building nor is it a forced attempt at assimilation. An individual expression must stand or fall according to its relationship to natural-ness of use, soundness of construction and inherent beauty of form not derived from superficial means by the copy of some known style.

The L-shaped plan and the wooden fence close in the rectangular corner lot. The enclosed space is to be garden so intimate and natural as to really become part of the living room which comes out into it by means of a concrete mat floor extending out in the form of a terrace. The garden may be said to come into the large floor to ceiling glass doors. Several brick masses (so natural to the material) rise up out of the ground serving as walls, fireplaces, ventilator ducts and chimneys. Binding these masses together are horizontal bands of wood (in the structural form known as board and batten) and glass with its delicate mullions webs itself between brick and wood, now in horizontal bands at eye level and then from floor to ceiling and again up against the sky to be opened for ventilation in the hot summer nights of this South Dakota region.

All spaces—living, study, dining, and sleeping have advantage of this scheme by breaking the otherwise flat roof up into a sawtooth to allow for the band of window ventilators over the rooms.

Within, furniture, rugs and hangings are designed to harmoniously contrast with brick and wood, which have come inside, blend to make the interior a quiet and charming whole. A place to live in, be it house work, quiet study, joyous play and fun, music and games, or rest. At one with the flowers and garden, complete in itself and yet embodying what the world has to offer in the way of materials and conveniences, suited to the best advantage, needs and desires of a particular family.

The art of architecture. The art of sculpture might take heed and do likewise.

BURTON J. GOODRICH

On Sunday, at 3 P.M. Taliesin presents at the Playhouse the Swedish film comedy: *Kvinnora Kring Larson* (*The Women Around Larson*). This promises to be delightful entertainment for Valentine afternoon, featuring the famous film comedian, Edward Persen—Sweden's most popular actor.

AT TALIESIN

February 20, 1937

In winter the sharp lines of the horizon along the ridges of our surrounding hills disappear and in the soft light of evening the valleys merge into the hills and the hills vanish into the sky. Trees upon the hills are patterned tracery. Pods of weeds, close by, are sharp edged black spots upon the white: staccato notes in the prevailing rhythm of quiet.

Snow: sharp, keen, icy, in billowing drifts or in long horizontal ledges, brings harmony to the landscape of our Wisconsin farmland: farmland that in summer is fenced in and fenced up and out by farm after farm of farmers who have worked out countless ingenious ways to characterize their acres of land. The boxed-in boxes of farmhouses, styes, coops, pens scattered about, hit and miss, over the countryside mar the land's native beauty.

We view—in winter—Wisconsin's hills as we saw the Arizona desert stretching off toward distant mountains: untouched, whole, clean.

What man could not do to the Arizona desert because of nature's protection, the winter snow has buried in Wisconsin.

As the hot desert sun decorates simplicity by sending color into the myriad lichens upon the patterned rock faces of the desert floor, so our winter sun flashes light and fire into the ice-jeweled thistles showing above the frosted earth in our own valleys.

And as the saguaro-cactus stands in heroic silhouette against the sunny southern sky, the ice clad Wisconsin trees crackle and shimmer: miraculous against the cobalt above.

What we went in search for to Arizona we have here around us: this harmonious union of natural things. A union here made supreme and impervious to harm by ice and snow: white and blue — silver and black. Again contrast and accentuation — in the distance a red spot — the Wisconsin barn.

EUGENE MASSELINK

On Sunday at 3 P.M. the French film *Crainquebille* will be shown. This film is based on Anatole France's story. A satire of the judiciary. Featuring Tramel and an excellent cast. There are unusual marionette sequences by Starevitch. "Powerful" — the *New York Sun.* "Remarkably well photographed and directed" — the *New York Times.*

AT TALIESIN
March 5, 1937

[Of the commissions that found the way to Taliesin during the "At Taliesin" years, the Johnson Wax building in Racine, Wisconsin, was unquestionably a major creation by a major genius. This column, William Wesley Peters' only known contribution, compares an earlier, equally significant work (the Larkin administration building, Buffalo, New York, 1903, still existent at the time of this column) to the more recent Johnson Wax design. The design opportunity came to Wright in the summer of 1936 with construction beginning later in the fall. Exterior walls were well under way at the time that this column was printed and only months prior to the now famous testing of the structural "petal" column design on June 5, 1937. The building was completed and opened almost two years later, in April 1939. Peters was closely involved in the project from inception through completion.]

In Buffalo in the third year of our century there stood completed a building so significant and so phenomenal that the world has yet only partly sensed the full implication of its existence. A building stark and affirmative, dedicated to the proposition that man may be master of his machines — of his environment. Strong noble master.

The Larkin building: a great sealed brick and glass enclosure. Its interior space the working quarters of the Larkin administration. The first air conditioned building; probably the first really fireproof one. The first building to provide for business as it should be: a relationship of human beings to human beings, individuals united preforming human tasks in a human manner. Towards this end the building was a great light room, so arranged so as to facilitate the various operations of its inhabitants and so equipped as to provide from within itself complete mechanical and functionary aids to these operations. The exterior is stern, even severe; but the building excluded by its very demeanor the industrial atmosphere of soot and grime from the vast work space within. Health, space, dignity: important physical requisites for joy in work. All these in the year 1903. The ornamentality of the period was rejected.

Today there is building in Racine another great office enclosure: a lineal descendant of the one which still houses the Larkin Co. at Buffalo. Built by the same architect 34 years apart, the two invite — compel — comparison.

The new home of the Johnson Wax Co. is rising slowly from its site, the walls nearly ready to take form, the footings, foundations and piers already a hint of what is to come. The sense of the great room as a general work space, secluded, the integrated development of all the features as parts of the whole, the inevitable "feel" of the existence of man in touch with his nature, these are characteristics which will indicate the familyship of the Johnson and the Larkin buildings.

As a positive statement the Johnson building will never surpass the Larking building. As a positive statement the Larkin building probably will never be surpassed. Does one noble tree surpass another? But the two represent wonderful growth and development. The Larkin building is primitive — primitive in its directness and straightforward strength: primitive in the sense of the radical — the "root," the stem, the spring whence starts the river. The Johnson building is civilization, civilization with all the beautiful significance that the word could—should—have. Refinement not disintegration. No less strong for all its grace.

Entrance to the Johnson building will be from the rear: the city street with its noises will be withheld from the interior workroom. A wide driveway, passing under a broad terrace—shelter above and lying between the main building and the covered carport will give access to the wide band of doors: the reserved entrance: the grand approach to the building—not from the streets but from its own ground. With dignity and calm these workers may enter their place of labor, enter the high lobby with the sight of the great room beyond.

In the Larking building we saw a high room, great rectilinear piers rising floor after floor, past working areas in balconies along the sides, finally ascending to the roof and skylights above. All strong, solid, direct, vertical.

Here the Johnson building. How different! The great room yet: but broad, horizontally spacious! Tall, slender columns, delicately tapering down to stand on bronze feet below, these shafts rise to flow out into a wide spreading "petal" or capital and merge with the ceiling slab. The slab itself is inter-pierced with light between the petals. And so throughout. The columns form the unit of construction, the vertical supports and the horizontal surface. The exterior walls exist in most places as brick and concrete screens, screens that insulate the interior from sound and cold, screens that admit light by means of continuous bands of glass held crystalline and bending up and back where wall meets roof so that the screens seem to float in air. The whole, again as in the Larking building, is a fireproof, extremely highly insulated, enclosure—a structure of great tenuous strength by way of its continuity: the concrete cores, the concrete slabs, welding the whole into structural unity. From the small private theater on the mezzanine floor to the garage and car port in the rear the building is essentially a brick-and-cork-protected monolith slashed by narrow rifts of sparkling glass that are continuous about the building: all subject to variations of form and shape in keeping with the varying conditions of use that occur within. Divisions of interior space where necessary are generally accomplished by means of light screens or glass partitions, imperma nent with regard to location and not serving to destroy the oneness of the whole.

Lighting, heating, the mechanical service, as in all of Mr. Wright's buildings are conceived as part of the building itself: they are functioning as conditions rather than as fixtures or gadgets. The heating, of especial interest, is performed by the floor of the large room. The floor itself is to be a low temperature radiant heating panel. Through the use of this principle the inhabitants of the building will be kept comfortable warm though the actual air temperature may be 15 degrees lower than that in building warmed in the customary manner. In addition to this phase, there is the whole air conditioning system. Fresh air inhaled by "nostrils" at the top where fresh—is prepared as to temperature, humidity, cleanliness, led by means of a simple but wonderfully contrived system of air passages in the structure itself through the various portions of the building and finally exhaled again to the outside.

Wonderful experience it is to see a great building like this grow. A building where once again after years of virtual disuse all the varying crafts known to man are called upon to really exert themselves in order to preserve a vast simplicity. Once again the master-builder is in control. Once again the various craftsmen look to him for direction in the weaving of a great fabric. No case here of "architect" decorating for the engineer.

Enough. Impossible to describe the infinite ramifications of simplicity inherent in this design. The significant fact in regard to the linking of the Larkin and Johnson buildings is this:

Were there but the one we should have a remarkable building. With the two we have a "line"—a flowering of the one from the root of the other—the essential linking with the past, the prophesy of the future that is inherent in natural growth.

WILLIAM WESLEY PETERS

Son of Mongolia, a recent film from the Soviet, will be shown at the Playhouse on Sunday. A film packed full of fascinating and informing novelties.

AT TALIESIN
March 12, 1937

This winter's Fellowship articles, so far, have been devoted to some of the new buildings being designed at Taliesin for people interested in organic houses. Let us turn this time to the surroundings in which these designs were made. Descriptions of Taliesin are familiar to most of our readers but for those who have not actually seen our workshop-studio-home I will describe it briefly.

Taliesin is as natural a crown for the hill it tops as the outcropping rock masses and trees are for the other hills around. Like the rocks, its native limestone ledge walls have their feet deep in the heart of the hill and its chimney wall and garden enclosures likewise fit themselves to the shape of the hill. Like the trees, gently sloping shingle roofs top the stone, meet it, or parting let chimneys and walls pass through above. Taliesin has broad overhanging roofs that shelter the walls and reaching out an arm here and there provide for stone paved terraces. Like the trees Taliesin is always changing, growing, suiting itself to the seasons. Because it grows naturally it is always beautiful. The new parts are related to the old. There is no unnatural grafting of alien branches to the native trunk.

Last summer saw quite a bit of this seasonal growth. Shortly after our return from Arizona it was decided that our kitchen was inconvenient and outmoded so that part of the house was soon suffering growing pains and in a few weeks emerged as a new top lighted laundry, a new heat room, pantry, a top lighted bathroom, and the kitchen completely redone. No new space was added but all this was reclaimed from the old kitchen, some vestigial hallways, storage room, and a rather inadequate bathroom. Taliesin had grown to meet new demands made on it by now conditions.

Next the opposite end of the house was found to be unsatisfactory in some ways. This wing which is passed first by the entrance drive had always turned its back on the approach but now sprouted a new branch to meet all arrivals. It took the form of a cantilever terrace high in the air commanding a magnificent view of the valley and provides outdoor sunny living space as complement to a sunny new bedroom, also developed from an old one, for Mr. Wright.

During the summer another one of the tower rooms for apprentices was enlarged and additional windows and ventilation was added. Space under the central wing which had been a storage room adjacent to the middle court yard was turned into a winter shop and much needed shower room.

Usually a tree stops growing during the winter and this is true of Taliesin too but the last two months have seen the studio equipment rearranged more suitably and some valuable new drawing file cases are being added to supplement the bulging old ones. Too much time was lost in searching for drawings.

Of immediate interest, too, is the remodeling of all heating systems at Taliesin just now being completed while the one in our theater was finished last week ensuring more than adequate heat there and at Taliesin for the rest of the winter season certainly—but more important, for the beginning of the next.

And so it goes—while one part of the day is spent on drawings for some new home for others, other hours will see us at work continuously bettering our own home.

NOVERRE MUSSON

On Sunday at 3 P.M., we are showing several extremely interesting films. Of especial interest is a cinematographical study by a young Dutchman, Joris Iveng called *Rain*. It is a record of nothing but a shower coming up and passing over and the sun showing again, and really beautiful. Refreshing as a bit of spring, it shows that from the beginning Iveng possesses that singular gift of seeming to get inside what he was photographing before he presents the outside of it. With this film will also be shown the famous short subject of the fight between the mongoose and the cobra: *Killing the Killer.* Also: Disney's *Mickey's Grand Opera*.

AT TALIESIN

March 19, 1937

The assertion concerning mural painting maintained by American lay people and regionalistic artists alike today that every available wall

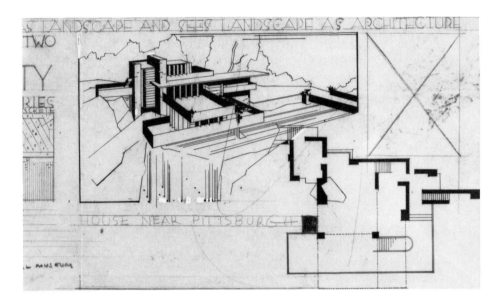

"So the house has grown, as something in nature" (Robert Mosher, "At Taliesin," January 22, 1937). *"Fallingwater,"* 1935 (preliminary graphic plan and perspective layout done for the unexecuted "Taliesin," vol. 1, no. 2, Broadacre City). Drawing courtesy of the Frank Lloyd Wright Foundation.

"God alone knows why the bees make up their honeycomb on the hexagon" (John Howe, "At Taliesin," January 29, 1937). *Hanna House,* 1936. Drawing courtesy of the Frank Lloyd Wright Foundation.

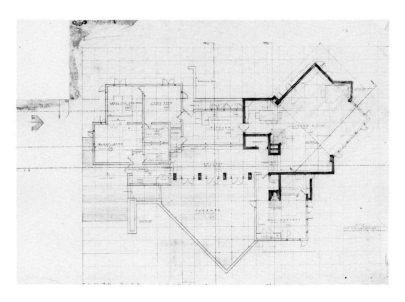

"The Roberts House. . . . it is not a type house, nor a style house, but is an individual house" (John Lautner, "At Taliesin," February 6, 1937). *"Deertrack," Roberts House,* 1936. Drawing courtesy of the Frank Lloyd Wright Foundation.

"It will stand as a thing of beauty in its own right, imitating no building or style of building" (Burton J. Goodrich, "At Taliesin," February 12, 1937). *Lusk House,* 1936. Drawing courtesy of the Frank Lloyd Wright Foundation.

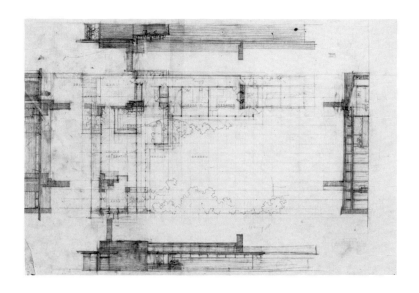

"Snow: sharp, keen, icy, in billowing drifts or in long horizontal ledges, bring harmony to the landscape" (Eugene Masselink, "At Taliesin," February 20, 1937). *Taliesin Hilltower Wing* (photo ca. 1930s). Photo courtesy of the Frank Lloyd Wright Foundation.

Apprentice William Wesley Peters, Frank Lloyd Wright and Herbert Johnson at Johnson Wax Construction Site (photo ca. June 1937). Photo courtesy of SC Johnson Wax.

"But now I must return to my model making—to craftsmanship—to cut clean straight lines and keep flat planes true to surface" (Burton J. Goodrich, "At Taliesin," July 19, 1935). *Apprentices Working on Models, Fellowship Living Room at Hillside* (photo ca. 1936; Hans Koch working on repairing model *in foreground;* Gene Masselink *on knees* constructing model of "Wingspread"). Photo courtesy of John H. Howe, Architect.

"Man and Machine Struck in the Mud" (John Lautner, "At Taliesin," April 16, 1937; photo ca. 1930s; Frank Lloyd Wright with apprentices pushing). Photo courtesy of the Frank Lloyd Wright Foundation.

"I was so taken with the little goat" (Svetlanna Wright Peters, "At Taliesin," May 21, 1937). *"Bittersweet" with Iovanna* (ca. late 1930s). Photo courtesy of the Frank Lloyd Wright Foundation.

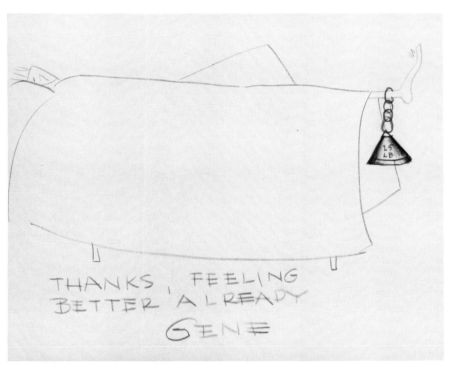

"They've been pulling my leg with a 25-pound weight and encased the broken part of me" (Eugene Masselink, "At Taliesin," June 11, 1937). *Self-drawn Caricature* (sent to past apprentices "George and Helen Beeeeeeeal," postmarked May 21, 1937). Drawing courtesy of the Kenneth Spencer Research Library, University of Kansas, "Taliesin Collection."

Taliesin String Quartet at Taliesin Playhouse (photo ca. late summer 1937; note Frank Lloyd Wright in shadows seated at piano.) Photo courtesy of the Frank Lloyd Wright Foundation.

"Our principal workroom—an abstract forest in oak timber" (At Taliesin, September 5, 1937). *Fellowship Drafting Room at Hillside, 1932.* Drawing courtesy of the Frank Lloyd Wright Foundation.

"The preparation of this issue was placed in the hands of Mr. Wright, and he and the Fellowship has prepared both format and contents" (William Cheaney, "At Taliesin," December 10, 1937). *Architectural Forum,* January 1938 (inside front cover; graphic representation of Johnson Wax administration building).

space in every American building is likely object for the regionalistic's idealistic, realistic, or modernistic conception of his own region — be it the southeast corner of Maine or the middle township of Wyoming — or the historians idea of an eventful past — be it the adventures of Daniel Boone or the escapades of Little Eva — this assertion has no place in the studied creative plan of the organic architect or in the mind of the painter trained in organic architecture.

In organic architecture, walls as walls have ceased to exist. Fenestration coming into its own more and more has done away with the old idea of a wall as an enclosing imprisoning feature in building. Wall surfaces — the muralist's meadow — bewindowed, bedecked, bepainted and paneled and papered is no longer the life-size canvas at the mercy of every aspiring vagabonding artist.

Wall planes in a room emphasize the roof and floor surfaces. By painting one or two walls one color and allowing the other walls to flow into the ceiling color a plastic effect is gained in a general harmonious unsymmetrical arrangement of the room.

Or when decoration, is conceived and executed architecturally — exactly as much a part of the architecture of the room and building as the structure itself is. Perhaps a plywood or glass mural: or painted in plaster, wooden strips heightening the brilliant abstract pattern. Always a related part to the organic whole.

Why not small moveable plywood screens in color and various designs to be placed about the room and moved in or out? Decoration would then become the alive thing it should be in our lives and not a static history upon our walls.

Easel painting has no more place as spots upon wall surfaces, kept in portfolios, pictures may be placed on exhibition easels from time to time in varying procession of interesting color and form — or put away and forgotten entirely.

Giotto, Cimabue, painted with architectural intelligence and retained the essential flat surface of the wall plane.

Those who followed up through the present day have invariably destroyed this flat plane. Nervous jittery history book stories writhe upon the walls of our buildings and the walls cease to be walls at all and become mere camouflage.

For those who would advertise history — give them the billboards that line our roadsides where advertising does its best work.

Leave American buildings at least the plain surfaces of what walls they have as a possible stimulation for some creative action in the future. Or against the time when freedom from the imprisoning wall will be characteristic of building in America by way of organic architecture.

EUGENE MASSELINK

[Unquestionably, Eugene Masselink's interest in art, painting, and graphic design flowered at Taliesin under the inspiration and tutelage of Frank Lloyd Wright and the Fellowship. In a letter dated March 12, 1933, to Karl Jensen (Mr. Wright's secretary before Masselink) prior to his entering the Fellowship, Masselink wrote, "More and more I have been feeling the need of some more significant expression in paint, something more than the futile, meagre and essentially egotistic so-called easel painting." Masselink came into the Fellowship as "a student of paint." However, he quickly grasped and excelled in the art of two-dimensional abstraction, based on nature, geometry, music, architecture, etc. In an earlier "At Taliesin" column (April 30, 1934) Masselink stated, "Association with the architectural life at Taliesin, however, does not bring disillusionment but enlightenment to a far greater art realization."]

On Sunday at 3 p.m. we will present *Picadilly Jim,* the American comedy starring Robert Montgomery.

AT TALIESIN

March 26, 1937

[The now-famous Usonian Jacobs House, designed in the late summer/early fall of 1936 with construction commencing two months after the following column appeared, was Wright's answer to the small-house problem in America. Its construction price of $5,000 (with the architect's fee taken out) was well publicized.]

Architecture begins and ends with the small house!

The first requirement of man included shelter—a roof overhead, warmth and rest from the days of toil. Amazing it is that after thousands of years of "progress," the cry for housing prevails throughout the land and most other lands too. Not enough homes, not good enough homes, not cheap enough homes for the families of the world.

When winter's frosty grip loosens its hold on Westmoreland slopes, Taliesin will plant a significant experiment on Madison soil. Wood board, common brick and glass, materials familiar to everyone, are combined to form one simple answer to the undying cry for fine, minimum houses.

New and unheard of materials are not necessary to solve the old small house problem. Many are the prefabricated house companies that can testify to that. This is not a betrayal of machine age architecture. It is a radical start where modern architecture can win or lose.

On the concrete floor mat of the Jacobs House in Madison there is apparent an idea that has been slowly growing for many years. It is the house itself—an idea of room planning, an idea of construction, an idea for family growth, and most important, an idea that combines these ideas into one. With the idea as a start and all the materials in existence as the means, the sky cannot define the extent and variety to which architecture can develop. Without the idea all the materials might just as well assemble themselves without the architect.

"Those who cannot tell the littleness of great things in themselves are apt to overlook the greatness of little things in others."

Simplicity has the quality of seeming effortless and undeliberate. So the Jacobs House will at first appear to be nothing to write home about. No chromium-plated gadgets or flashy sales points, no buttons beside an easy chair by which you preform all the duties of the day. But rather, a direct answer that makes one wonder why it has never appeared before. Just too simple, I suppose. Even the contractor discovers more each week—that walls occur in specific places for as good a reason as no walls occur in other places. He recognizes the fact that this little house has had considerable thought and experimental predecessors. A great step with even greater possibilities.

With most of our time being still spent "at home," it is no wonder that while steel bridges span unheard of distances and sweeping

expanses of well designed office buildings, factories, etc. become apparent, we return to the humble little house and ask,
"What about our own homes?"

BENNIE DOMBAR

On Sunday at 3 P.M., will be shown a recent Gaumont British production: *River of Unrest,* a story of the Black and Tans during the Irish rebellion in 1922.

AT TALIESIN
April 9, 1937

In the rear studio at Taliesin on a site of ⅝" plywood four fellows are building from its cardboard foundations a model. Pins and pen knives are the tools and cardboard and glue are the materials.

A few weeks ago the plywood site was innocent of all but the unit lines which later determined the position of and size of the model. The walls were glued in place and floor slabs laid. Then came a long wait for those not working on the model — no progress was seemingly made but in that time the "super-structure" of the building was being constructed and painted ready to be set into place: a finished unit. That is how models are built at Taliesin. Unit by unit, each unit completely fabricated before it is added to its brother on the finished model.

Visitors in the model studio frequently smile knowingly when they see a fellow struggling to glue several small pieces of cardboard together: to them it is glorified paper dolls with all of its pitiful connotation. But to us the model serves a dual purpose. It provides the client with plans and elevations of his building at a glance, making it a reality that can be understood rather than a confusion of lines that may cloud the architect's superlative conception in the client's mind.

At the Fellowship the model is the analyzing ground for those who hope to perpetuate the spirit Mr. Wright has given to architecture. We build in cardboard the design created by the master that we may see why a building is inter-related and correlated as it is.

Models must be changed when the drawings are changed. This adds interest and confusion to an already interesting and confused model room. It is quite unnerving to change a basic part of a nearly finished model.

A few weeks ago nothing but plywood—today, units ready to be put into place—tomorrow, changes, perhaps, in completed units. All of this gives a model personality that only those behind it can feel.

LAWRENCE LOW

The outstanding event at the Taliesin Playhouse two years ago in December was the showing of the great foreign film that had won the international first place in Venice: *The Blue Light.*

Produced in the Italian dolomites it contained some of the most beautiful scenic photography made for the screen and woven about a beautifully fantastic tale.

As a revival we are again showing this picture for the public on Sunday: at 3 P.M. We hope our friends will not miss seeing the eventful revival.

AT TALIESIN

April 16, 1937

Man and Machine Stuck in the Mud, or Springtime

You've sunk too low—no traction—no tread—no cleats,
You're in the wrong rut, in the wrong direction, in the wrong car,
You're out of gas,
You're out of juice,
You're resting on your end,
You need to be jacked up,
You need direction,
You need traction,
You need fuel,
But that's today. You're stuck again tomorrow.

JOHN E. LAUTNER

Sunday, April 18, 3 o'clock in the afternoon—*Ziguener-Baron*, or *The Gypsy Baron*. The delightful operetta by Johann Strauss combined with the acting of an excellent cast makes the famous story of the Gypsy baron unusual entertainment. An UFA production with English titles.

Coffee and cakes will be served by the fireside. Come and enjoy a pleasant afternoon.

AT TALIESIN
April 30, 1937

Americans pride themselves on being Americans. No matter what their antecedents, French, English, German, they are now Americans and glad of it. They are proud of the streamline trains, the electric stoves, the planes and automobiles, movies, the countless machines for making anything man dreams of. Yet in their buildings Americans are neither American nor modern.

Americans are all business men. They spend their days making money, their evenings playing bridge, their weekends playing golf. Each one thinks he is "smart." He is absorbed with business deals and sure that no one can put anything over on him. Yet—look at his house. It shows him up for what he is. It proves he is neither smart nor a good business man.

All over the United States today there are new houses on exhibit, each mechanically perfect—but a modern heating system doesn't make a modern building. All the shinning equipment in the kitchen only emphasizes the pseudo-antiquity of the rest of the house. Great steps forward have been made in developing adequate machinery for the home, but the home itself has been left behind. The quaintly designed cottage kitchen was never designed to hold an electric refrigerator nor a gas stove, nor was the colonial living room ever meant to be disturbed by a radio or a radiator. Certainly the Norman dwellings never had streamlined gadgets, automobiles, bathrooms or electric lights. Combine these things, the old and new, and the result is a generous display of mongralism.

In a recent issue of women's magazine is a design for a suburban home "In the Tasmanian Tradition." Why Tasmanian or France or

Colonial England? Why not "In the American Tradition?" The answer is simple: because it isn't yet recognized. The buildings that are called American are not that, but are Tudor, Mediterranean or Colonial.

The western house is Spanish, the eastern house in English, the middle-western a confounded mixture that is nothing at all.

Too much emphasis has been laid in "styles." Americans change their houses the same way men change their hats, and women change their skins, and for no better reason than the fact that the "style" was changed. There are changing fashions in furniture and houses because the designs are not good to begin with and one is soon tired of them. A really fine piece of furniture, an old Japanese screen, a perfectly proportioned vase — these things are never tiresome, never can be replaced or copied. To create is the greatest gift of man, to imitate, the most unfortunate.

To produce a native architecture for America, there must be creative efforts. So far, there has only been effort to imitate. Bernard Shaw, speaking of adapting plays to the modern stage, said that the process was not "one of masterly amelioration, but one which must necessarily be mainly one of debasement and mutilation when the adapter is inferior to the author." Adapting houses of another age, built by people with another way of life, is most certain to result in debasement and mutilation.

America does not lack creative spirit, but does not recognize it. It knows that imitative spirit though, and accepts it. Not until America builds its own buildings each one appropriate to its place and use, each designed for a particular person or family, not until machine and house are integrated for modern use, will there ever be American architecture.

MARYBUD LAUTNER

Sunday, May 2, three o'clock in the afternoon: Taliesin announces the first program of an extremely interesting and valuable series of motion pictures collected and circulated by the Museum of Modern Art Film Library. A short survey of the films of America.

This first program is the development of the narrative: *The Execution of Queen Mary of Scots,* produced by the Edison Company, made for the peepshow or kinetoscope.

Washday Troubles—1895. Comic incidents like this were improvised from the earlier days and developed later into slapstick.

Queen Elizabeth—1911. Miss Sarah Bernhardt headed this illustrious cast and the fact that she consented to act for the movies did much to diminish prejudice against them.

AT TALIESIN
May 7, 1937

A state of war exists between organic architecture and eclecticism. Recent uprisings in the eastern states over the proposed memorial to Thomas Jefferson have been reported to result in only minor injuries to date. Skirmishes and ambushes in the west and south are continuous.

The latest important news from the front in the middle west is the invasion upon the state of Michigan last week. Organic architecture conquered the state in four strategic points: the Furniture Capital of the United States; a small cultural city; a liberal and leading architectural academy; and the center of the chemical revolution in the country. As a result of this invasion Michigan has lain down its eclectic standard and has hoisted the banners of an organic architecture. At least, this is according to the report of the official aide-de-camp who accompanied Mr. Wright on a lecture tour when he addressed five organizations in four days.

The first: an art-teachers club in Grand Rapids. An informal group in the afternoon gathered after tea to discuss culture in America. Shocked at the deplorable state of culture in the country, the teachers vainly tried to rally around the flag of their school system, only to be told that it was that very "system" that made any indigenous culture in America impossible. In the evening Mr. Wright spoke to a thousand of the citizens in the same city continuing the discussion in terms of the "new reality" in America.

The next day we advanced to Kalamazoo where the people have been generously endowed with "art" in several of their civic buildings. They filled the "civic auditorium" and responded enthusiastically to the revelation which creative thought in terms of building opened up for them, making what they had as "new" in architecture dated and only modern because "a-la-mode."

At the Cranbrook Academy of Art in Bloomfield Hills, the following evening, a hundred or two were turned away from the doors of the crowded small auditorium. Sixty came up in a bus from the university. After the lecture the students of the richly endowed Academy gathered about to discuss their work, stoutly upholding their point of view and way of working. Richly equipped with looms, with which they have furnished their halls and rooms with beautifully woven and designed tapestries and rugs; printing presses; a large library; everything you could possibly need along with a large maintenance staff and excellent guidance in architecture and the arts, there seems nothing they lack toward the development of an architecture. The argument was, that having everything to work with they have little indigenous or creative tradition and inspiration to work toward. Nevertheless notwithstanding, Taliesin and Cranbrook could benefit each other greatly. We both hope the Michigan invasions and Wisconsin visits may continue and our relationship strengthens.

After the final lecture in Midland, where the home plant of the Dow Chemical Co. is located and where Alden Dow, a former apprentice at Taliesin, is building many buildings, we returned to Taliesin: the storm center about which the battle between organic architecture and eclecticism is fought.

"Sic transit gloria mundi."

EUGENE MASSELINK

Taliesin is proud to announce the showing of the great film of 1936 *Carnival in Flanders* at its spring opening Sunday at 3 P.M.

Carnival in Flanders, or *La Kermess Heroique,* won the international film prize in Venice. It is a gay colorful comedy, a saucy and impudent farce of how the women of Flanders took the men's places and cunningly saved their town from the Spanish invaders.

The *New York Herald Tribune* says: "It will inevitably rank as one of the important classics of the motion picture."

On the special occasion there will be music and refreshments.

[Newspaper accounts of Wright's Michigan lectures of April 1937 provide interesting reading. The *Grand Rapids Herald* reported that in the Saint Cecilia Auditorium on Tuesday evening, April 27, Wright suggested that "culture is a matter of realization. Until we face the new realism of contemporary life, we will not have a culture worth the name." And on the following evening in the Kalamazoo Civic Auditorium, as reported by the *Kalamazoo Gazette,* Wright stated that "finding that success has handicapped America because it has dulled thought which produces a consciousness of sound realities." It went on to say that Wright predicted "it would take at least five generations to get over the befuddlement." On his final evening he spoke in the Dow Auditorium in Midland. The *Midland Daily News* quoted Wright as saying, "I believe three-fourths of our marriage failures are due to the utterly stupid conditions under which people live. . . . its all a mess — you all live in heaps!"]

AT TALIESIN

May 21, 1937

She was born in a stable on the coldest night of the year. Next morning when we found her, her breathing was almost imperceptible and her little ears were frozen stiff. She looked like a jack-rabbit than a little goat. I bundled her in my coat and took her up to the kitchen by the big wood range — and there we taught her to suck on a cloth, dipped in milk and finally on a bottle.

Then there was a problem of a place to sleep for her — and by that time I was so taken with the little goat, whom we named Bittersweet, that nothing seemed worthy of her, except our room. So, she had a little box by the radiator and then for a week or 10 days she did nothing but sleep — which was fine. "But, when she awoke" we found it not a joke. So soon (though not soon enough) hustled her off to the stable.

But meanwhile I had been milking the mother goat — Odi. She was quite a problem to me at first, for I couldn't make her stand still while milking. At first she put her foot in the pail, but I found a way to prevent that — then she tried making a grand dash for freedom and succeeded in pushing me off the stool. By that time I felt the only thing to do was to tie her up while milking her — she merely laid down then and nothing I could do would make her stand up. Then, by mere accident, I discovered that gentle sweet words kept her quiet at last. So now I always talk to her sweetly, calling endearing names, while she stands perfectly still. The others tried to milk her, but no one seems to please her as well as I do now. As a result I am the only one who is privileged to milk her.

We find that goat's milk tastes delicious and much sweeter than cow's milk. When I ask my friends if they'd like to taste goat's milk, they look slightly worried. I can see what they imagine as they raise the glass to their lips — goats — queer beings with those strange owl like eyes. And ever so slightly our friends pause before the glass touches their lips, and after they tasted all, without exception, exclaim it is wonderful, it tastes better than the cow's milk.

When Carl Sandburg was here he told us about his little farm and the goats he has.

We had just a couple of goats at that time. We really listened with wonder to his beautiful tales about them. He seemed to have lots of fun with those goats. And now we understand him thoroughly. We too treasure the rare, life-giving quality of the milk. We think that the cheese we make is far the best we have ever tasted.

We love to watch our goats climb the rocks, their horns silhouetted against the sky. They are so clean and neat. There is a small square window in their stable, just big enough to put their heads trough it. Sometimes, when we walk by in the twilight suddenly we see in the window frame a motionless head with transparent eyes. There comes a sensation of centuries past, of eternal Pan, of fairy tales of all nations with the same mystical image of the goat. But it quickly leaves us, for someone will say "look at Alma," or "look at Odi — does not she look snobbish?" Little Bittersweet will run out and chew at our heels. Then they become the familiar characters of our animal world.

They defend themselves beautifully against enemies' attack. Except for our poor little Charity, three days old. The Russian wolfhound, Doushan, got her. But we trained Doushan never to touch a goat as long as he lives. The other day Alma butted him so hard that it served him as initial force to jump over a six-foot wall. Our goats are safe now.

S. W. P. [Svetlanna Wright Peters]

Sunday at 3 P.M. the Playhouse will present the Swiss prize-winning screen achievement, *The Eternal Mask*. The production won high rating from the National Board of Review.

AT TALIESIN
June 11, 1937

[Sometime mid-May 1937 apprentice Eugene Masselink was running (his brother remembers him always running) between Hillside and Taliesin, caught his foot in a gopher hole, twisted his leg and broke his hip. He spent the next two months recuperating in Saint Joseph's "Sister's" Hospital in the nearby town of Dodgeville (which he wrote fondly of in a subsequent "At Taliesin" column).]

It was a fairly good hip as hips go, and as hips go this hip went. Consequently ever since (5 weeks or 5 years it seems the same) they've been pulling my leg with a 25-pound weight and encased the broken part of me in a weatherproof plaster cast. Consequently again ever since I've been practically invulnerable to further injury.

Invulnerable, that is, all except my mind which started out with some high ideals about how to pass time constructively and even creatively. It worked for a time but as the weeks and years have passed complexities have given away to simplicities. I might say just simple.

My excuse: Paths of least resistance are inevitable when one is being pulled and encased at the same time.

The greatest simplicity of all is sleep.

But easily the next greatest is the radio, my most constant companion. After this is all over and I'm selling apples on some street corner, this radio will sell apples with me. My mind has become so controlled by its direction that any sudden break from its super vision would be fatal.

The life problems of Bill and Mary and Susan and Jim of all the Tom Dick and Harrys radio story tellers can think of are my problems now. And let me say that these problems are without parallel in the history of literature. Each day fresh heartaches and new situations keep the agony of life constantly on the run and bring vicarious sorrow into the lives of Americans, incidentally make my own hip-problem only the most minor consideration for me to think of.

And then the News, Pebecco Tooth Paste, Beatrice Lillie, Granger Pipe Tobacco, Symphony Concerts periodically, Boake Carter, Alexander Woollcott, Ford, General Motors, Major Bowles, Chrysler, Ad

Infinitum, Ad Nauseam: the radio is a continuous glorious circus entanglement of the finest and the worst America can think of to hear.

It has opened the walls of this tiny room to a world many times removed and I maintain wherever I go it shall go.

It's love me, love my radio from now on.

EUGENE MASSELINK

Sunday at the Playhouse at 3 P.M. Program V: *The Talkies* is a survey of the Film in America circulated by the Museum of Modern Art Film Library, *The Jazz Singer* and *All Quiet on the Western Front* and *Steamboat Willie,* the first Mickey Mouse. Coffee and refreshments.

AT TALIESIN
July 16, 1937

Taliesin. Remarkable name for a remarkable place: America! The America which a young, freedom-loving German son of the greatest order of this country, the order of the "Sons and Daughters of Steerage" (an American society still to be organized) thought to find when he arrived on these shores years ago: democratic in the sense of a Walt Whitman, libertarian in the sense of a Henry Thoreau, philosophical in its outlook and conception of world and life in the sense of an Emerson, and all loving in the sense of that legendary poor soul who did not know where to rest his head, Jesus Christ, no doubt a son of "the Order of Steerage" — post mortem.

How long a time it takes to reach the land we set out for in youth. Thirty years! Everything here at Taliesin moves on a higher level. But it does not lose its firm hold of the earth. It is an earthbound place. Life "defacto" if we perceive it philosophically right. Life integral: in its manifoldness life as a whole.

Great comprehension of these things, it seems to me, is fundamentally underlying Taliesin in everything it stands for. The sense of the whole pushes itself distinctly through in all its activities, its teachings, works and enjoyments.

Young perspective architects plan, plow the fields, sow the harvest, work the gardens, tend and build the roads, maintain the water supply, the power plant, the heating system, tend to their own rooms, do the cooking and kitchen work, plan, tear down and build up, carpenterwork, masonry, plasterwork, design and build their furniture, arrange their programs and operate their theater and do their technical studio work—planning. There are no servants at Taliesin, seldom hired men. It is self-sufficient.

Taliesin, the integral, wherein a master communicates with deep educational insight and ability his own growth, or continuous becoming, to his apprentices.

It seems to me unthinkable that without this great conception and feeling for life as integral there could have been created by Mr. Wright his great contribution to art, his integral indigenous architecture. Nothing comes out of empty souls. They don't make even good "eclectics" any more.

I always thought a town, a county, a state must be proud of a homegrown genius and the remarkable place his creative spirit built. But we are not so far advanced yet as we like to pet ourselves, and our time, in our thoughts. For there are only the few, strewn over this big country of ours, who reach the mental elevation to understand and give due esteem to great work.

So much was the fate of the pioneer from long ago, and still is. What fate then for genius?

Often I linger around an hour and like it. That is always the time in which I look around and into corners of the Taliesin studio in hidden shelves and drawers rummaging after hidden valuables. What I bring to light is always unexpected in beauty and boldness of conception.

Much as the world already knows out of the workshop of Frank Lloyd Wright, more still lies hidden and unknown in those shelves and drawers piled with drawings and manuscripts in which I am sometimes rummaging. If that should ever come to the light of day sometime in the future, say in a work called "The Unexecuted Buildings and Ideas of Frank Lloyd Wright," that would cause a sensation and surprise. And the blessing would be immense.

What a great honor if many sons of such a work grow to characterize a country.

HANS KOCH

[It is rather astonishingly prophetic of Hans Koch to realize and note the future importance of the unexecuted buildings and ideas of Frank Lloyd Wright.]

The Taliesin Playhouse presents on Sunday the adventures of a Czechoslovakian Robin Hood in a highly entertaining and beautifully made film, *Janosik*. Refreshments will be served at 3 P.M.

AT TALIESIN
August 13, 1937

[Frank Lloyd Wright traveled to Russia in June 1937 to attend and participate in the First All-Union Congress of Soviet Architects, held in Moscow. This, of course, wasn't Wright's only contact with Russian culture, as many Russian films were shown in the Taliesin Playhouse during the "At Taliesin" years (and after). In one of his earlier "At Taliesin" columns (manuscript dated May 25, 1936) Wright stated, "The silliest scares gratuitously handed out to Americans today are the 'red menace,' ergo Russia, and the 'yellow peril,' ergo Japan." Wright goes on to admit that they (the Taliesin Fellowship) "have recently been accused of Russian propaganda at the Taliesin Playhouse. We are sincerely interested in the art of the cinema as we are in other arts and to leave Russia out of our widening horizon would be like throwing Hamlet out of *Hamlet* because we didn't like Hamlet." (Interestingly, he also stated that "facts are, there is no possible threat to America from Japan . . . I am not so sure we are no threat to Japan.") Wright's trip abroad to Russia certainly added fuel to the already smoldering fire burning in southern Wisconsin. In addition to the *Racine Journal Times* August 5 editorial, referred to in the following column, he, too, was (mis)quoted in the *Capital Times,* upon his return from Russia, as asserting that "our so-called Communists running around in our Universities are mere racketeers, unaware of what is going on in Russia." This, of course, raised the ire of the University of Wisconsin Faculty Branch of the Communist Party. Wright replied, "My Dear University Communist" — in another "At Taliesin" (manuscript dated August 2, 1937) column, with which he attempted to clarify his views — "Comrades, please do not put me up against my country as a reproach to the country. I've been pretty 'trying,' you know. Am 'trying' still."]

Reply to an editorial in the *Racine Journal Times:*

From The Editorial: "We wonder if Mr. Wright doesn't realize that his statements (concerning Russia) are likely to have this country's leading "red hunters" down around his neck. Men have been called hired hands and accused of plotting the overthrow of American government for saying less."

Mr. Editor: Yes, I realize that telling the truth concerning the Russian struggle for freedom lays me "liable." But I early assumed, ever since acting upon the assumption, that truth is not only a man's best defense or offense but, in any real showdown, his only safety. This "red" menace I see as a special creation of a very bad social consequence in our country and just about as valid as the "yellow peril" started echoing down the columns of the press by the late Kaiser. My country cannot fairly question my loyalty nor doubt my service. The value of my contribution to American culture is a matter of record around the world.

My discretion is another matter. But everyone is getting so damned discreet nowadays that truth, for sometime past, has been getting a bad break. Concerning this affair of "discretion:" I may honestly say that I never talk unless asked to do so nor answer an attack unless I feel the truth demands a reply.

Concerning this matter of truth: it was bad luck for our citizens when the big corporation newspaper took over the crusading editor and his spirit passed away.

The big newspaper, the big interests, big institutions of every kind—they are now the real menace to candor and veracity of every sort not favorable to the profit-motive. "Bigs" have given the truth concerning the Russian spirit and what it is doing, a bad slant. And you can often hear their silences lie much louder than their words.

I believe the American citizen is slowly learning to know big-advertising and how it affects his "news."

The *Racine Journal Times* editorial again: "Some folks being critical might want to argue certain points with Mr. Wright. They might inquire why since everything is so peaceful and lovely among the people of Russia so many keep dying of 'lead poisoning' after being lined up against a wall. The curious might ask what kind of 'constitution' it is that promotes such shooting parties, forbids free speech, free press, etc."

To the Critical Folk:

Why forget that the infant U.S.S.R. is the product of revolution — as were the Republic of France and our own U.S.A.?

We know that it takes half a century to clear up the blood-stream after such fevers. The Russian Revolution was only about 15 years ago.

I conjecture (all the press can do notwithstanding its "it is learned from well informed quarters," is "conjecture"), that "lead-poisoning" in the Soviet Union is emergency antidote to internal poison: a hangover from revolution. Press criticism of Soviet court-procedure is no proof that the life of the union is not being wisely protected by a wise, if relentless, leader.

And I suspect that the union feels that if emergency practice in that respect had prevailed at the times Trotsky was let go free — many lives might have been saved. That suspicion may or may not be well founded. As a consequence of our own wild revolution we spilled some blood ourselves without apology or explanation to the inimical neighbors.

I like the tenet in Russia's constitution: "From every man according to his ability — to every man according to his contribution." A traitor's contribution? Well, perhaps lead-poisoning against a wall is antidote. Who knows?

But I prefer to take the spirit and practice of the life in Russia I actually see. What I have said has the character of first-hand observation and applies to the Russian people.

FRANK LLOYD WRIGHT

On Sunday at 3 P.M., we will show the Austrian film *Truxa* — circus extraordinary.

Coffee and cakes will be served at 3 o'clock and there will be special music: The A Minor Quartet by Kreisler, by the splendid quartet: the Taliesin String Quartet, now in residence at Taliesin.

AT TALIESIN

September 5, 1937

The project at Taliesin most interesting to visitors and of first importance to the Fellowship itself is the rehabilitation of the buildings begun four years ago at Hillside to eventually house the major group of the Fellowship. Attention last week was focused once more upon this work when John Lautner took charge as chief for two weeks and is encouraging the apprentices enlisted to carry out the work of finally completing the big drafting room.

For four years we have looked forward to the time when the big drafting room would be an alive and active workroom surpassed by none, and we need the working space. For a long while for various reasons it was just outside our grasp—unfinished and empty: filled with a strong clear light from the north, perfect for the work we anticipate doing there. We would walk through it regretful, waiting for the day when we could be at work on it.

Now we are entering into what we hope to be the final phase of construction and the end of a long waiting. Two months of continual and concentrated group activity by the Fellowship should announce the fact that our principal workroom—an abstract forest in oak timber and sandstone—is in order. Then watch our dust!

On several occasions recently we have listened to music by the Taliesin Quartet, music in unique and beautiful circumstances. Once in the evening on one of the terraces they played for the first time a quartet by Gustav Hoffman, the Chicago composer who recently visited Taliesin. Unfortunately the composer was not here, otherwise he would have heard for the first time himself his interesting work— outdoors under a full moon.

Again another time at a Sunday picnic out in the country on a craggy hillside under an aged oak surrounded by the Fellowship sitting or lying about, the quartet brought their instruments and played a Beethoven quartet—Opus 18. The sound carries perfectly out of doors. The surroundings were in absolute harmony with the music. Just as Whitman is best read out of doors, so Beethoven is best played outside under the trees where the eyes may dwell on a beautiful vista.

Sunday evenings after another Beethoven quartet they played an expressive Borodin quartet which was a revelation to many of us; Borodin to whom they erected a statue as chemist not knowing how much greater he was as a musician.

Gradually the time of the quartet at Taliesin is drawing to a close and we intend to arrange a final concert program which they will present at the Playhouse on Sunday afternoon, Sept. 12. Full announcement concerning this program will be made next week so the Taliesin's friends may share in the festival.

At the Playhouse on this coming Sunday we are showing *Paris Commune* an epic of Paris during the Franco-Prussian War and the historic Paris Commune of 1871. Years of research and preparation with the brilliant direction of G. Roshal have produced a stirring historical film worth going far to see for those to whom the cinema is more than a superficial entertainment.

The Taliesin Quartet will play music by Borodin and Glasonov next Sunday afternoon at 3 at the Playhouse as usual.

AT TALIESIN

November 12, 1937

[Walter Gropius lectured to a "crowd of 700 Madisonians" on November 8, 1937, in the Great Hall of the Memorial Union on the University of Wisconsin (Madison) campus. His lecture, entitled "New Horizons in Architecture," began the 1937 Madison Art Association lecture series. A European-born "modernist," Gropius was both an architect and an architectural educator. Known for his founding of the German Bauhaus (1919–28), he had recently taken a position in the United States as a senior professor in the Department of Architecture at Harvard University. While in Madison, Gropius had hoped to meet Frank Lloyd Wright and visit Taliesin. However, as was reported in the *Wisconsin State Journal* on November 9, Wright was quoted as having said, "I am not in the habit of entertaining guests of the University." The article went on to describe an unplanned, "cool meeting" that actually took place at the site of the Wright-designed Jacobs House in Westmoreland (now Madison). In the same article, shortly after that coincidental meeting, Wright went on to say about Gropius, "He's a very nice man, but he came along after all this (modern architecture) got started."]

It was interesting to listen to the comments of the audience as it left Prof. Gropius' lecture on "Modern Architecture" last Monday night— especially those of the older listeners, most of whom were laymen in architecture and at least superficially interested to learn from a noted authority what modern architecture was and why it should exist. One scholarly gentleman was saying, "It was all over my head"; a superior-looking woman complained, "But there was nothing I could really grasp"; another asked, "What was his argument for such buildings?" Nowhere was there to be felt any enthusiasm either for or against the lecture; rather boredom, bewilderment and general apathy were everywhere evident. Afterwards I met some very intelligent people and asked them what they really got out of Dr. Gropius' lecture that either provided a rational basis for his "Functionalism" as a style of modern architecture, or any reason why building in America should follow along this direction. And not one was able even to remember the words of the lecture, much less its intended significance or meaning!

Those of us who attended from Taliesin were left equally at sea — but our disgust was aroused by the whole performance. We were well acquainted with the examples of work shown and with the theories behind them, and had long ago discounted the spirit as one of negation and self-evident impotence and the examples of the so-called International style as merely one more inorganic and arbitrarily imposed style — examples perforce lifeless and inorganic. But we at least expected a more brilliant exposition, a more concrete analysis, and a more constructive program from Dr. Gropius, one of the leading figures of the movement who had been forced from Germany because of his professed Socialistic sympathies. Especially did we expect more when he was discussing the housing problem. Instead we listened to a long historical survey of the movement illustrated by slides, each properly dated and catalogued.

We heard the Bauhaus movement sought the essence of style inherent in materials and scientific methods and did not seek to impose an arbitrary system of design (although the pictures shown of buildings all over Europe seemed all alike to detail); we were told nothing of the urgency of the housing problem and no more definite plan for the solution of the over built city than to space the buildings farther apart so that green strips of grass might intervene (even Herr Gropius feels the need of something of nature to look at from his machines-for-living); and we finally lent a dull ear and deadened mind to the plea that America give up its imitation to past styles and develop one of its own—a good safe proposal in 1937 when one knows that the advanced creative thought of the country did just this thing long before any of the Internationalists including the speaker were even born!

And so Prof. Gropius ended. No appeal to the finer sensibilities had been made by the illustrations, no response either of imagination or instinct evoked by the lecturer; the mind had not even been stimulated to consider any of the aesthetic, social, or philosophical issues at stake—if, indeed, such considerations are involved at all. No wonder the layman was left at a loss! The student must have fared far worse: any enthusiasms or illusions he might have had for the modern European movement or any understanding of its value to human life and culture certainly must have been blasted forever. To us at least, Herr Gropius' talk was as good a piece of evidence as needed against his own cause, which stood forth in all its importance, superficiality and barrenness in the illustrations.

CHARLES SAMSON

On this Sunday, Nov. 14, at three in the afternoon, we are showing *The Wave,* photographed by Paul Strand in Mexico. It was initiated by Carlos Chavez, famous Mexican composer and conductor. The English titles are by the noted American writer, John Dos Passos.

George Seldes says of this Mexican film: "One of the great achievements of the camera, superior to almost everything ever done in the United States, ranking with the 10 great films of all times and all countries—a work of art and emotion."

AT TALIESIN
December 10, 1937

[The architectural magazine of national circulation referred to in this column was the *Architectural Forum.* Its January 1938 issue was unprecedented and totally devoted to the new and unpublished work of Frank Lloyd Wright (of the thirty projects represented in the issue, fifteen were projects designed since 1930) and was designed and written by Wright with the assistance of the Fellowship and the *Forum* staff. Previously written off by the Museum of Modern Art and Henry-Russell Hitchcock in 1932, its publication helped greatly to reintroduce Wright's reemergence as the preeminent leader in the architectural world.]

Last month at Taliesin was spent in preparation of a forthcoming issue of an architectural magazine of national circulation—an issue to be devoted to Mr. Wright's work of the last few years. The publication of this issue is of signal importance for it is the first collection of Mr. Wright's recent work—work of great architectural value which should be as widely known as possible. The preparation of this issue was placed in the hands of Mr. Wright, and he and the Fellowship have prepared both format and contents. Since the importance of the publication was realized, every effort was devoted to making it as complete and significant as possible.

Every apprentice was busy at his table in the studio, preparing plans, perspectives and elevations of buildings which Mr. Wright has designed in the last few years. The wonderful plans of the buildings built—and of some never built—were taken from the filing cases and pointed up or copied for reproduction in the magazine. Two secretaries spent long hours at the typewriter getting the written matter ready. Professional photographers scurried over several states to get pictures of the houses and also did much work at Taliesin. Two young editors of the magazine sent out to help Mr. Wright were worn to a frazzle. Telegraphs and airmail communications were sent at frequent intervals.

Mr. Wright filled the role of supervisor and organizer with characteristic energy and artistry. He revised the usual format of the magazine, introduced changes of a constructive sort, individualized this number of the magazine by designing both front and back covers. He tossed aside publication difficulties with a facility which left the two young editors white at the gills. Desiring that this issue should do more than give a graphic presentation of his latest work, he included in it a resounding forward and sprinkled it with apropos quotations from Thoreau and Whitman whom he considers among the greatest of Americans. He also included articles in which he describes the houses and the principles working in them.

Besides doing these things, Mr. Wright was ever busy in the studio—showing apprentices how to clarify drawings, doing decorations and revisions himself. He trekked over Taliesin in bitter weather to supervise the work of the photographers. At a breathless last moment he managed to secure plans and photographs of his work which he had taken to Soviet Russia with him last summer from custom officials. He is now in New York checking up on the issue before it goes to press.

The result of all this effort is going to be something extremely worthwhile despite the comparatively short time for preparation. Nothing like it has heretofore appeared from American sources: for the first time a monograph of our greatest architect will be presented by an American publication for the American people. This issue should be a clarion call to young architects—as a record of the greatness of a mature but ever-developing genius who, with supreme talent and unflinching devotion to principle, has long been the leader in modern architecture.

WILLIAM CHEANEY

AFTERWORD

This account of the "At Taliesin" column series abruptly ends during the final days of December 1937. There were very few columns written after that primarily because of the realignment of priorities in the early part of 1938 when the Fellowship left for Arizona to construct Taliesin West outside of Scottsdale. Some apprentices remembered also that interest in writing the column began to lag in 1937 owing to the added work load and the pressures of the growing number of architectural commissions at Taliesin (i.e., writing the "At Taliesin" column became less important as the architectural work increased). Wright's relationship with the local press continued at full force, however, as evidenced by the fervor created by the Madison Monona Terrace controversy (a project begun by Wright in 1938 and still, to this day, seriously considered for potential construction). Both Madison papers took sides in the issue of the project and Wright as its architect. The *Capital Times* was his staunch supporter; the *Wisconsin State Journal* opposed his involvement. Wright's warm relationship with the editor of the *Capital Times*, Bill Evjue, continued for the rest his life. After Wright's death, Olgivanna Wright began a new column in the *Capital Times* entitled "Our House."

The significance of the "At Taliesin" column series has usually been misunderstood and underestimated. On the surface, the columns are oftentimes seen collectively as a historic diary or even a graphically written "home movie" of Taliesin life during the four short but eventful years of the Fellowship's infancy. On a deeper and more important level, however, the "At Taliesin" series of 1934 through 1937 spans one of the most critical periods of Frank Lloyd Wright's life and career and thus can provide a valuable and unique insight into those years that began in crisis but ended in an explosion of renewed creativity.

In 1934 Wright had barely a commission and was basically written off as having already done his best work. To the architectural world his importance and worth had been proven, his position of eminence secured. And so as he approached his seventies, Wright was thought to be headed toward inactivity for the remaining years of his life. But by 1938 he would set that world of architecture on its ear once more and reestablish himself as America's architectural leader and living legend.

Starting with *An Autobiography;* then the Taliesin Fellowship in 1932; picking up steam with Broadacre City, "Fallingwater," the Johnson Wax administration building, and his Usonian House concept during the mid-1930s, Wright was full speed ahead again as the "At Taliesin" column series came to a close. As William Drummond expressed to Wright in a letter dated January 18, 1938, "Have not seen *Forum* as yet but *Time, Life* and your own form letter, so strong and able, have been a refreshing treat to me—to the casual reader must seem astounding. For behold—one frail man thought to have been downed perhaps or shut away—hath he not like the giant of old, stepped forth again with redoubled strength and faith and purpose to have his say in the teaching of a distraught world and to take his rightful place in the larger affairs of reconstructing that world?" Betty Cass also congratulated Wright, regarding his "rebirth" in a letter dated January 26, 1938, "but at least it will prove to you that you aren't just a has-been as you said to Olgivanna and me that gloomy October afternoon last fall when you felt so low. I told you all you needed was one of Pop-eye's cans of spinach! You're still IT!"

In the January 1938 issue of the *Architectural Forum,* in his "Foreword Concluded," Wright wrote, "I have at least ten years more (unless I get a Ford up my back, or something) in which to practice the basic principles of an organic architecture." Wright lived over twenty more years and, as he promised, practiced within those organic principles until his final days on earth. Dozens of Wright's most-famous architectural creations came forth after the "At Taliesin" years. Taliesin West was built as the Fellowship's permanent Arizona camp; many forms and variations of the Usonian House concept were constructed; several derivations of earlier designs were actually built (i.e., St. Marks-on-the-Bowery found form, although modified, as the Price Tower; the Standardized Modern Gas Station was built later for R. W. Lindholm in Cloquet, Minnesota); the Guggenhiem Museum; the "Mile High" skyscraper; Florida Southern College; the Marin County Governmental Center complex; ad infinitum.

Wright's death in Arizona on April 9, 1959, did not terminate the Taliesin Fellowship. Quite to the contrary, the Fellowship has continued to "practice the basic principles of an organic architecture" just as Wright had promised earlier. The traditions, philosophy, and practices set forth during the early Fellowship years (and written about within the "At Taliesin" column series) are still alive today, and the Frank Lloyd Wright Foundation is committed to inspirit and enliven the legacy left by Wright for the present apprentices within the Foundation, the Taliesin Architects, and the students within the Frank Lloyd Wright School of Architecture for perpetuity.

APPENDIXES INDEXES

APPENDIX A

"Frank Lloyd Wright Realizes Another Dream
at Unique Theater Opening at Taliesin Tonight"

[Frank Lloyd Wright provided the *Capital Times* a personally guided tour of the very-soon-to-be-completed Taliesin Playhouse, constructed within the original walls of the Hillside Home School gymnasium. The following is a reporter's account of that tour replete with dialogue by Wright (the *Capital Times,* Wednesday, November 1, 1933).]

Frank Lloyd Wright Realizes Another Dream at Unique Theater Opening at Taliesin Tonight — Building Constructed by Apprentices from Native Materials

by Mary York (of the *Capital Times* staff)

When the Taliesin Playhouse, latest addition to the Taliesin foundation near Spring Green, Wis., opens tonight at 7, another of Frank Lloyd Wright's visions will have taken definite form. A huge artistic building, made from stones of nearby hills and rough woods of nearby forests, it seems to be a part of the surrounding landscape. It is the only theater of its type in this part of the country, and probably the only one of its kind in the world. Located on the opposite hill from Taliesin, home and studios of Mr. Wright, it has been remodelled from the old gymnasium of the Hillside School, founded in 1886 by the Lloyd-Jones sisters, aunts of Mr. Wright.

Work on the building has been done almost entirely by Taliesin foundation apprentices—or Mr. Wright does not call them pupils. They have felled the trees, sawed them into lumber, quarried rock, and burned lime to lay the rock in the wall. The sawed lumber has been turned into structure, trusses and furniture. Walls have been plastered and frescoed; all by Taliesin apprentices.

One enters a little foyer of stone, with the mask of Taliesin (meaning shining spirit) and the motto: "So works the artist to make form as God does one with the Spirit." — Richard Hovey.

Taliesin Playhouse Entrance at Hillside (Playhouse *right;* Dana Gallery *far left*). Photo courtesy of the State Historical Society of Wisconsin (John H. Howe Collection).

"Some of the removable seats and the stage, with its moving picture screen. The stage also may be used for drama. Under the upper stage is a lower stage for musicians" (original photograph caption accompanying article, the *Capital Times,* November 1, 1933). *Taliesin Playhouse at Hillside* (photo ca. November 1933). Photo courtesy of the *Captial Times.*

One is first impressed by the general color harmony. The brown of the rough woods, the unusual structure of the seats, their rose denim cushions, the curtains, of monk's cloth with their designs of vivid red, green and blue, make a gorgeous color symphony.

Taliesin Playhouse has a double stage. The under stage is for musicians. On the upper stage either motion pictures can be shown or drama played. An amplifying apparatus is built very much as sound is built into a cathedral. One can hear in the farthest corner as easily as one can hear from the front seat. There is a director's chair in the front row, with an electrical telephone connecting with the projector's booth and all dressing rooms.

Mr. Wright, a picturesque figure clad in a big brown suede trench coat, green corduroy trousers tied around the bottom, wool socks, heavy woolen gloves, a yellow and red woolen muffler and a small, foreign looking hat jammed on his grey hair, came to escort us around. He led us to the back of the theater and showed us the big stone fireplace (fireplaces are a feature at Taliesin) with its carved Welsh motto: "Gosod by Galon Ar Addysg," meaning, "The soul without knowledge is not good." Tea will be served here, on tea tables from plywood by the apprentices, between acts, while the play is reviewed and criticized.

"Our first play will be a motion picture, *The Merry Wives of Vienna,*" he explained. "We can seat 200. And if you will note, the seats can all be separated and moved back for dancing or other amusements."

Mr. Wright led us back stage. There were green rooms and electrical rooms. Below are dressing rooms. A crew of apprentices worked as we watched. Some sawing boards, some doing the finer work of finishing tables, some painting. There was the sound of a piano in the distance. Some of the boys sang as they worked. All seemed happy, and they looked healthier and clearer of eye than the average group of city bred students. "Well, why shouldn't they sing while they work?" Mr. Wright said in answer to a question. "They are happy because they are doing what they want to, and they have an ideal. We live what we do here."

The Playhouse is not the only addition to Taliesin. There are many others in process of construction. These buildings must be finished before the many pupils on the waiting list, 27 of them college graduates, can be admitted to apprenticeship.

We went across an enclosed bridge to the drafting room, where apprentices in architecture may work under Mr. Wright's guidance. "There are 18,000 feet of wood used in this room," he explained, as we grazed in amazement at the unusual lighting system in the ceiling. "There will be no crowding here, and there will be plenty of light."

"This wood was hewed from the forest for the benefit of the human mind — it is not being sacrificed in vain," he said gently.

There are many hundred feet of wall space where drawings may be hung. At one end of this room is an enormous baronial fireplace, with an entrance on either side to a courtyard. "You will note our architecture is different," Mr. Wright explained. "We believe in organic architecture — we build from the inside out, while others build from the outside in. Also, we believe in building in complete harmony with the landscape."

A sculptors' studio, with a ramp to bring in live animals for modeling; a painters' studio with north ceiling lights and a big fireplace; and a long study hall and boys' dormitory are being completed. A unique feature of these rooms is a balcony running around all, where music may be played while the students work if they so desire. Music, Mr. Wright believes, is an inspiration.

A girl's dormitory, which will have a matron in charge, is also in process of construction, a separate building from the study quarters.

Another feature is a boys' and girls' living room, which is being built as a memorial room to Richard and Mary Lloyd Jones, grandparents of Mr. Wright. On the six sides of a balcony are carved verses from the book of Isaiah. Another stone fireplace, 18 feet long, with andirons modeled after Welsh hats and couches on either side make this a homey room.

"You see the balcony above," Mr. Wright said, waving a sturdy arm, "that is the library. There will be no books there, but works of art. We will have embroideries, Japanese prints, etchings, tapestries, and other things our apprentices can gather information from first hand."

Taliesin is devoted to architecture and the allied arts. It is concerned with the impotence that is the consequence of what Mr. Wright calls a "gamble in education," believing young America over-educated and under-cultured; sex over-emphasized, present social differentiations absurd or obscene. He believes that we have been cut off from the life-giving sources of inspiration by the very means we take to find and reach them. There are no courses, no credits, no examinations, no teaching at Taliesin. Apprentices arise at 6:30 in the morning, and retire at 10:30 at night. They work in the saw mills, the electrical plant, in the fields, and in the studios—as they see fit.

When they reach a certain degree of perfection, they are at liberty to undertake projects which pay them, working with Mr. Wright's supervision. Several now are at work on architectural projects. "Our textbook is the book of creation itself. Our classrooms the workshops of the artist," Mr. Wright explained.

Apprentices at Taliesin do not lack for amusement. They are capable of supplying their own music, but frequently hear artists who wish to play for them. Recently a string quartet from Milwaukee played for them, also Miss Jane Dudley, well-known Madison violinist. Lecturers and statesmen come to speak to this intelligent group of apprentices, ranging in age from 17 to 36. Robert Einstein has promised to speak to them when he comes to Chicago shortly. And now that they have their theater, there will be many other guests.

Among Taliesin apprentices are: Ernest Brooks, instructor at Taliesin in music, and composer of many compositions played by the Philadelphia symphony orchestra, from Tulsa, Okla.; Frederick Langhorst, Elgin, Ill.; Louis Stevens, Milwaukee, Wis.; Robert Bishop, Swarthmore, Pa.; Alfred Bush, N.Y. Vernon Allen, S. Dak.; Charles Wells, Wis.; Martha Asire, graduate of the University of Michigan, from Ann Arbor, Mich.; Henry Schubart, New York; Abe Dombar, Cincinnati, O.; Robert Mosher, Bay City, Mich.; Philip Holliday, Fairmond, Ind.; Charles Edman, Montevita, Cal.; William B. Fyfe, Oak Park, Ill. Emanuel Sandoval, Nicaragua; Edgar Tafel, New York; William Bernoudy, St. Louis, Mo.; Paul Beidler, graduate of the University of Pennsylvania, Leighton, Pa.; George and Ruth Dutton, San Francisco, Cal.; Stanhope and Sally Fricke, Davenport, Ia.; Alden and Valda Dow, Midland, Mich.; Thomas Weighle, Detroit, Mich.; Van Elston, Muscoda, Wis. Yen Liang, Peking, China; Irving Shaw, Minneapolis, Minn.; John H. Howe, Evanston, Ill.; John Henry Lautner, of North States Teachers' College, Marquette, Mich.; Mary F. Roberts, Smith College, Marquette, Mich. Two apprentices who are shortly expected are Karl Knappe, a sculptor from Germany and Elizabeth Barnsdall, daughter of a wealthy oil magnate from Hollywood, Calif.

APPENDIX B

"Taliesin is Refuge From Modern University, Wright"

[The following discourse by Wright appeared on the editorial page of the *Capital Times* (Sunday, February 4, 1934), the same week that they printed the first "At Taliesin" column. It was also subsequently published in the March 1934 issue of the *Wisconsin Magazine of History*. (Wright signed that publication with "by Frank Lloyd Wright, '89." His attendance at the University of Wisconsin was only as a "brief" student for two terms in 1886.) He writes about the generally dismal condition of American education, architecture, the Fellowship idea, and his hope for the future—not only the future of Taliesin and the Fellowship (now one and the same) but his hope for the future generations that may be improved by Wright's living experiment of organic life.]

Taliesin Is Refuge From Modern University—Wright
by Frank Lloyd Wright

Paper inflation and over-production has characterized education in our country for a half century or more. We have manufactured white-collarites, both sexes, by the million, and they are on our hands now, "for better or for worse." Textbooks and classroom education by way of "credits" and "degrees" has inflated utterly commonplace intelligences far beyond their merits. And this inflation of the unit, this mass production of the candidate for a white collar job somewhere, some-how, is more serious than we seem to imagine. I do not know how far the machine, once man's slave, has conquered its master, but I do know the old traditions are broken or breaking down and thousands of young men and young women are wandering about the states with little hope of the good life enjoyed by their forefathers. Every day it is becoming more difficult to be a decent failure, the prevailing success is so outrageous. By "new deal" and ultimatum, to get the system started again we are trying hard to make all the sad mistakes all over again and at the slightest sign of improvement there is a selfish rush to play the game once more. The game has many angles and incidents but only one net result as the result of the gamble in education—more impotence, and as a result of the economic gamble—more poverty.

Taliesin is concerned with the impotence that is the consequence of the gamble in education, believing young America over-educated and under-cultured; sex over-emphasized, present sex social differentiations absurd or obscene. Nor does Taliesin believe the "artist" has any special claim to divinity such as he arrogates to himself. As the usual "graduate" is educated far beyond his capacity, so the "artist" sacrifices manhood to a bag of tricks, a mere pose or seeming. Both are significant—there is no health nor any strength in them. Personality gets in the way of the quality of individuality genuinely divine in man and that relates him nobly to all men. The being that is unconcerned with seeming has found in our life little soil in which to grow. As the "American" people our ingenuity is unquestioned. Intellectually we function in the glittering generality pretty well and for certain specific purposes very well. But where the deeper needs of men are concerned (we speak of these needs as Art and Religion)—we beg or borrow or steal what we have and assume the virtue we have not. Nor do I doubt that, in the large, we have been cut off from the life giving sources of inspiration by the very means we take to find and reach them. Take youth away from the ground, put growth on hard pavements and pigeon hole it in the city—and the first step has been taken toward future impotence. Herd youth in schools and colleges, textbook and classroom the growing period, and what have you but vicarious power in the hands and a cigarette in the mouth? Send the more self-indulgent, egotistic youth to art institutes and again the vicarious life and the insignificant "me." Technique and nothing to do with it. Men of vision? Men of deep feeling? Men to create life anew and the strength to meet defeat in that cause? Not much of any of these qualities. Our youth runs more and more to journalese and the wisecrack. Stimulants an invisible craving. And youth will have to function in fashion, the critical faculty stimulated with no valid basis for criticism; choice predetermined in various shallow or narrow grooves; personality more and more mistaken for individuality; mechanical horsepower or kilowatt mistaken for personal power. Noble selfhood run down into ignoble selfishness. The salt and savor of life that is joy in work soon runs stale in any academic formula whatsoever or in any attempt at "institution." A stale sap is the consequence. How can this knowledge-factory-education really culture any individual for the wrestle with machine-leverage owned by selfish interest, or encourage in man the interpretation of life in an era unprecedented in all the essential factors of the artifex? Education has gone on until, dropped from the present scheme of things, are these two great inner experiences, fructifying sources of good life — Art and Religion. Both by way of education, have gone to seed. Seed on the barren soil of capitalistic centralization has become where man-growth is concerned.

Architecture is the harmonious nature of all structure whatsoever, and a sense of valid structure in our culture is what we most lack. In steel, pulp, glass, and in the multiple powers of machinery and the basis for life they should bring with them, we have greater resources for new form than ever existed before and greater facility for failure. And it is a knowledge of architecture in this broad, organic sense that is essentially not only the salvation of twentieth century life but it is the natural opportunity for a great culture. The very basis of our future as a civilization. An architect of an organic social order would then be our statesman. The poet and philosopher would be an architect of our spiritual life. The architecture of sound it was that intrigued Bach and Beethoven as music and this will inform our musicians. The architect himself on this natural or organic basis is necessarily the useful interpreter of the life of his era. Search for new forms is particularly his because we live in them and we live by them. If we had them we would be only too happy to live for them. Painting and sculpture are features of such architecture. As for literature, the writer committed to the literal knows less of architecture in this sense — and unfortunately this writer is almost the only writer we have. By way of him the literal has invaded, confused and corrupted the plastic arts. In all artists must lie these deeper appreciations and realization that consciously or unconsciously, have always recreated, refreshed and lifted life above pleasure into joy. Our society knows pleasure but knows so little joy; knows excitement but knows no gaiety; has lost innocence of heart in exchange for an arid sophistication that may debunk anything but can make nothing but machinery. Reverence is dead. Even reverence for money is dying. To machine-power we do reverence, still, but essentially human powers and human values are in the discard while we pretend to do them honor, expecting to get around them again someday — somehow.

Well, Taliesin believes the day has come for art in this more simple organic sense to take the lead in this thing we miscall "education;" believes the time over-ripe for a rejection of the too many minor traditions in favor of great elemental tradition that is decentralization; sees a going forward in new spirit to the ground as the basis for a good life that sets the human soul free above artificial anxieties and all vicarious powers, able and willing to work again as the first condition of true gentility. Taliesin sees work itself where there is something growing and living in it as not only the salt and savor of existence but as the opportunity for bringing "heaven" decently back to Earth where it really belongs. Taliesin sees art as no less than ever the expression of a way of life in this machine age if its civilization is to live. Yes we must go forward feet on the ground, with all our mechanical leverage made more simple and effective, to a new realization of human values in everything. By simple measure of the man as a man and new standards of human values in "success" it expects to measure the man for a nobler environment and beget in him a better correlation of sense and factor. Taliesin is not a back-to-the-land movement. No. Nor is Taliesin interested in art for art's sake. Not at all. But means to go forward, feet on the ground, seeing art as man's practical appreciation of the gift of life by putting his sense of it into the things he makes to live with and in the way he lives with them. When he makes them he must make them his own and make them worthy of his spirit. When he does that he will know well how to live with them to greater purpose and with greater satisfaction of the demand real men make upon themselves.

The language of an ideal? Guilty. The moth, rust and corruption that have broken in and stolen are not so easily defeated? Yes easily defeated, but not by Utopia. It takes only faith and the ideal to defeat where there is good work to be done and the capacity definitely to do it. Neither Faith nor ideal are yet dead in our country although we have done our academic dollar-minded best to kill them, seeing both as the sentimentality they have mostly become. But Faith and the Ideal are alive at Taliesin in spite of the system and in some ways more alive because of it not insensible of what has been achieved in the way of useful tools but determined to make better use of efficiencies for the humanity that has bought them at a terrible price. As a people we may see, now, that they have cost too much. The Fellowship is an experiment? Inevitably an experiment. But one that knows direction definitely from experience. The experiment may fail but if a failure, even so more valuable to life in our extremity at the end of this epoch than so many of the successes we have acclaimed or achieved in the past. A few more such successes and we will know no future!

As to the young men and women who are voluntary apprentices; watching their work—I was about the new group of buildings when several apparently well educated people came up and, all together, asked: "Can you tell us what they are building here?" "Yes, they are building a refuge from the universities. There is now no place to lay one's head," and walked away to let them figure it out for themselves. And I suppose the impertinence does come to something like that. A group of volunteers: no courses, no credits, no examinations, no teaching. A work in progress and many refugees from "Education" doing always all they can do to help it forward wherever the work lies and whatever it may be. Meantime they are being as natural and kind as is possible to intelligent social human beings designing and creating a new integrity in the atmosphere of environment conscious of the design of the whole as organic. Conscious of the design of the whole together with old masters in their crafts, they are falling trees, sawing them into lumber, quarrying rocks and burning lime to lay the rock in the wall. Laying the hewn stones in the wall. Sculpturing likely stones and carving likely blocks of wood. Turning the sawed lumber into structure, trusses and furniture. Plastering walls, frescoing them. Digging ditches, working in the fields with the ground. Washing dishes, caring for their own rooms. Planting and harvesting. Making roads. Farming, planning, working, kitchenizing and philosophizing in voluntary co-operation in an atmosphere of natural loveliness they are helping to make eventually habitable. A consistency seldom seen in any country. Here is building, painting, music, sculpture, motion as good work. All together working out a greater correlation than they have known, toward an end dimly foreseen, it is true. But why not relax, work hard, and enjoy the journey? What worthwhile ideal was ever reached except to find realization still—beyond. It was the poet and philosopher Cervantes who said—"the road is always better than the inn." So Taliesin is a way of life. Action is a form of idea and idea is as surely a form of action in that life.

But action in the sense known at Taliesin is unthinkable as "academic." Good correlation, a good background, sane feeling for what we call the work of art and ability to work with some initiative are the essential qualifications for the apprenticeship which is a practical form of the co-operative competition that is growth. Individual initiative must awaken in the apprentice or he will lose himself in unaccustomed freedom and become a nuisance or a betrayal. And yet, in this freedom—sometimes seeming chaotic—here are being made better plans for all the special buildings needed by the farm, factory and countryside so badly, if we are ever going to get started again, rational, appropriate forms and better and more sensible furniture and utensils. More honestly significant painting and sculpture and music. We must have a better use of our industrial achievements where the user is concerned and more sane and beautiful ways of using our new tools and synthetic and natural materials and we must have true and more rhythmic and free interpretation of life in all those things we live with and live by, most of all in ourselves. Fellowship at Taliesin is either making the necessary new forms or is going to make them soon, not blind to the sociological changes necessary if they are to become property effective to society.

Music is architecture at Taliesin just as architecture is a kind of music. Music, being modern, is necessary to existence. Perhaps music as we already know it is the only modern among all the arts.

And Taliesin has a tradition—that of an organic architecture for America. A center line for a valid culture. Love, sincerity, determination, and courage not reserved for heroes but the common sense basis of any life worth living. As for economic basis this relaxed and more or less spontaneous activity in which the novitiate may be lost or find himself, the Fellowship has a two hundred acre farm, and as another— there are yearly fees fixed at about what a medium grade college education would cost plus what work the apprentice can do. Eventually, paid services to industry in architectural research will contribute substantially to put the tools needed into the hands of the workers and reduce or eventually abolish the fee so worthwhile young men and women may work for their living not as education but as culture. Out of this endeavor is coming an appropriate — somewhat cosmic — place in which to live and in which to work for and with America. And play, although when work is play — mere play becomes rather irksome at times. The margin of leisure here is no problem, nor is over production, nor is the length of the working day. Competition is a form of voluntary co-operation. Institution and routine is avoided where possible. Here is a workplace, rather, and a decent way of life as spontaneous as still may be so that growth may be joy — not the too much pain it has become in current effort. Our textbook is the one book of creation itself. Our classrooms are the various workshops of the artist.

APPENDIX C

"Making Light of the Times"

[Ernest L. Meyer (1892–1952), newspaperman, author, editor, and columnist, wrote a daily column for the Madison newspaper the *Capital Times* during the early "At Taliesin" years. His "Making Light of the Times" column featured three excellent accounts of his own personal experiences with Frank Lloyd Wright and the Taliesin Fellowship, the first of which appeared Tuesday, February 13, 1934.]

Making Light of the Times
by Ernest L. Meyer (*Capital Times* staff columnist)

Taliesin . . . "shining spirit . . . ," merely a lovely name, until I saw it Sunday. A monastic community, almost, sawing wood instead of telling beads. A score of apprentices and instructors here labor with head and hand under the guiding genius of Frank Lloyd Wright, rebel against the shoddy, the stilted, and the sanctimonious. What tutelage, and with what unconquerable energy! Ill winds once blew the Taliesin hilltops; calamity and fire took their harvest, and a man less brave than Wright would have surrendered on the ashes. Yet here he is, striding once more the soil where his ancestors labored, and once more the valley is astir with dynamic enterprise.

The fragrance of fresh-hewn wood is in the wind, the smell of plaster, and the pungency of stone-dust under the chisel. Here is the uncompleted and vast drafting room, where eighty architects can labor under the north light. Here the dormitories. Here the public Playhouse, newly built, and there the sculptor's studio, the painter's studio, the study hall . . . Phoenix in many forms winging out of the ashes of mischance. And the ashes are artfully mingled with the new. Buddhas and Chinese goddesses, snatched from the fire that once left Taliesin a husk, look from their perches in the new stone walls, unblinking witness of a miracle. Tradition, fealty to Welsh ancestors have, too, their place in the cloister, "Gosod by Galon Ar Addysg," reads the motto on the great stone fireplace in the Playhouse, meaning "The Soul Without Knowledge is Not Good." And on another, a chiseled stanza from Gray's Elegy, the favorite of Mr. Wright's mother, and on her lips when she died.

This is impressive: the new not overlaying the old, but intertwining with it and creating an harmonious entity. The new Taliesin is bizarre and beautiful; in all the world there is nothing like it. And all about the studios are models and plans for fresh wonders in skyscrapers, palaces in the mesa, even humble gasoline stations done into things to delight. Yet permeating this pioneering is always a spirit of venerated yesterdays; what was good and sound in the old has been preserved; old loveliness has not been sacrificed to the gods of novelty . . . Taliesin overlooks the distant river, and like the river it has its restless drive, its eternal questing, but, too, its lore and traditions that brood over the waters and the hills.

Thirty of us are gathered in the master's great living room. Twenty apprentices, resting after a week in the studios, in the sawmill, in the field and woods. One, who has been felling trees, plays Brahms on the grand piano. Another, who has been hewing stone, sings folk songs. A third, a Chinese, has left his palette to play for us a melancholy flute. Logs sing in the fireplace. The mistress of Taliesin looks to our comfort graciously, while her young girl-child perches in her observation window, watching dusk steal over the ridges of the still-naked river bluffs.

The master is quite silent; this is the boys' night, a night for song and for laughter . . . Tomorrow there will be mortar to mix, timber to saw, nails to hammer. Tomorrow there will be plans to be drawn for a house on a hillside. Tomorrow there will be new patterns for the loom, new acid for the etchings, new designs for the screen . . . Tomorrow and tomorrow . . . each day too short to bring to fruition each day's gigantic dreams, yet each day ripe with rewards and the knowledge of good work done. The master stands, rugged as a sound tree, among his apprentices. They seem a radiation of his own strength, his own aspirations. They seem a promise that willing hands and hearts will not be wanting to call forth harvests and to bring grandeur to the long tomorrows of Taliesin.

[In a letter to Wright dated June 7, 1934, Meyer enclosed the following poem and noted, "Dear Mr. Wright: You asked for 'more poetry please.' The enclosed is sincere, but inadequate" (*Capital Times,* Thursday, June 7, 1934).]

Making Light of the Times
by Ernest L. Meyer (*Capital Times* staff columnist)

To Frank Lloyd Wright
Out of the ruck and squalor of the earth,
Sometimes, in sundown skies, a brilliant spire
Points to new stars, new planets finding birth
Where faint moons circle in the farthest fire.

Just so, you stand, you point, your prophet eyes
Fixed on vast distances, and, with you, we turn
To scan the promise of the pregnant skies
Where new words quiver and where new worlds burn.

How like you are to your own honest work,
How like the massive mansions you create;
Still standing, proudly, in that Orient murk
Of quake and smoke and flames, unscarred and great,

Your building towered. So you tower, too!
Though fires of fate thrice burned your hillsides black,
Though knives of malice stabbed you through and through,
You stand, serene, above the yapping pack.

Myself you told: If you would thrive, keep young, —
Live perilously, with the salt of danger on your tongue.

[In late July/early August 1934, the Meyers spent a week "vacationing" at Taliesin, living and working alongside the Fellowship apprentices. The following three-part column (*Capital Times,* Tuesday–Thursday, August 7–9, 1934) describes his fond memories of that visit. In a letter to Wright dated August 9, 1934, Meyer writes, "Dear Mr. Wright: The enclosed pieces fall far short of what I had projected, but inspiration lags in this terrific heat. At any rate I hope they convey the notion that I enjoyed tremendously my short stay at the Fellowship, and will do whatever I can to aid it. Rarely have I lived among a group of young people so free of affection, so life-loving."

Making Light of the Times
by Ernest L. Meyer (*Capital Times* staff columnist)

Taliesin, Wis. — Last night I saw the Devil. Opening my dormitory window to cool my cheek in the night-wind, I saw him clearly, hoofs, horns and all, starkly outlined against an uptilted moon, rising late over the long roof-tops. The vision troubled me, for it was in line with the morbid mythology which has for years darkened this valley of Welshmen, and which causes burghers of the countryside to wag their heads and point with sinister fingers at the Taliesin walls hugging the brow of a great hill. So I shoved my shoulder over the windowledge, and gazed intently at the thing on the roof thirty feet away. Far from dissolving, it was now more clearly defined, especially the horns, which now held the moon on their tapering prongs. For a long moment the Devil thus reared himself against the stars and then, suddenly, he vanished behind a gable, and I heard, or thought I heard, the staccato of his cloven hooves.

This odd and ominous tap-tapping persisted even when I had gone to bed; now near, now far, the Devil seemed bent on prowlish enterprise, and my dreams were made uneasy by the vision that he would claim me as rightful tenant in his domain and conduct me personally to the pit. At daylight, I struggled to recapture the night vision against the moon and had all but persuaded myself that I had dreamed the whole episode when I arose and looked again out of the window.

There, not ten feet away, with the chewed fragment of a tether-rope around its neck, was a billy-goat. Gazing at me vaguely with its curious horizontally black-slotted eyes. The roof-climbing goat of Taliesin, which so I was informed when I had related the Devil episode to an uproarious audience, mistakes the gables for Alpine peaks and cannot be restrained from adventuring on midnight tyrolean explorations. And if you inquire how a goat can climb a house wall, then I must confess that the thing sounds incredible, but there it was. Almost as incredible as the spectacle four of us had beheld the day before: a black-snake, five feet long, slithering up with precision and ease the rough, perpendicular stone wall of Frank Lloyd Wright's residence, and being disappointed in its probable quest of a bird's nest under the eves.

The story of the Devil apparition is an anecdote slight enough, but it seemed to me in the morning when daylight had dissolved the specter, that the episode held in it something illuminating. For, just as the satanic illusion could not maintain itself against the searchlight of the sun, so all the apparitions with which local lore peopled the Taliesin hills vanished under scrutiny in daylight. Many and fantastic the tales woven hereabouts by idle tongues, but all of them are blown away like the foggy emanations they are when the dawn breeze and brightness slide into the valley.

I am here on vacation from the newspapershop and I am living with the apprentices, and like the apprentices, of Taliesin Fellowship. With wife and child—and others among the thirty apprentices have wives and children—I occupy two little, airy rooms in a wing of the dormitory. Our windows overlook the strip of garden, the round stone-seat and bird-bath, and the giant vine climbing a tree that half hides the long, low roof of the master's residence. A cooling and calming vista, cheerful with bird and human voices. The getting-up bell rang at 6:30, and now the apprentices are already in the courtyard, snuffing the mocha aromas from the kitchen. We look at them in astonishment, for these surely cannot be the well-groomed and gowned young men and women we had seen yesterday (Sunday) entertaining visitors in the master's living room, and sitting primly in the Taliesin Playhouse while the movie-reels unwound a romance of old Vienna. Sleekness has passed with the Sabbath; they were girded for work though not overgirded. One youth wore shorts and shoes; a girl shorts, jersey and sandals, another girl pajamas, and a chinese youth only swimming trunks and a look of Oriental ateaseness. Their bodies were tanned to the color of fumed oak; health rippled in young muscles, cheerfulness sounded in laughter and morning greetings—a Taliesin day was beginning.

Breakfast at 7 in the half open-air dining rooms. Breakfast cooked by apprentices, served by apprentices, eaten by apprentices, and shared by the master and his family who had risen with the same bell. It is a grand thing to sit at the tables and listen to the chatter about today's projects, about yesterday's accomplishments, about tomorrow's long dreams. Nothing moody or brooding, nothing bookish or banal;

but active minds concerning themselves with active things, workers fitting the day's task into the design of a comprehended whole, and so finding in the day's labor not only pride but purpose.

Apprentice Earl is today's job-giver. Earl assigns four of us to tar the roof of the great studio building at Hillside. Earl scans my costume, halting at my shoes, my good shoes, my only shoes.

"They'll be ruined by the tar," he says.

"They're the only pair I have."

"Go barefoot," says Earl, simply.

Dutifully I remove my shoes, yet I look with some misgivings at the roof we are to tar. Already the sun is beating on the roof. I teeter apprehensively on my tender toes.

Frank Lloyd Wright comes to have a look at us apprentices tarring the roof of the studio building. The building is enormously long. Not having done any manual labor for 22 years, I decide after half an hour of scrubbing tar with a chopped-off broom that the sloping roof is fifteen miles in length, ten in breadth, and of an exceeding hotness. Hopping barefooted on this Sahara, we speedily become splattered and smeared with tar. Apprentice Earl, who has scooped the tar in luscious bucketfuls out of the barrel, attains the complexion of an Othello, with some of the Moor's melancholy.

"You look," I suggest, as he wipes a blob of tar from his cheek, "like Tarzan."

Mr. Wright chuckles. He offers a few suggestions crisply, then climbs down the ladder to superintend the laying of a stone floor in the main hall of the studio. He is a man of astonishing energy. He has need of it, what with thirty apprentices to direct, to instruct, to inspire, and what with a half dozen vast buildings to repair, keep in running order, and another half dozen to erect as part of the expansive enterprise he projects. To that enterprise there will be no end; his creative vigor knows no boundaries, there is never a "finis" at the end of his chapters, but forever and ever the restless promise: "to be continued." . . .

Plop, plop!—we daub the gummy and redolent tar on the hot roof.

"I begin to sense dimly the import of Mr. Wright's teachings," I observe to the three apprentices, "His revolt, I gather, is against pure book learning. The pallid stuff one digs out of tomes in college before one is dumped into a world with whose stuff and texture one is entirely unfamiliar. He wants you, in other words, to face that world with shrewd and willing hands, and minds sharpened by actual wrestling with its million problems. That is a splendid theory, but I must confess that today's lesson in tar is a little — well — exacting. Are the lessons sometimes more dramatic?"

"Hah," laughs Apprentice John. "You should have been here last week. There was drama. Mr. Wright was dissatisfied with the interior of our Playhouse. Too cluttered, he said. Problem: to make it more spacious without enlarging the walls. So the whole gang of us pitched in and in a week the Playhouse was transformed. We ripped out sections of the balcony. We tore out beams. When the thing was torn apart and lay in messy and tangled fragments, Mr. Wright gathered us around and said: "There it is. Now what in thunder will we do with it?" Well, we got more out of that week in practical engineering problems than we would have got in a library of theoretical learning. In the end, at Mr. Wright's suggestion, we began to yank out a series of supporting pillars and substituted a single cantilever. The floor will crash, we said. Knock out the last pillar, Mr. Wright ordered calmly. We did, holding our breath, waiting for the walls to quake. Bang! Down went the last support, and nothing happened. Nothing but our snorts of relief, and Mr. Wright's chuckle. There she stands."

There she stood. From the roof where we stood we could see a corner of the unique Taliesin Playhouse, with the sun bright on its red plywood shades. Drama!

"Sometimes in shaping practical problems," says Apprentice Henry, "we are helped by even turtles."

"Turtles!"

"Yes. Not long ago all the lights at Taliesin went out. We have our own plant, you know, run by a turbine at the artificial lake over there. There was a job — to locate the difficulty. We finally did locate it — a big snapper, caught in part of the turbine, and its shell half ground away by the mechanism."

As they chatted I caught a cross-section glimpse of the life at Taliesin. Work and work and work. Work in the fields, the 200 acres of pasture and provender. Work in the quarry, work at the sawmill, work in the sand and gravel banks. Work at the draughting tables, at the loom, at the easel, at the piano, fiddle and flute, and at the steaming sink and kitchen range.

Work and work with evening leisure to ease the ache out of bones and with ever-recurring crises to lend a savor to life. Things going wrong to be righted. Wood running short on zero nights, and foraging expeditions over the windy hills. Water system falling. And righted again. Drought burning up the pastures and borers in the corn. Wherever one turned, in this community striving for self-maintenance, foes to be faced and overcome. And forever . . . work.

"Whenever I see a pile of gravel on the roadside," said Mr. Wright to me as we drove toward town one day, "I long to put it to work. Whenever I see an idle pile of lumber, I long to shape it into something. . ."

Scrub! Scrub! We dip our stubby brooms into the tarpail, and daub the roof. Only an item, this roof, in the long tally of things to be done. These boys are not apprenticed to a master, but to a chain of endless tomorrows, to which they dedicate their vigor and in whose assured fecundity they will share.

Teatime in Taliesin is an interlude between work and work. No gowns, formality and fragile talk at a Taliesin week-day tea. At 4 the apprentices troop in with the clanging bell. The dust of their labor is still on them; they come from the fields, stone-heaps and carpenter benches, and drink pitcherfuls of ice-tea in the round stone-seat under the trees. Today most of us have been picking lima beans, sweet corn and digging onions in the hot sun. Two hours work in the morning; two in afternoon—this much of the apprentices' time goes into the maintenance and productivity of the Fellowship estate. After that tea, and then labor less strenuous with paint and brush, piano and T-square.

For myself, unused to farm labor, I drowse in the shade on the hilltop, every bone aching. Bones will ache in the breaking-in period making sleep a double boon. Through my drowse float pleasant sounds: someone is playing Brahms on a distant grand piano; someone is playing a melancholy tune on a flute; the dog, King, is barking at sheep in the orchard over there where Apprentice Yvonne is busy with palette and oils, and the roof-climbing goat is clip-clupping on the dormitory eaves. The good sounds of humans and animals actively happy, peaceful. The hills, too, peaceful, with the white wands of the birches lifted against the sandstone outcroppings of the hills, and the river in the distance weaving darkly through the silver shields of the sandbars. There is in Wisconsin no spot more beautiful than Taliesin.

After supper, the master invites all apprentices to the newly-completed art gallery. He lectures on Japanese prints drawing from Oriental art illustrations for his theory of craftsmanship. He pleads with his apprentices to see — as the Japanese masters saw — more than the surface of the world around them. They must study to master the texture and core of things; to learn the peculiar genius or essence which makes a pine tree what it is and which makes an apple bough what IT is. Once they have probed the complex texture of the world, he says, they can begin to interpret it through art and through building, creating stuff more vital, more true, more eternally significant than the placid mirrorings which characterize bad paintings, bad sculpture, bad architecture.

He speaks quietly, convincingly, directly, and with power. That is the essence of him, whether he deals with plastic wood or plastic word. His style in each is unmistakable: Frank Lloyd Wright and no one else.

After the lecture, lights out at 10:30, and bed. A good day. A full day. The roof-climbing goat will not arouse me tonight and my sleep will be dreamless. A cool wind blows over the hilltop roofs of the Taliesin colony.

I had almost said, "monastery." But monastery? In the sense of discipline, of communal life of subjecting individual whims and wishes to the leash of a collective ideal, a monastery, yes. But not in the deeper sense of withdrawal from the world, and of feeling lost in the welter when once outside the monastery gates. For this IS a world in the making with all the world's diverse enterprise. Here one may master the secrets of corn and cookery and cornice, of Beethoven and bricks, of Gaugin and cantilevers. So that Taliesin is not a relinquishing, but a getting; not a withdrawal from the world, but, in a sense more profound than that employed by dusty schoolmen, a preparation for life.

APPENDIX D

"Madison: Day by Day"

[Betty (Willoughby) Cass (1900–1977) was a writer, newspaperwomen, columnist, and radio personality. During the "At Taliesin" years she wrote a lively daily column for the *Wisconsin State Journal*. A frequent guest at Taliesin, her "Madison: Day by Day" column featured Wright's name often. The following captures an "up close and personal" glimpse of Mr. and Mrs. Wright's unique and special relationship (*Wisconsin State Journal*, Tuesday, July 30, 1935).]

Madison: Day by Day
by Betty Cass (*Wisconsin State Journal* staff columnist)

. . . Finally, for Saturday, there was the affair of the stringed instruments.

Just as a late afternoon peace had settled on the household a truck loaded with musical instruments came up the winding driveway to the back courtyard and dumped them beside a lily pool.

One of the apprentices came running into where Mr. and Mrs. Wright were sitting and cried excitedly, "Oh, Mr. Wright, the truck's just come with your instruments!"

"What?" Mrs. Wright asked, startled, a faint frown appearing on her brow as she sensed another extravagance of her famous husband. "What did you say?"

"Never mind . . . never mind!" said Mr. Wright and hurried out, pushing the confused apprentice before him.

But in a few minutes he was back, a beatific (albeit cat-caught-in-the-cream) smile on his face, his grey beret pushed jauntily to one side, affecting a gay swagger — AND strumming a guitar (or maybe it was a viola) like a wandering minstrel of old serenading his lady love.

It didn't thaw Mrs. Wright, however. She merely glanced at him disdainfully out of the corners of her black, black eyes and went on with her wool embroidery.

Mr. Wright laid the instrument down and went out without a word
. . . and in a minute he was back with another, striding with a springy
step, humming to the little tune he was making — this time on a violin
held like a guitar.

Mrs. Wright embroidered. Out went Mr. Wright again . . . and
again . . . each time bringing in one of the instruments, each time
strumming and humming a gayer, more carefree tune. And Mrs.
Wright continued to embroider and remain aloof — but when he
finally came in with the last one, a bass viola larger than he was, a
regular Paul Bunyan of an instrument, his twinkling eyes just peeking
over the shiny brown side of the giant he was trying to strum, she
could remain aloof no longer.

She laid down her embroidery and laughed until tears ran down her
face. And the crisis was over. Taliesin had been completely equipped
with string instruments and there had been no casualties. But Mr.
Wright is sorry now that he didn't get a flute, too, while he was about
it. It was all so easy, after all.

APPENDIX E

Contributors to "At Taliesin"

The following list provides brief descriptions of the contributors to the "At Taliesin" newspaper column series. An asterisk indicates column(s) written by the contributor are included herein. A bracketed number is the total number of known columns written by the particular contributor. Education listed is prior to entering Fellowship.

* **Margaret Crouse (Asire) Allen**   October 1933–May 1934

[1]   Westerville, Ohio; received B.A. degree from University of Michigan in February 1933; entered Fellowship at the age of twenty-three; October 1933 Fellow; married Vernon Patrick Allen in the first official Fellowship wedding in Unity Chapel on February 4, 1934.

Vernon Patrick Allen   October 1933–May 1934

[1]   Miranda, South Dakota; married Margaret Crouse Asire in the first official Fellowship wedding in Unity Chapel on February 4, 1934.

* **Everett Burgess Baker**   1935–1936

[2]   Milwaukee, Wisconsin; attended University of Wisconsin (engineering); entered Fellowship at the age of twenty-six; used "Everett Burgess" as his stage name; Fellowship application listed interest in the "art of the marionette."

* **George Malcolm Beal**   Summer 1934

[1⅓]   Lawrence, Kansas; architect and professor at the School of Engineering and Architecture, University of Kansas; entered (at the age of thirty-five) with wife, Helen, as special "summer only" apprentices; wrote article regarding the Fellowship after leaving Taliesin.

Paul Beidler   1933–1934

[3]   Lehightown, Pennsylvania; attended University of Pennsylvania; entered Fellowship at the age of twenty-six; October 1933 Fellow.

* **William Adair ("Billy") Bernoudy**   October 1932–1935

[1]   St. Louis, Missouri; high school only; entered Fellowship at the age of twenty-one; October 1932 Charter Applicant.

* **Robert ("Bob") Bishop**   July 1932–March 1935

[2]   Swarthmore, Pennsylvania; received bachelor of architecture degree from Swarthmore College; entered Fellowship at the age of twenty-four; October 1932 Charter Applicant.

* **L. Cornelia Brierly**   September 1934–Present

[12]   Pittsburgh, Pennsylvania; attended University of Pittsburgh, Cornell, and Carnegie Tech; came to Taliesin to join her sister, Hulda.

Ernest Brook   Late 1933–July 1934

[2]   Tulsa, Oklahoma; October 1933 Fellow; 1934 musician-in-residence (pianist and composer).

* **Alfred ("Alfie") Bush**   Summer 1933–Fall 1935

[3]   Brooklyn, New York; three years high school; entered Fellow-ship at the age of sixteen (at the time he was the youngest apprentice until Peter Frankl entered the Fellowship); October 1933 Fellow.

Jesse Claude ("Cary") Caraway   1935–1942

[½]   Texas; University of Texas.

* **William Fletcher Cheaney**   August 1937–December 1937

[3]   St. Louis, Missouri; while at Taliesin acted as an assistant secretary to Frank Lloyd Wright; came to work on "book project."

* **Abrom ("Abe") Dombar**   October 1932–September 1935

[6]   Cincinnati, Ohio; attended University of Cincinnati College of Architecture (two years); entered Fellowship at the age of twenty; October 1932 Charter Applicant.

* **Benjamin ("Bennie") Dombar**   July 1934–August 1941

[10]   Cincinnati, Ohio; high school only; entered Fellowship at the age of seventeen; joined brother Abrom.

Blaine Drake   December 1933–Summer 1941

[3]   Ogden, Utah; attended University of California at Berkeley (fine arts); entered Fellowship at the age of twenty-three; married fellow apprentice Hulda Brierly in the Taliesin living room May 1936.

James ("Jimmie") Drought   1932–October 1934

[1]   Milwaukee, Wisconsin; attended University of Wisconsin (landscape architecture); entered Fellowship at the age of twenty-three; October 1932 Charter Applicant.

Charles Edman   November 1933–Summer 1934

[1]   Monte Vista, California; attended Northwestern University (one year); entered Fellowship at the age of twenty; October 1932 Charter Applicant.

* **Earl Friar**   Summer 1935–1937

[2½]   Gibsonville, Ohio; raised on a farm and "milked the cows" at Taliesin.

* **William ("Beye") Fyfe**   June 1932–September 1934

[2]   Oak Park, Illinois; attended Antioch College and Yale University; entered Fellowship at the age of twenty-one; October 1932 Charter Applicant; nicknamed "Beye" by Wright because there were too many "Bills" in the Fellowship already (Wright knew his mother and that her maiden name was Beye).

* **Burton J. ("Burt") Goodrich**   August 1934–1942

[13]   Exeter, New Hampshire; received B.S. degree in architecture from University of New Hampshire; entered Fellowship at the age of twenty-three; remembered as a "wonderful model maker."

Frederick S. ("Fred") Gram

[1]   Not Fellowship apprentice or associated with Taliesin; secretary to Wisconsin congressman (and frequent guest at Taliesin) Thomas R. Amlie and worked for the *Racine Day* newspaper; wrote positive review of the Broadacre City model exhibit seen at the Mineral Point County Fair; review was reprinted as an "At Taliesin" column.

Philip ("Phil") Holliday   October 1932–August 1934

[2]   Fairmount, Indiana; received B.S. degree in art education from the University of Wisconsin; entered Fellowship at the age of twenty-one; October 1932 Charter Applicant; interest in painting.

* **John Henry ("Jack") Howe**   September 1932–September 1964

[10]   Evanston, Illinois; high school only; entered Fellowship at the age of nineteen; October 1932 Charter Applicant; the Fellowship's most-gifted and prolific draftsman.

Ellis Leon Jacobs   July 1937–Summer 1941

[1]   Des Moines, Iowa; entered Fellowship at the age of seventeen.

Karl E. Jensen   1929–Fall 1934

[6]   Copenhagen, Denmark; indicated in list of October 1932 Charter Applicants as "Taliesin Man"; secretary to Frank Lloyd Wright prior to Masselink.

* **Hans Koch**   Summer 1935–1936

[3]   New Brunswick, New Jersey; German craftsman and Taliesin master carpenter; also known as "poet, philosopher, free thinker, and citizen of the world."

* Frederick L. ("Fred") Langhorst   October 1932–May 1934

[4]   Elgin, Illinois; received B.A. degree from Cornell; entered Fellowship at the age of twenty-seven; October 1932 Charter Applicant.

* John E. Lautner   October 1933–1939

[9⅓]   Marquette, Michigan; received B.A. degree in English from Northern Michigan University; entered Fellowship at the age of twenty-two; October 1933 Fellow; married fellow apprentice Marybud Roberts January 1, 1934; apprentice superintendent for Roberts House during "At Taliesin" years.

* Marybud L. (Roberts) Lautner   October 1933–1935

[8]   Marquette, Michigan; entered Fellowship at the age of twenty-one; October 1933 Fellow; married fellow apprentice John Lautner January 1, 1934; daughter of future Frank Lloyd Wright client ("Deertrack").

Larry Lemon   November 1937–?

[1]   Falls Church, Virginia; landscape architect by training; with wife and daughter received scholarship to be Fellowship cook(s).

Max Levin   1937

[1]   Milwaukee, Wisconsin.

Yen Liang   October 1932–October 1934

[4]   Peking, China; received BFA degree from Harvard (also attended University of Pennsylvania and Yale); entered Fellowship at the age of twenty-four; October 1932 Charter Applicant; lived in the uppermost apprentice room in Taliesin hilltower.

Marya ("Mary") Llien   January 1936–Summer 1937

[2]   Poland.

* Lawrence Wesley Low   October 1936–?

[3]   North Canton, Ohio; attended College of Worchester (Ohio, three years); entered Fellowship at the age of twenty-two.

Kevin Lynch   September 1937–Spring 1939

[1]   New Haven, Connecticut; attended Yale (two years); entered Fellowship at the age of nineteen; interest in city planning.

Charles Grey Martin   1934

[1] Bedford, Iowa; October 1933 Fellow.

* Eugene ("Gene") Masselink 1933–1962

[28] Grand Rapids, Michigan; received B.A. degree from Ohio State University; entered Fellowship at the age of twenty-three; October 1933 Fellow; secretary to Frank Lloyd Wright; painting background (later took charge of Taliesin graphics and publications); second-most-prolific writer of the "At Taliesin" columns; died and buried at Taliesin.

Karl J. Monrad Summer 1935–Spring 1936

[1] Little Falls, New York; attended University of Michigan (two years); entered Fellowship at the age of twenty-one.

* Mabel Morgan 1934–?

[1] Dodgeville, Wisconsin; daughter of mason who helped build Taliesin.

* Robert Keeler ("Bob") Mosher 1932–1942

[12] Bay City, Michigan; received B.S. degree in architecture from the University of Michigan; October 1932 Charter Applicant; apprentice superintendent for "Fallingwater."

* Noverre Musson September 1935–June 1937

[3] Findlay, Ohio; attended Ohio State University (with Eugene Masselink); entered Fellowship at the age of twenty-five; friend of Eugene Masselink.

Lucretia Nelson 1934

[1]

* Nicholas-Ray (stage name) 1933–Summer 1934

[2] (Raymond Nicholas Kienzle); LaCrosse, Wisconsin; attended University of Chicago (one year) and University of Wisconsin (one year); entered Fellowship at the age of twenty-two; October 1933 Fellow; interest in theater and film.

* Svetlanna Wright Peters

[1] Daughter of Olgivanna Wright by previous marriage; married William Wesley Peters in 1935.

* William Wesley ("Wes") Peters October 1932–Present

[1] Evansville, Indiana; attended Evansville College and M.I.T.; October 1932 Charter Applicant.

Charles Poore

[1] Not Fellowship apprentice or associated with Taliesin; wrote a

positive review of *Architecture and Modern Life,* published in the *New York Times,* that was reprinted as an "At Taliesin" column.

* Sim Bruce Richards   May 1934–September 1935

[3]   Phoenix, Arizona; attended University of California at Berkeley (fine arts); entered Fellowship at the age of twenty-six.

* Charles Felix Samson   October 1936–1942

[2]   Dobbs Ferry, New York; received B.A. degree from Harvard; entered Fellowship at the age of twenty-two.

Kornelia ("Kay") Schneider   September 1935–Present

[1]   Beloit, Wisconsin; three years high school; entered Fellowship at the age of seventeen; father (mechanical engineer) knew Wright.

Henry A. ("Hank") Schubart   September 1933–October 1934

[2]   Ossining, New York; high school only (abroad); entered Fellowship at the age of seventeen; October 1933 Fellow.

Pauline Schubart

[2]   Ossining, New York; mother of Henry Schubart; wrote "At Taliesin" columns while at Taliesin caring for injured son (farming accident).

* Edgar Allen Tafel   October 1932–1941

[14]   (Also known as "Peck's Bad Boy" or "Joke Boy"); New York; attended New York University (one year); entered Fellowship at the age of twenty; October 1932 Charter Applicant; apprentice superintendent for several projects; subsequently wrote *Apprentice to Genius.*

* Donald Thompson   November 1934–Summer 1935

[3]   Cleveland, Ohio; entered Fellowship (with wife Mary) at the age of twenty-seven; mechanical engineer.

Mary Thompson   November 1934–Summer 1935

[1]   Cleveland, Ohio; entered Fellowship (with husband Donald) at the age of twenty-six.

* James McArthur ("Jim") Thomson   October 1934–1939

[3]   Farmington, Connecticut; entered Fellowship at the age of twenty-two.

* Frank Lloyd Wright

[31]

GENERAL INDEX

FILM INDEX

Randolph C. Henning was born in Madison,
Wisconsin, and is an architect living in Winston-Salem,
North Carolina. He has lectured on Frank Lloyd Wright,
researched Wright's Florida efforts, and is the author of
The Frank Lloyd Wright Designed A. D. German Warehouse:
A Rehabilitation and Adaptive Reuse Design (UMI, 1985).
Mr. Henning has a bachelor of design degree from the
College of Architecture at the University of Florida.
He received his master of architecture degree from the
School of Architecture and Urban Planning at the
University of Wisconsin-Milwaukee, where he also
independently researched Wright's Wisconsin work.